Only the Strong Survive

A publication in the
Black Music and Expressive Culture Series

Portia K. Maultsby, Series Editor
from Indiana University's Archives of African American Music and Culture

Only the Strong Survive

MEMOIRS OF A SOUL SURVIVOR

Indiana
University
Press
Bloomington
& Indianapolis

Jerry Butler
with
Earl Smith

This book is a publication of

Indiana University Press
601 North Morton Street
Bloomington, IN 47404-3797 USA

http://www.indiana.edu/~iupress

Telephone orders 800-842-6796
Fax orders 812-855-7931
Orders by e-mail iuporder@indiana.edu

The paper used in this publication meets the minimum
requirements of American National Standard for Information
Sciences—Permanence of Paper for Printed Library Materials,
ANSI Z39.48-1984.

Manufactured in the United States of America

Library of Congress Cataloging-in-Publication Data

Butler, Jerry.
    Only the strong survive : memoirs of a soul survivor / Jerry Butler,
with Earl Smith.
      p. cm.
    Includes bibliographical references and index.
    Discography: p.
    ISBN 0-253-33796-8 (cl : alk. paper)
      1. Butler, Jerry. 2. Soul musicians—United States—Biography.
I. Smith, Earl, date II. Title.

    ML420.B899 A3 2000
    782.421643"092—dc21
    [B]

                        00-032002

1 2 3 4 5 05 04 03 02 01 00

Title page photo by Sam Costanza

For Annette

The trouble with writing a book about yourself is that you can't fool around. If you write about someone else, you can stretch the truth from here to Finland. If you write about yourself, the slightest deviation makes you realize instantly that there may be honor among thieves, but you are just a dirty liar.

—GROUCHO MARX

Thus when I come to shape here at this table between my hands the story of my life and set it before you as a complete thing, I have to recall things gone far, gone deep, sunk into this life or that and become part of it; dreams, too, things surrounding me, and the inmates, those old half-articulate ghosts who keep up their hauntings by day and night . . . shadows of people one might have been; unborn selves.

—VIRGINIA WOOLF

A great biography should, like the close of a great drama, leave behind it a feeling of serenity. We collect into a small bunch the flowers, the few flowers, which brought sweetness into a life, and present it as an offering to an accomplished destiny. It is the dying refrain of a completed song, the final verse of a finished poem.

—ANDRÉ MAUROIS

Contents

Contents

Part IV.
The Motown Years and Beyond

Part V.
The Political Years

Acknowledgments

First and foremost, we are deeply grateful to Robert Pruter, whose timely suggestions and diligent research were invaluable. Without him, this book would not have been completed.

Our gratitude also goes to Dr. Portia Maultsby and Ed Bradley for their help in keeping us focused, especially Ed Bradley, whose amazing balancing act of reading the manuscript, attending to his *60 Minutes* duties, and finding the time to get back to us with frank and constructive comments was absolutely awe-inspiring. We are deeply indebted.

We also are indebted to Herbert Oscar Allen, of Columbia College, for his thorough, thoughtful editorial work and insightful comments. Sue Cassidy Clark has our gratitude for allowing us to use excerpts from some of her interviews and for tracking down some very hard-to-find people. The same goes for Mable Dorsey, Suzanne Flamdreau, Terry Stewart, and Don Beiderman for their immeasurable contributions.

Also, we would be remiss if we did not acknowledge the painstaking work of the fine people at Indiana University Press, in particular Joan Catapano, Jane Lyle, and Sue Havlish.

Lastly, much thanks and love goes to my wife, Annette, for her patience, love and, understanding throughout the whole process.

Introduction

From the outset, Jerry and I felt that, instead of writing a tell-all book about his personal life, as so many celebrities in his situation are wont to do, we would broaden the scope a bit and concentrate on what was going on at different stages of Jerry's career, taking into account the political, social, and personal forces impacting his life as well as the world around him.

With that framework in mind, we concluded that what we were really up to was writing a book about our generation—the Silent Generation—the "people who finally brought you civil rights, an unparalleled national wealth in the arts and in commerce, and unimaginable advances in science and technology," as one observer described the generation born between 1925 and 1942.[1] The comment was in reference to William Strauss's and Neil Howe's brilliant book *Generations. Generations'* basic hypothesis is that there are four different generational types: civic, adaptive, idealistic, and reactive. Further, it contends that each generation has two cycles: awakenings and crises. Awakenings are like "the dawn of the Golden Age of rock and roll," while crises are larger events, such as the Vietnam War.

In our own examination, however, we found that African Americans, the least silent of the Silent Generation, experienced altogether different awakenings and crises than their white counterparts. For example, while white teenagers in our generation were "awakening" to the discovery of a new musical form called rock and roll, black teenagers were awakening to the realization that the music they had invented was no longer theirs, and, importantly, they could not profit from it. Newcomers like Elvis Presley, Pat Boone, and the McGuire Sisters could profit—and did—from the same music deemed too crude for Top 40 radio stations when performed by black artists.

As for crises, the civil rights struggles of the fifties and sixties were our, black people's, crises. That is, while young black men were contributing disproportionately to the deaths and casualties in Korea and Vietnam to save those countries for democracy, back home their siblings were being beaten and hosed in the streets for trying to save some semblance of democracy in America.

Lost in all of that were the stories of some of the people who created the music that Harry Turner, a self-styled music historian, calls "the original American music." We felt compelled to tell a few of those stories in *Only the Strong Survive,* while also bringing to light some little-known facts about Jerry's many careers, including his soon-to-be new career, teaching. In light of our discussions about this book, as well as other matters, I believe that teaching will probably be Jerry's most rewarding career. He is ideally suited for it. With more than forty years in show business, interspersed with several years as an entrepreneur and ten years as an elected official, and as the holder of bachelor's and master's degrees, Jerry has much to teach about life, about music, about business and politics—and about survival.

But Jerry's first love is music, and it is music that is the driving force, the raison d'être, of this book. By telling the stories of people like Little Willie John, for instance, we felt we might at least mitigate some of the hurt from the slight by modern-day practitioners of rock and roll. As chairman of the Rhythm & Blues Foundation, Jerry has addressed that issue head-on, along with people like Bonnie Raitt, Ruth Brown, Etta James, and Chuck Jackson. In the Epilogue, we discuss some of the problems faced by past and current rhythm and blues performers.

In closing, please understand something: We did not set out to write a book about race relations in America. In all sincerity, we tried very hard to avoid discussing race altogether, hoping to focus attention on all the wonderful music and all the great people Jerry encountered throughout his forty years in public life. It was not to be. As with most things in America, race seems to color everything. It definitely is unavoidable when discussing or writing about America's musical heritage.

EARL SMITH
SEPTEMBER 1998

Prologue

Get up in the mornin'
Take the Highway 49

—Lyrics from "Highway 49 Blues"

I always get a tight, uneasy feeling in my stomach when I go back home to Mississippi. It's not that I hate or dislike Mississippi. After all, it's where I was born. The thing is, whenever I travel in the South, especially to and from Mississippi, I invariably think about all the misery, all the suffering black people had to endure in that part of the world for so many years—just to survive.

The last time I visited Mississippi was in the summer of 1997, when I was hired for a weekend show at the newly opened Casino Magic hotels in Bay St. Louis and Biloxi. Huge crowds—made up mostly of black people—crowded the casinos each night. They were loyal fans, people who had grown up with my music. I took my wife, mother-in-law, and brother-in-law Earl along on this trip, partly because Earl needed to do research for this book, and partly because I enjoy their company immensely. We always have a lot of fun when the four of us get together; it's one laugh right after another. Another reason was that we all needed to get out of Chicago for a while. My father-in-law had passed the previous month, and with the exigencies of work and other responsibilities, I, like my in-laws, needed time and distance from the sadness—time to reflect on how much "the old man," as we liked to call him, had touched our lives, and distance from the pain evoked by his loss. The gig in Mississippi was a godsend; it gave us all a sense of renewal. We learned how to laugh again.

But there was very little laughter on the way back home to Chicago. I was in a very somber mood, which probably had been brought on by the dark, overcast sky that greeted us when we awoke that Sunday morning, Getaway Day.

The downpour came just as we turned onto Highway 49, heading toward Sunflower County, where I was born. According to my mother, I was born on the Yellow Dog River, six miles from the town of Sunflower, near the infamous Highway 49.

From Gulfport on the Gulf of Mexico to Sumner in the extreme north-west corner of the state, U.S. Highway 49 meanders snakelike across Mississippi. Along the way, it connects with other highways and roadways, including the legendary "Route 66" and Highway 61, which has been dubbed the "Blues Highway" because of the many sad and tragic stories of people who lived near or traveled on it.

As we zoomed down Highway 49, I was immediately struck by the raw beauty of this part of the Mississippi delta: the green lushness of the countryside, with its ubiquitous vines and cypress trees, offers vivid testimony to God's power and brilliance. One can readily see why Robert Penn Warren once described this place as having a "sad and baleful beauty."[1]

But then, striking with equal force, is the incongruity, the paradox that is Mississippi: How is it that in a land of such beauty, some of the most vicious and grotesque forms of man's inhumanity to man can coexist? I would venture that for every magnolia, every daffodil found throughout the countryside, there is a story of horrible pain suffered by one group of human beings at the hands of another. I remember thinking, How many mutilated bodies lie at the bottom of these tranquil rivers? How many innocent souls are crying out for justice, for solace? Billie Holiday's haunting, mournful "Strange Fruit" suddenly came to mind:

> Southern trees bear a strange fruit
> Blood on the leaves and blood at the root
> Black bodies swaying in the southern breeze
> Strange fruit hanging from the poplar trees.

The images of Bessie Smith and Emmett Till also flashed into my mind. Were their spirits roaming among the dispossessed, the innocents? Their stories are uniquely American stories, especially the story of Bessie Smith, "Queen of the Blues."

On the night of September 26, 1937, after appearing at a juke joint in Sunflower County, Smith and her fiancé were driving west on Highway 49, heading toward Memphis, when their car was struck head-on by a truck. Bessie's fiancé suffered only minor injuries, but Smith's right arm was nearly severed. Bleeding profusely, she was taken first to several "white only" hospitals, but was denied treatment. By the time she arrived at a "colored only" hospital in Clarksdale, Mississippi, it was too late; she had died from loss of blood.

Till's story is even more tragic. His hideously decomposed body was found floating in the Tallahatchie River on August 27, 1955. He was only fourteen years old. Investigators theorized that Till's alleged murderers—a grocery store owner and his half-brother—used Highway 49 to transport Till to a barn in Money, Mississippi, where he was tortured and murdered and then dumped into the Tallahatchie. His body was found two miles from Highway 49. An all-white jury acquitted the two men, even after their admission of abducting "a little nigger boy" whose only "crime" had been whistling at the store owner's wife.

These two stories, and hundreds like them, underscore why the blues genre has survived as an art form. The low moan of an Otis Redding, for example, touches something deep inside us. Call it "race memory" if you'd like, but in Otis's moans and guttural wails, I can hear the primal scream of an African ancestor and feel the pain of an Emmett Till or Bessie Smith. It is visceral, cathartic, real.

And it's not just me. Several people have expressed similar experiences. This vicarious feeling, manifested in song, cuts across racial, social, and economic lines. None of us can run from it, because it's in our blood. It's even there in our love songs. Someone once said, "To understand the pain of unrequited love, one must first experience the pain of loving too well." Bobby Blue Bland's "You've Got to Hurt Before You Heal" is reminiscent of that.

Madly in love or simply mad, this is the kind of love that soul, pop, country, and even opera singers sing about. As for the latter, I challenge anyone to listen to Luciano Pavarotti's—or even Aretha Franklin's—rendition of "Nessun Dorma" from the opera *Turandot* and not be moved.[2] Good music does that to you.

As we drove back to Chicago, I thought about all of that, about what my life had been up until then; about how much I owed to those who came before me; about how far we had come as a nation and how much farther we had to go; about my life in music and politics. I began to see life with new, clear, and focused eyes. Mostly, I listened to voices from the past—voices from my generation—that implored me to tell their stories. I returned to Chicago and began to write.

JERRY BUTLER

Part I.

The Early Years

1.

The Beginning

I am fed up
With Jim Crow Laws,
People who are cruel
And afraid,
Who lynch and run,
Who are scared of me
And me of them.
I pick up my life
And take it away
On a one-way ticket—
Gone up North,
Gone out West,
Gone!

—"One-Way Ticket,"
a poem by Langston Hughes

Making My Grand Entrance

Two events that did not affect me directly did, however, have a profound impact on my mother and father when I was born: World War II and the Great Depression. When the armies of the Nazi Third Reich attacked Poland on September 1, 1939, three months before I was born, it caused a shock wave not only across Europe but throughout the rest of the world, even along the Yellow Dog River in Mississippi as I was preparing to make my grand entrance. Although the economic depression of the 1930s preceded the war in Europe by several years, the two events were intertwined, one a corollary to the other. Had Germany recovered economically from the first world war, there never would have been a second world war. Had there been no depression or world wars, I probably still would be living in Mississippi, earning a living as a sharecropper.

My parents were at the tail end of what has been called the "Great Migration" of African Americans who began leaving the South at the turn of the century to search for work in the northern industrial cities of Chicago, St. Louis, New York, and Philadelphia.

The Great Migration marked a major change in where African Americans chose to live in the United States. According to E. Marvin Goodwin, "In 1900, of the 8,883,994 African Americans living in the United States, only 911,025 (nearly ten percent) lived in the North. Most lived in the deep South—Georgia, Alabama, Texas, Mississippi, Florida, and the Carolinas. Due to rural poverty, racism, and segregation, men and women—young and old—began to set out for the promise of a better life in the cities of the North."[1]

The Discovery Channel's five-part documentary series *The Promised Land* estimates that some 5 million blacks moved up north from the South between 1940 and 1970. The documentary called the mass movement "the greatest peacetime migration in American history."

Many of the migrants were, like my mother and father, sharecropping farmers who picked cotton on large plantations and shared their meager earnings with plantation owners. Cheating was common. Add to that the segregated lifestyle that blacks had to endure and their lack of political power, and life in the South became not only intolerable but dangerous for most blacks.

Oddly, though, racism wasn't the main driving force behind the mass migration of hard-working African Americans to northern cities. It was a tiny insect from Mexico, the boll weevil, that forced the issue. This cotton-loving insect showed up in the South during the early 1900s and began devouring the cotton plant. In its wake, it staggered the South's cotton economy, finally destroying a way of life that had brought so much misery to so many.

Among those happy to see the demise of cotton was Ira Gates, my drummer for the past twenty-nine years. Ira grew up in Belzoni, Mississippi, and picked cotton from the age of nine until 1969, when he joined the Scott Brothers' blues band headed for Chicago.

"There are three seasons for cotton," Ira explained. "First, you plant it, then you chop it with a hoe. When you chop it with a hoe, you get blisters on your hand. After that, you pick it.

"A cotton ball is made like a ball. It opens up in the spring and kinda fluffs out like popcorn. The cotton ball itself is wedged inside a pod surrounded by sharp stickers. You have to run your finger down between each one of the stickers. They cut your fingers to hell. It's a painful ordeal.

"You start pickin' at six in the morning and work until six in the evening. Cotton is light as hell. You would be amazed at how much cotton it takes just to make a hundred pounds or even twenty. When I left Mississippi, some guys were pickin' two to three hundred pounds a day."

The boll weevil may have administered the coup de grâce to the southern way of life, but it was the gathering whirlwind of racism that finally uprooted the South's most precious seeds and blew them northward. The two forces, working together, were key in spurring the Great Migration, which in turn created a virtual explosion of black culture in northern urban ghettos. Among the blues artists who migrated up north to Chicago following World War II were Muddy Waters (1947), J. B. Lenoir (1952), Howlin' Wolf (1953), Elmore James (1953), Walter Horton (1954), and Sonny Boy Williamson (1955) —all from Mississippi. From other southern states came blues masters Little Walter (Louisiana, 1947), Robert Nighthawk (Arkansas, 1948), Johnny Shines (Memphis, Tennessee, 1950), Junior Wells (West Memphis, Arkansas, 1953), and Willie Nix (Memphis, Tennessee, 1953). All helped develop the Chicago "down-home" blues style, the closest link with the country blues of the Delta.[2]

The Chicago style, not to be confused with the more sophisticated Memphis-style blues, was influenced by people raised in both Memphis and the Delta.[3] They include Elmore James, who made his first records, accompanied by Sonny Boy Williamson, in Jackson, Mississippi, in 1952. He also spent some time in Willie Nix's band in Memphis, while alternating between Chicago and the Delta. Howlin' Wolf first recorded in Memphis in 1948, where he had some success as a singer and deejay before moving to Chicago in 1952. Sonny Boy Williamson was also popular in Memphis and the Delta as a singer and disc jockey. He recorded in Jackson, Mississippi, before going north. Both Willie Nix and Walter Horton recorded and performed in Memphis before going to Chicago. Most of the other Chicago down-home singers made their first records in that city.[4]

Recalling the oppressive social climate that precipitated our move to Chicago, Mama said, "We had to go. We had no choice." Things had gotten so bad, she said, that it was like walking on eggshells when black people were around whites. "No one knew what to say anymore."

What finally prompted them to take action was an incident involving a father-and-son doctor team. The way Mama tells it, Papa, who had a long-standing relationship with the elder doctor, was told to make an appointment with the nurse to see him the following week. "Just tell her that you want to see the old man," the venerable doctor said. He didn't want to confuse things with his son, who had recently begun his practice. When my father arrived for the appointment, he casually told the nurse that he wanted to see "the old man." Maybe it was the way Papa said it, but it definitely didn't go over well with the nurse or the other people in the office. To them, it was a serious breach of protocol. In those days, black people simply did not refer to whites as "the old man." You used "Mr. So and So" or "Doctor" or some other title of respect, never "the old man." To do so would suggest that you, a black man, were equal to a white man. People were lynched for lesser offenses. In Papa's case, he was refused service.

Ira Gates tells a more poignant story:

"I remember one time this policeman slapped my mother," he began. As he told the story, tears welled in his eyes. Even now, nearly fifty years later, you can see that the pain is still there.

It all started at the movies. "In those days the whites sat downstairs and the blacks upstairs," he said. "They would throw shit up at us and we would throw it back down. We couldn't see who was throwing it up, and they couldn't see who was throwing it down.

"One Saturday, this police thought that me and my brother had did it. He came to my house and asked my mother how long we had been home. She said all evening. She wasn't lying. But he kept on askin', kept on askin'. Then this sonofabitch just hauled off and slapped her.

"Can you imagine seeing a white man—any man—slapping your mother? My father couldn't do nothin' about it. If he had raised his hand, they woulda shot him Johnny on the spot. I swore then that if I ever got a gun, I was gon' kill the sonofabitch.

"I was raised up with that in me. When that honky died, I felt like I was cheated. I wanted to kill him myself. I'm not saying I hate white folks, but this was one I wanted to kill myself. He died from cancer. I was ten years old when he slapped my mother. I was a grown man when he died."

Ira was nearly thirty years old when he left Mississippi. I, on the other hand, had just turned three when my family—Mama, pregnant with my little brother William; Papa; my oldest sister, Dorothy; my youngest, Mattie; and me—packed everything we owned and joined the throng headed north.

Also fueling the exodus of blacks from the South were the steady stream of editorials in black-owned newspapers encouraging African Americans to "Go North! Go North!" The *Chicago Defender,* the most widely read black publication of the time, led the way. The *Defender,* which billed itself as the "World's Greatest Weekly," literally became the bible for black migrants seeking "The Promised Land."

Many of the migrants viewed Chicago and other northern cities almost in biblical terms, some of them going so far as to call Chicago "heaven."[5] It's understandable. For one thing, the two world wars had sparked an upsurge in factory jobs, creating a demand for black workers, especially black women, to fill in for the men who went off to Europe and Japan to fight. For another, the stench of Jim Crowism had not reached the North, although segregated housing patterns were the norm in northern, eastern, and western cities. Black people could actually own businesses in the North, and they could sit next to white kids in integrated schools and eat at the same restaurants as whites. They could even talk back to their white bosses without fear of being lynched or humiliated in front of their families and loved ones. To people who had known only subservience for most of their lives, the North indeed seemed like heaven.

We left Mississippi a year after President Franklin D. Roosevelt delivered his famous radio address formally announcing that America was at war with Japan. He made the announcement on my second birthday, December 8, 1941. "Yesterday, December 7, 1941—a date which will live in infamy," the president began his now-famous speech.

In leaving Mississippi, my parents left behind not only the bleak life of sharecropping, but the only life they had ever known. For some, like my mother, it was a bittersweet departure. On the one hand, she was about to embark on a journey whose ultimate destination would mean salvation for her family; on the other, she was leaving behind friends, family, and all that had made her who she was.

Jerry at four years old

Arvelia Butler

My values, my outlook on life, most of who and what I am today, can be attributed to my mother, Arvelia Agnew Butler, who I consistently went to for advice and counsel throughout my life, even into adulthood. My father died when I was fourteen years old. So it was left up to Mama to fend for us kids, counsel us, and teach us the ways of the world.

While I learned from Mama, she in turn attributed her values—and mine—to the Church of God in Christ (COGIC) "holiness" training she received at my great-grandfather's log cabin church located deep in the back-woods of Sunflower County, Mississippi. He called the church Evergreen. At Evergreen Mama accepted the Spirit, received the Holy Ghost, and became a "saint." In COGIC terms, you become a saint after a personal vision in which you actually feel the healing power of God. Mama never revealed when she actually accepted the Spirit, only where. Daniel Wolff's extraordinary book *You Send Me: The Life and Times of Sam Cooke* goes into more detail about COGIC, tracing the history of the church from its founding in 1895 as the Church of God to its heyday in 1937, when more than eighty black COGIC churches sprang up in the delta town of Clarksdale alone.[6] COGIC went on to become the largest black Pentecostal sect in the world. The Church of God, Mama explained to me once, is "half truth, and Church of God in Christ is the whole truth."

Mama was born April 28, 1910, in Monroe County, some forty miles from Tupelo. Her parents, Amos Monroe Agnew and Carrie Moore, were converted Baptists and devout members of COGIC.

The Agnews were from Alabama, and "anything people wanted to know," according to Mama, "they'd go and ask Uncle John Agnew, or John Bush," as most people in those parts referred to him. John Bush was on her father's side.

On her mother's side was Henry Moore, my great-grandfather, an erst-while Watusi chief who was robbed of his birthright by people quoting obscure biblical scripture as their moral authority for enslaving African people. "He was snatched at twelve years old," Mama said, describing how my great-grandfather was abducted from his small African village and brought to America. Signifi-cantly, in all my talks with Mama about my great-grandfather, I don't ever recall her referring to him as a slave, or herself, for that matter, as the grand-daughter of a slave. Alex Haley, in his famous book *Roots,* wrote that everyone in his family always referred to his great-grandfather as "the African" or "Kunta Kinte," never as a slave or former slave. I have my own opinion about this. I think it's because the elders knew that if they accepted the word "slave" it meant,

A rare opportunity to dance with an African princess. The occasion was one of my thirtysomething birthday parties. Princess Arvelia and I are joined by then Mercury president Irving Steinberg and his wife.

in effect, accepting the ultimate dehumanization of African people. To be a slave somehow got construed in the mind of the racist to mean that African people themselves were at fault for their predicament; that human sacrifices in the cotton fields of Mississippi were a small price to pay for an idealized southern way of life; that bondage in America was preferable to freedom in the Gambia or Ghana or Sierra Leone. To their credit, despite their lack of education and total cultural deprivation, my ancestors held on to their dignity, their pride in their heritage, refusing to give comfort to people like George Washington, this nation's first president, and Thomas Jefferson, author of the Declaration of Independence, who bought and sold human beings like cattle.

Henry Moore's father was a chief, and before his son was abducted, he gave him a necklace made of shark teeth, signifying that he was a prince, nobility. He wore the necklace around his waist. "I saw it," Mama said, even though he was "way on up yonder," her way of saying he was tall. "If I had been a boy, I would have been a prince, too. Instead, I was a princess. That's what he called me, his 'little princess.'"

The interesting thing about this is that several black families probably come from a royal African lineage:

> The commonly held notion that the population of the United States is derived from lower- or middle-class origins may be true enough for whites and Asians, but it is often not true for African Americans. Given the wide-branching nature of inheritance, by now a majority of black Americans may have the blue blood of African royalty and aristocracy mixed in their veins.[7]

When Mama was five years old, my great-grandfather gave her a watermelon for her birthday. "I never will forget that," she said, "because that's all he had to give. All of his possessions, all of his subjects, were in Africa." On that memorable day my grandmother had made Mama a "red-checked gingham dress with black buttons," and my great-grandfather brought in the watermelon from the fields. He said it was just for her. "When he cut open the watermelon, it was red with little black seeds to match my dress.

"But I fell out with him over it. He cut a small piece of that watermelon for me and gave the rest to the people. I had to sit there and watch all the other people eat. He told me, 'That's what an African princess has to do. She has to feed her people first.' The chief or the queen of the tribe had to support their people.

"I loved my granddaddy. Once, when I went to our family reunion, I looked for the bandanna he wore around his head. But they told me they threw it away."

Mama passed shortly before this book was finished. But I know she's still with us, feeding her people with her abundant spirit, whispering wisdom on the wind, enjoying the company of saints.

2.

Starting Over in Sweet Home Chicago

Hog Butcher for the world
Tool Maker, Stacker of Wheat,
Player with Railroads and the Nation's Freight Handler;
Stormy, husky, brawling,
City of the Big Shoulders.

—EXCERPT FROM CARL SANDBURG'S POEM "CHICAGO"

When we arrived in Chicago in the winter of 1942, the war was still raging in both Europe and Japan. Chicago, meanwhile, was enjoying a brief respite from what had become known as the "Capone era," a period in the city's history in which more than five hundred gangsters died violent deaths.

Al "Scarface" Capone, a former dishwasher from Brooklyn, New York, was twenty-one years old when he and his cousin Johnny Torrio arrived in Chicago to run the outlaw enterprises of their uncle, Big Jim Colosimo.[1] Their arrival coincided with the passage of the 18th Amendment in 1920, which prohibited the manufacture and sale of alcoholic beverages.[2] Capone, who served with the U.S. Army in France during World War I, was to amass an income estimated at $300 million a year by the late 1930s, mainly through a highly sophisticated—and deadly—bootlegging operation. By the end of the decade, Capone had consolidated his power and his hold on Chicago and nearby Cicero, Illinois, putting him in virtual control of all illegal activities. The *Chicago Daily News* estimated that Capone controlled more than six thousand speakeasies and two thousand bookies, and that his combined revenue from these and other illegal activities was estimated at $6.2 million a week.

When we arrived, Capone already had been successfully prosecuted for tax evasion and had served seven years in federal prison. He was released from Alcatraz on good behavior in 1939, suffering from neurosyphilis. He died from it on January 25, 1947.

Capone left his mark on Chicago, lasting to the present. It wasn't until 1983 and the election of Harold Washington, Chicago's first African-American mayor, that people abroad stopped identifying Chicago with Capone-era gangsterism. Seemingly overnight, Washington's election transformed the image of Chicago abroad from machine gun–toting gangsters going "ratta-tat-tat" to the cosmopolitan "City of the Big Shoulders" immortalized in Carl Sandburg's 1920 poem "Chicago."

Still, you cannot begin to put Chicago in historical perspective without at least acknowledging Capone's legacy of organized crime and influence peddling. Corrupt politicians and union bosses spawned by Capone's Prohibition era "mob" touched nearly every aspect of Chicago's day-to-day life, including the recording industry. Many a day I saw reputed mob figure Philip (Milwaukee Phil) Alderisio walking the halls of my first record company, Vee Jay Records. Why he was there, I don't know. I didn't ask.

At the height of his power, during the mid-1920s, legend had it that Capone was so brazen, so sure of himself, that he kidnapped fellow New Yorker Fats Waller, held him for three days at his Cicero hideout, and forced the derby-wearing piano man to perform exclusively for Capone and his henchmen. Fats was paid well for his inconvenience—one hundred dollars a song—a handsome sum in those days or any day.

When Capone went to jail, the organization that he had helped create suffered a few setbacks, but it eventually grew and prospered under Frank (The Enforcer) Nitti, Capone's successor. Nitti steered the organization into new activities: narcotics, business and labor racketeering, as well as the numbers, or "policy," rackets in black areas of the South and West Sides of the city.

In the years prior to the Great Depression, Chicago was especially attractive to indigenous black migrants and European immigrants because of the abundance of good-paying jobs. By the forties, Chicago had become the railroad capital of the nation and the home of the largest meatpacking companies. It also was the location of the world's first, and biggest, mail-order catalog companies, as well as the nation's printing center, and a leader in making steel. Men's clothing, machine tools, telephones, and farm equipment also were produced here.

Against this backdrop, a continuous influx of immigrants from Europe and black migrants from the South converged on Chicago, creating in the process a dynamic, culture-rich society. Chicago's Sicilian immigrants settled mostly in two neighborhoods: the Sedgwick Street area on the Near North Side, where my family also chose to settle; and the Near West Side Taylor Street area, aptly called "Little Italy," where my future wife's family settled. The Irish settled farther south in an area known as Canaryville. The Polish, like the parents of recording pioneers Leonard and Phil Chess, lived to the west, and Lithuanians were mostly to the north. The majority of black migrants, meanwhile, moved south to an area known as the Black Belt.

As these diverse groups of immigrants and migrants converged on the city, they built communities close to where they worked and where they were familiar with the people, the language, and the food. Sometimes these isolated neighborhoods would erupt in hostility between people in different communities. The Chicago riots of 1919 were among the bloodiest race riots in the nation's history. Twenty-three blacks and fifteen whites were killed following false reports that a black youth had been stoned to death at a beach in a predominantly Irish neighborhood. More than 290 people were wounded and maimed in five days of rioting.[3]

The riots created little, if any, disruption in the progress of Chicago toward its destiny: becoming one of the nation's largest industrial and training centers. Aircraft factories and shipyards, as well as military training facilities, proliferated. As hopeful workers flooded the city, the population grew to nearly 3 million by 1945, leading to Chicago's becoming known as the "Second City" after New York, with its nearly 8 million population. Housing and transportation facilities were scarce, resulting in the building of wartime public housing projects and passage of the first ordinances protecting African Americans against discrimination in housing and employment.

This was the climate in Chicago that cold December night in 1942 when our Illinois Central train pulled into Chicago's Grand Central Station.

❉

"Chicago!" the conductor yelled out as he stood in the doorway of the car. There was a lot of movement as people started getting their things together. Mama shook me, not knowing I was already awake. She began fussing over me the way mothers do when they are nervous about their child's appearance: pulling up my pants, pressing out the wrinkles in my shirt with her hands, and doing a general mop-up job with a tiny handkerchief from her purse.

Papa found a redcap who helped with our bags and put us all in a cab. "Eleven-oh-two North Sedgwick," Mama said to the cabbie. She did most of

Johnny and Pearlie Bennett, the uncle and aunt we lived with when we moved to Chicago

the talking and reading because she had a better education than Papa. And though he would never admit it, Papa's eyes were bad, giving him another reason to let Mama do all the reading and writing. Mama had gone only as far as the eighth grade, but when I recall all the things I learned from her and how she made my homework seem so easy, either she was a genius who did not have the opportunity to reach her potential, or the schools that I attended were poor in comparison to those one-room Mississippi schoolhouses where she received her education.

The cab pulled away and we were on our way to the home of Aunt Pearlie, one of my father's older sisters, who had moved to Chicago many years before.

I recall looking out the window of the cab and marveling at the seemingly millions of lights gleaming from the never-ending skyscrapers that touched the nighttime sky. It was magical! At age three, I certainly couldn't recall ever having seen anything so beautiful. A light snow had fallen the previous day, making the scene even more awe-inspiring.

Moments later, we arrived in the area where I was to live for most of my young life: the Near North Side of Chicago. Much has been written about my old neighborhood, the area known today as Cabrini Green. Bounded by Wells Street on the east, Larrabee on the west, Division Street on the north, and Chicago Avenue on the south, this small tract of land is where it all began for me. This is where I spent my formative years, where I learned the values that sustain me even today, where I found hope, made lifelong friends, went to school, fell in love, and nurtured my passion for cooking and music.

3.

Learning the Basics

Church of Emotion

My earliest recollections of music being performed live were of the church and tent revivals that Mama and Papa took us to. These services were of the Apostolic or Sanctified Church of God In Christ.

I remember this one night Mama had talked Papa into going to a revival meeting, probably hoping that he would get carried away with the service and join the church. The outing took on a very festive mood. Mama and Papa looked beautiful together. She was dressed in a long white dress, with white stockings and shoes, and her hair, hanging to her shoulders, was newly pressed. She wore no makeup except for powder, no lipstick, no rouge. Papa was dressed in his best blue serge suit. It had to be his best; it was his only suit, with a white shirt and tie, and the same light-gray hat he had worn the day we came from Mississippi. Mama had Mattie in her arms and I was holding Papa's hand as we crossed Oak Street.

As we went inside the tent, it seemed as if my mom and dad had been duplicated a hundred times. Most of the women were dressed in white, and all of the men were neatly dressed in dark suits. But to me, Mama and Papa looked the best.

On this particular night the Reverend Moncreif, a sixteen- or seventeen-year-old prodigy, was preaching. I didn't know what he was screaming and marching and wiping his face about, but Mama and the rest of the congregation must have understood it all, because they were waving their hands, crying, and shouting "Hallelujah!" "Yes, Lord!" and "Have mercy, Father!" after everything he said. Before long, the tent just exploded with music. There was a man whipping a guitar in a frenzy. And then there was this tall woman, dressed in a white robe, with a big cross around her neck. She would sing "I'm a soldier," and the audience would answer "in the army of the Lord." While she sang, she slapped a tambourine with one hand and shook it with the other, all the while stomping her feet. I was hypnotized by the rhythm created by the drums, the guitar, the hand-clapping and foot-stomping, and that tambourine. Soon people were shouting and jumping up and down and dancing in the aisles. Some people got so overcome that they actually passed out. The Reverend Moncreif started dancing close to one of the poles holding the tent up and shaking his head back and forth with such abandon that I cringed, thinking he might hit his head against a huge wooden pole in the middle of the tent. Mama was right in there with them, shouting hallelujah and jumping up and down.

It had gotten to Papa, too. I could see tears rolling down his cheeks. But that was all they would get from him that night.

Many years later, I realized what I had witnessed. That night these people had spiritually gone back to their African roots. Yes, the songs they were singing were about Christ—and in English—but the rhythms and the dances, the shouts and call responses between that woman and the congregation, were African. Imamu Amiri Baraka (LeRoi Jones) wrote about that in *Blues People:*

> The Negro church, whether Christian or "heathen," has always been a "church of emotion." . . .
>
> In Africa, ritual dances and songs were integral parts of African religious observances, and the emotional frenzies that were usually concomitant with any African religious practice have been pretty well documented, though, I would suppose, rarely understood.[1]

✸

My introduction to secular music began in the neighborhood surrounding Wells Street, which was an exciting place even in those days. It was loaded with taverns, pool halls, policy players (numbers runners), pimps, whores, and other wild life. There was even a taxidermist down near Oak Street and Wells. I laugh at myself now, having long since discovered that a taxidermist has nothing at all to do with cabs or transportation.

Every Saturday night along Wells you could see, for the price of a drink, Muddy Waters, Howlin' Wolf, Lightnin' Hopkins, and other blues greats who, after years of doing it for blacks, were being discovered by the nouveau hip rock society. The difference between Wells and Sedgwick Streets was small, except that on Sedgwick there were no taverns, and the only music I remember on this street usually came from a loudspeaker outside the little record shop across the street from our apartment building. Or from the radio, with disc jockeys Jack L. Cooper and Al Benson, who played everything from gospel to jazz. WLS-AM, meanwhile, played country music and directed its programming to the "prairie farmer."

❊

Papa found a bigger apartment in Old Town, Chicago's version of New York's Greenwich Village, San Francisco's Haight-Ashbury, London's West End, and Paris's Left Bank. Old Town was the meeting place and home of Chicago's literati, intellectuals, artists, and musicians, who on any given day could be found in nearby Bug House Square haranguing over everything from Bach to Bird, from Marx to Martin Luther. The blustery Bohemian lifestyle gave the neighborhood vibrancy and its own unique character. It was the ideal setting for someone like Ernestine B. Curry, my fifth grade teacher at James A. Sexton School.

Mrs. Curry, a disciplinarian but real down-to-earth, was extremely proud of her African heritage and spoke proudly of it long before it was popular and fashionable to do so. She taught everything—math, English, music, history, etiquette, and even how to box, which in our neighborhood was just as important as the three R's. I appreciate her so much more now because she taught the black history curriculum that so many high school and college students are crying for now. For example, she made it mandatory for everyone to read the works of Countee Cullen and W. E. B. DuBois and other great black writers. We also learned about the achievements of Mary McLeod Bethune, Prince Hall, George Washington Carver, Booker T. Washington, Nat Turner, Duke Ellington, Louis Armstrong, Jack Johnson, the famous and notorious. Mrs. Curry gave us a sense of pride and dignity that has carried me and many other of her students through life. I was sad to learn recently that she passed away in 1990.

As I look back now, I can see how I was exposed to more types of music than children are now. The age of specialized radio had not taken hold then, and stations played a little bit of everything: Louis Armstrong, Louis Jordan, Sarah Vaughn, Ella Fitzgerald, Big Mabelle, Frank Sinatra, Nat King Cole, Billy Eckstine, Homer and Jethro, Tex Ritter, Paul Whiteman, Kate Smith, Hank Williams, and, of course, the Five Blind Boys, Brother Joe May, and the music of the Harmonizing Four, and all the great gospel groups, known and unknown.

Overall, going to school was fine, except for a dude named James, the neighborhood bully, who used to take my lunch money, bust me in the nose, and all that stuff. I finally got tired of it and smacked him upside the head with a handle from a cast iron stove. I have to confess, though, that even after that I was afraid of him, because I didn't know if, when, or how he would try to get even.

Running Buddies

Fred Jeter became my first real running partner. He was a year or so older than me, but we were in the same grade. And then there was Fred Hudson. We became such good friends that we used to lie about being related. Both Freds were light-skinned, but Jeter differed from Hudson only in terms of size: Jeter was short and skinny, and Hudson was nearing six feet and husky. At twelve years of age, it made Hudson a definite attraction to girls and a distraction to anybody who wanted to get down wrong.

I was about eleven or twelve when I started thinking about sex in any real sense. Running with these guys, chasing the girls and whatnot, was really the beginning of my coming of age. All of a sudden we were thinking about big pretty bikes, which neither of us could afford, so we had to get jobs.

I got a job working with Bobby Faulkner, who lived a couple doors from me, delivering papers over on the Gold Coast, so named because it is probably the most exclusive neighborhood in Chicago, comparable to New York's Park Avenue. Today, most of the mansions that once graced the area have been replaced by high-rises. I mainly delivered papers in the Drake Hotel and other luxury high-rises overlooking the lake.

When I took the job, I really thought Bobby was a great friend—that is, until I realized it was December. There ain't no place in Chicago, or in the world, I think, much colder than Lake Shore Drive on a winter night in Chicago, at about 6:00 P.M., and all you have is a wagon and about three hundred newspapers to deliver.

That same year I went to summer school, not because I had to, but because there wasn't too much else to do. I only had to go to class for half a day for six weeks in order to advance a half-grade. The following year, like most of the guys in my age group, I became very clothes- and girl-conscious, which I guess was the reason for the sharp clothes in the first place.

Knowing that Mama and Papa couldn't afford to do much more than they were doing already, I lied about my age and got a Social Security card. It wasn't difficult, because I was big for my age, and for some reason I always acted older than I really was. Both Freds were two or three years older than me, so it was natural for me to act their age rather than my own. After I got my card, with Mama's permission, I took a couple of days out of school and went job hunting.

I went to an employment agency, which promptly sent me to this plastics company that was growing so fast the owners were working day and night to fill orders. They were so anxious for help that, even though I looked too young, the guy hired me anyway. The job paid about $75 a week. I worked the evening shift, from four until twelve midnight, five days a week, and was paid time and a half for working on Saturdays.

So there I was, going on thirteen, running a plastic injection lathe, making soap dishes and plastic in my sleep. I had nice clothes, but nobody saw them, except at school and on Sundays; the rest of the time I was working.

I kept the job for about three months and quit—not because the work was too hard; I just got bored with working eight hours a night and on weekends while all my friends were having fun. Fred Jeter's sister, Frances, was about to get married, and her fiancé, Joe Saffold, needed a job. I took him to work and introduced him to my boss, who promptly gave Joe my job. When I quit, Papa hit the ceiling. I thought he was very inconsiderate at the time, but now I understand. After all, there he was, a man who needed the kind of work I was doing, but couldn't get it because he could neither write nor read; and there I was, with the education he needed, walking off a good-paying job because I wanted to play.

In March 1953, I took another full-time job working at night. This time it was to help my folks out. The job was in a dingy mattress factory, where I packed mattresses and Hollywood-style beds.

One night a young man was hired to help me pack the mattresses. It was his first night there, and since he was about eighteen years old and the only other young person in the place, we struck up an immediate friendship. His name was Terry Williams, but everybody called him T.C. I never knew what the C was for.

Some nights later, T.C. and I were talking about the things we enjoyed, and he told me that he used to sing with this group of guys on the West Side. I told him I enjoyed singing, too. About two or three weeks later, he invited me to go to his church.

Sunday rolled around, and we went to a little church in the heart of the West Side. It was in the basement of an apartment building on a little side street about a block east of Western Avenue. The building was painted blue, and on the front window, in big white letters, were the words "Traveling Souls Spiritualist Church." When we got there it was about five or six o'clock, and the day's services had long since been over. That night, however, they had planned a special service.

As T.C. and I entered, a few people who had remained were milling around talking and just having a good time in general. There was a little potbellied stove in the back of the church and a door behind, which I guessed to be the toilet.

There were maybe forty or fifty seats facing the pulpit, with about four or five chairs behind the rostrum. Off to the right of the pulpit were five or six more chairs, and over by them were some young guys sitting around talking to an older man, who was about 6'2" and rather stocky for his height. His name was Charles Hawkins, Sr. The youngest of the group, who appeared to be about fifteen, turned out to be Charles Hawkins, Jr. The others were Tommy and Eddie Hawkins, who looked to be about seventeen. I found out later that Tommy and Eddie had been adopted by this wonderful family.

When we reached them, they began hugging T.C. and making a fuss over him. I could see he was embarrassed. The woman's name was Mercedes Hawkins, Mr. Hawkins's wife. Another woman walked over proudly, with her fist balled up, and thumped T.C. on the chest. As she hugged him, she fought back tears. Her name was Annabelle, but she was better known as the Reverend A. B. Mayfield, the mother of Mercedes Hawkins, the natural grandmother of Charles Hawkins, Jr., and the pastor of the Traveling Souls Spiritualist Church.

In a few moments, everyone in the church had surrounded us, and T.C. began introducing me: "This is Annabelle" (which was what her family and all her friends called her), "This is Mercedes," "This is . . ." Among those I met that day was a nine-year-old kid whose name would forever be linked with mine— Curtis Mayfield.

After the excitement of seeing T.C. again had passed, they all went back to what they had been doing before we arrived. I wound up in a corner of the room with T.C., Charles Sr. and Jr., Tommy, and Buddy (which was Eddie's nickname). After a while we began singing spirituals and having great fun. Before I knew it, it was eleven o'clock and everyone was saying good night and heading for home.

In the months that followed, I was at the Hawkins home almost every moment of my free time, having become a permanent member of the group and the family. In fact, I was with these people so much that Mama started to complain. But Papa said, "They seem like good people, and if the boy is singing, hell, he can't get into any trouble." Mama held her peace and I kept singing.

Traveling Souls Spiritualist was really an appropriate name for the congregation because we were always going somewhere. "Uncle Charles kept us running," said Curtis, recalling those halcyon days at his grandmother's church. "Whether we were in the city or on the road, we were moving quite a bit. We were running, playing the cities, trying to keep our little group up." We traveled, on a bus purchased by the church, to places such as Detroit, Cleveland, Louisiana, and, in the summer of 1953—when I should have been graduating from summer school—Tampa, Florida. Mama had a fit about me going so far away from home at age thirteen. But Papa said, "Let the boy go and see some of the world while he has the chance."

So, with $60 I had saved, I got on board the bus. I didn't need the money because the church paid for everything, and with me being one of the lead singers in the quartet, I had to go. It was a long ride on the bus, but for a boy of thirteen it was a great adventure.

On the way to Tampa we stopped at a little roadside fruit stand, where I met one of the most beautiful girls I have ever seen. I can still see her even now, in that pink dress that had little, if anything, under it.

We arrived in Tampa early in the morning, and as we drove through the downtown area, a group of white boys looking for trouble threw things at the bus, made faces, and called us "sanctified niggers." It was my first experience with the callousness and ignorance that characterized the attitudes of some southern whites toward blacks from the North.

We were in Tampa to attend the National Spiritualist Convention, which was held at the Pallbearers Union Hall. We sang every night. It was the first time I experienced how a guy doing any kind of singing, in any kind of limelight, could attract pretty girls who would to do anything, even have sex with you, just to say they were in your company.

The local black boys in Tampa proved just as callous and ignorant as the white boys. They seemed to know only one phrase: "You ain't shit, man." Overall, though, the trip to Tampa was something I would not have missed for the world. The good times far outnumbered the bad.

I brought a lot of gifts back from Tampa, and I was going to really put on a show for the whole family, including Dorothy's kids, Margaret and George, who were raised in our house and were treated as our sister and brother. But in my hurry to get home and tell of my adventures, I left all the stuff in a cab. I cried.

❊

The following September, I entered the freshman class at Washburne High School. Located on the corner of Division and Sedgwick Streets in Chicago, Washburne was one of the most highly accredited vocational high schools in the city. And though it was in a predominantly black neighborhood, it was attended mostly by whites.

One reason for this was that the school had only one team sport, basketball, and most black students went to Wells High School, which had teams in almost every sport. There were only 9 black students in my freshman class of about 140. The student body numbered approximately 1,000; of those, probably fewer than 200 were girls.

I was assigned to Division 132, a print shop. Mr. Trautwein, the division teacher, was a tall German with a very thin face and deep-set eyes. He walked slump-shouldered and seemingly glided down the halls. He made it very clear that he was not going to tolerate our cutting classes and being late. He informed us that he would help anyone who wanted to learn, and that he would help get rid of anyone who didn't.

Howard Toney, Curtis Cade, James Lowe, and Thomas Morgan were the other black guys in my division. Coming from the same general background, we eventually gravitated toward one another. Curtis and James were sixteen and were there to learn a trade. They would be twenty when they graduated. Thomas Morgan was fourteen and, like me, told everyone he was older because being young was square.

Curtis and Thomas lived on the West Side, near Homan and Carroll Avenues, just down the street from the Smiths, my future in-laws. James lived across the street from me on Wells. Howard lived across the street from the school. Thomas, Curtis, James, and I became the problem students right away, just by each of us trying to appear hipper, badder, and gutsier than the other three. Each of us, in the first semester, had to bring our parents to school, and we each got suspended about the same number of times.

I was still singing at the Traveling Souls Spiritualist Church, where we had formed a quartet called the Northern Jubilee Gospel Singers.

4.

Reality Sets In

Coming of Age

A week before school let out for the summer, June 14, 1953, I was getting ready for bed when the phone rang. It was Aunt Pearlie. "You'd better come quick!" she told Mama. "J.T. is sick!"

Later, her eyes red from crying, Mama sat down on my bed and said, "Junior, your daddy is dead."

It didn't register at first. All I knew was that Mama was crying, and that was enough. Everyone in the house was up now. Dorothy was crying. So were William and Mattie. Oddly, even with all that crying going on and people moving about, the voices sounded as though they were in an empty house. There was an echo of screams. Relatives appeared; the phone began a constant ring; everything was strange, and everybody, seemingly, was a stranger.

The man who we'd seen only passing through on his way from one job to the next (he worked two jobs most of his life) would not be passing through anymore. I realized there would not be any more hymns at 5:30 in the morning. No more "Get a good education, son," and "Don't grow up to be dumb like me." No more "I'm working my ass off and y'all just want shit like money grows on trees." No more "Y'all gonna miss me when I'm gone." No more "Boy, you ain't got enough sense to pour pee out of a boot and the directions right on it say 'turn up.'" No more "Take your hands out of your pockets, son. You'll never get to be a man with your hands in your pockets." No more "Pray that God lets me live 'til Junior's fourteen. He'll be able to handle it then."

Perhaps God was impatient. I was thirteen and a half when Papa died. The hospital said Papa died as a result of coronary thrombosis, a massive heart attack. But I think he died of a broken heart, stemming from his frustrations at being uneducated and unable to give his family all the things he wanted them to have.

At Papa's funeral, a long line of cars followed the big black hearse from Johnson's Funeral Home. Mama and Mattie sat in the back of a black Cadillac limousine, crying. Dorothy was crying, too. William looked confused. I don't recall if I cried at Papa's funeral, but I do recall trying to sort things out: What was the meaning of death? Where do you go when you die? Was Papa in heaven? It was my first experience with death, and I probably handled it badly.

Two weeks after Papa was laid to rest, I awoke to see him standing at my bedroom door. He spoke to me: "I'm going to work now. You take care of your Mama and your brother and your sisters." I do remember crying then. Mama said I saw him in a dream. Maybe she was right. But at the time, it seemed awfully, awfully real.

Everything was coming apart: Papa's Social Security check got held up along with his insurance, pension, and welfare funds from his job at Illinois Central Railroad. Bill collectors started banging at our door. And the welfare folks were asking a lot of questions. Mama, still grieving, didn't know what to do.

Shortly before Papa died, my oldest sister, Dorothy, had married Andrew Clark, nicknamed "Tee," a short, muscular man with hands like hams and feet to match. After the funeral, Dorothy and Tee moved in with us to help out. Aunt Pearlie and Uncle Johnny offered their help, too. I remember them telling Mama, "As long as we can eat, y'all can eat." Tee, with his big hands and his big heart, said, "Don't y'all worry." I imagine every family goes through these defining moments following the death of a loved one, where someone steps up to be strong. In my family, Tee, Dorothy, Aunt Pearlie, and Uncle Johnny were the strong ones who held things together while the rest of us got our bearings.

Still, I was confused, scared. I had to become a man quick—not next year, not tomorrow—right then. Where was that job that pays $75 a week and time and a half on Saturday? Why are these people taking away furniture that was nearly paid for? Why does Mama cry herself to sleep at night? Why did we move to a place where the houses are built so close together? Why did Papa pray to live until I was fourteen?

Being fourteen is difficult enough for most people, but for me it was hell. At best, my condition could be described as being caught in some kind of limbo, where I was either too old for this or too young for that. And all of it was compounded by the fact that most of my friends thought I was sixteen or seventeen, causing me to lie a lot. Not only that, I had a super chip on my shoulder.

To top everything off, the racism at Washburne had become oppressive. And no one personified that more than Mr. Hamilton, a music teacher who nearly turned me against music. I loved music, but I hated his class. Many of the black students in the class felt the same way, particularly Joe Brackenridge. Joe had an excellent voice and played piano as well by ear with one or two fingers as anybody I've ever heard. He played with two fingers because he had lost two of his other fingers in a machine shop accident at Washburne.

The reason Joe didn't like music period was that he, like the rest of the black students in the class, was forced to sing old racist standards like "Old Black Joe," "Swanee River," and "My Old Kentucky Home," songs that glorified an era that blacks—especially young blacks—wanted to forget. We all felt that those songs were out of step with the times. We believed that Mr. Hamilton favored those types of songs for racist reasons rather than to teach a musical style. Almost every black in his course started cutting the class.

Music period wasn't a total loss. We would go in the boys' room and sing all the latest doo-wops and listen to our voices bounce off the tile and porcelain. Thomas Morgan sang bass, Curtis Cade tenor, Joe Brackenridge tenor and lead. I sang baritone and lead.

It was during this period that I learned that if you really wanted to sing lead, all you had to do was sing out of key in the background. When the rest of the group got tired of singing your note to you, someone would say, "Hey, you sing lead and I'll sing your part to you." At least that's the way it was until they realized what I was doing. Just for kicks, we called ourselves the Toileteers. It was our own private joke.

Miss Ridge

As I reflect on it now, had it not been for my young age and Miss Ridge, I might never have finished high school. Miss Ridge was a little red-haired Irish lady in her thirties, who tried to be tough but always gave herself away by show-ing genuine concern for some reason. We became good friends, I think partly because she made me feel great when I accomplished something and, I guess, in a real sense, because in her class we got to read poetry, which at the time was a thing that I really dug.

One day she came up with the idea of starting a school newspaper, and because of our friendship and my straight A's, I was drafted as editor. That was really a psych on me because now I had to straighten out my act all over the place. As editor of the paper, it wouldn't look right for me to be in trouble. Fur-thermore, how could she justify my being editor of the paper to Mr. Portal and Mr. Moehle, the assistant principal, if I kept getting into trouble? Thus be-gan the rehabilitation of Butler, which was what I was called by students and teachers alike.

By the time I was going into the end of my sophomore year, I was getting A's and B's in most of my subjects. The one subject I wasn't too keen on this time was auto shop, which I was supposed to take for two periods. Those were two free periods for me, and it was strange but it was one of the few classes I had to cut alone, because for some reason all my buddies really dug auto shop.

Mr. Forestier

I guess if it hadn't been for Mr. Forestier, I would know a lot more about cars than I do today. Mr. Forestier was the instructor of the culinary arts class at Washburne. At that time, part of Washburne was attended by adults under the GI Bill. Classes in lithography operations, cabinetmaking, carpentry, ma-sonry, and culinary arts were offered under this program.

Mr. Forestier was a portly man in his early fifties who wore this three-foot-high chef's hat, checkered pants, a white cotton double-breasted jacket, and an apron with towels tied around it. And when he walked fast, as he always did, the apron and towels would flap up and down, giving him the appearance of a strange fat bird about to take flight.

Once, while I was cutting auto class and roaming the halls, I stopped over by the chef's training school. I was digging what they were doing when Mr. Forestier busted me. I started to run when I saw him coming, but it was too late.

"Hey, you, boy! What're you standing outside this door for?"

"Oh, nothing. I was just looking."

"Well, if you really want to look, come in and take a good look."

I went in. "This is a chef's school," he said, as he gave me the cook's tour. "These men are all learning to cook—not like you cook at home, but for hotels and fancy restaurants and ships. They'll spend two years here and cook their own meals, make up their own menus, wash their own pots and dishes, and pay for anything they mess up."

There were two black men in the class, and they only had half a year to go before graduation. After he had shown me the whole thing, he asked where I was supposed to be. He said he had seen me hanging around outside the door before, and that was why he asked me in. We spoke for a while, and he asked me if I would like to spend the time I was supposed to be in auto shop in his class. I said yes, and he took me to the principal's office.

Mr. Portal, the principal, after a long discussion, asked me to bring Mama to school. I did, and he explained to her that I would have to pay $30 a month, which was what all the GIs paid to cover the cost of the food and stuff used in learning the trade.

Mama was agreeable to everything, but wasn't quite sure where the money would come from. I told her I would earn the money, and I took a part-time job at the YMCA.

Mr. Forestier never paid any special attention to me, which I thought kind of strange, since I was the first high school student ever allowed to take that particular course.

Most of the men in the place called me "young blood." That was cool, because being fresh back from the Army and all, they had slang names for everyone and everything. For instance, Mr. Forestier was the "old man"; creamed chipped beef was "shit on a shingle"; hors d'oeuvres were "whores de ovaries"; and cream of potato soup was "cream of pot [marijuana] soup."

Danny Terlikowski, who I met in the class, used to crack up about all that. Danny, a couple of years older than me, became a real good friend. We had a lot of fun.

Mr. Forestier was used to dealing with cutups, though, and whenever we got out of line, he would be there with his jaws hung in our buns. He didn't bother with threats having to do with the principal or sending for Mama or suspension. He just gave us a good old-fashioned ass chewing.

"You boys asked to come here," he would say, "but while you're here, you will do what I say and shake your asses doing it! And if you don't like that, you can get the hell out of here, because there are other people who would like to take advantage of my knowledge. I have no time for foolishness."

His ears and nose would get red, and you knew he wasn't jiving about his knowledge or his time. He had gold cups and trophies from three or four World's Fairs and cooking competitions. He was a master at his craft. Most of the major hotels in Chicago were waiting in line to pick off students from his classes. Eddie Doucette, then chef at the Drake Hotel, Chicago's finest, would often come to our class and lunch with us. The chef's school is now located over on Kedzie Avenue near 35th Street. I don't know if Mr. Forestier is still there or not. Maybe I'll run by one of these days and see.

Lawson YMCA

The job I took to help pay that $30 a month tuition was gotten for me by my Aunt Juanita, the sister next in age to my mother. Aunt Juanita had been working at the Lawson YMCA ever since she ran away from her husband, Harry, sometime around 1947 or 1948. She was a beautiful woman, with a heart as big as they come. She had a hearty laugh and could curse as good as anybody.

I'm told that in her youth she could fight pretty good, too, typified by the night she, Aunt Sarah, and my sister Dorothy went to this bar and some man tried to pick them up. Legend has it that the man kept pestering them, and Aunt Juanita became so enraged that she picked him up and threw him behind the bar.

She got me a job as a busboy in the cafeteria of Lawson Y. It was a pretty easy gig, and because she was there watching, I wanted her to be proud of me. I knew she was going to report to Mama, so I worked hard and fast. Pretty soon I was working on the dishwashing machine. From there I graduated to the garbage room to pot washer to cook's helper level. This was simple cooking for working-class people. What I was learning at school was an art.

The one thing I hated most about working at the Lawson Y was that it cut into my staying on the basketball team. Coach Podraza was never too enthused about my playing because I was too short for a forward and too slow for a guard, but usually when we were far out in front or hopelessly behind, he would put me in. Most of the time it was because we were behind. We were in the same division as Wells, Crane, and Marshall High Schools, which were the basketball powers when I was in high school. The only reason we even looked respectable against them was because of a man named Hosie Thurmond, who for his height, a mere 6'2", was probably the best center in the city. If Hosie had studied harder, he probably would have been a basketball star.

The biggest kick I ever had in high school sports was the day we played Gordon Tech. I think I scored 14 or 16 points. But the *Chicago Sun-Times* got me and a guy named Archie Butler mixed up and credited me with 26 points. I got my name and picture in the paper as a result. The mix-up occurred because I played on the freshman team that won. Archie played on the varsity team that lost. I didn't care, because my name and face were in the *Sun-Times* sports section. What was a real drag, though, was after I quit the team to go to work, Washburne began recruiting some fine sisters for cheerleaders. Rah! Rah! Rah!

✤

Both Tommy and Eddie Hawkins were army crazy. I mean crazy. Eddie was in the R.O.T.C. and the National Guard. Tommy was just in the National Guard because he had dropped out of school. It looked like a lot of fun, and I was sixteen and you only have to be seventeen to join. One more lie wouldn't hurt, so I talked with Mama. She said it was okay if I wanted to go, so I lied about my age, forged Mama's signature, and joined the 178th Infantry Battalion, D Company, at 35th and Giles.

Tommy took me to my first drill. I looked on in awe as several contingents of recruits, toting M-1 rifles and carbines, marched in cadence. Here and there, smartly dressed officers and enlisted men snapped curt, efficient orders in commanding voices. I didn't know what was going on, but it sure was fun. I remember thinking, I'm going to have all this fun every Wednesday night from now on and get paid $33.50 every three months on top of it. Wow!

One of my most vivid memories of Guard practice, after I settled into a routine, was when this little man and I were racing to the water fountain. He beat me but I was bigger, so I pulled him away and drank first. Suddenly I went into a whirl. Something had happened. What's this, I'm on my ass and he's drinking water? When he finished drinking, he turned to help me up—me, The Butler! I found out later that I had challenged the judo instructor. That little episode taught me that the measure of a man is not related to his size, but to his skill, his knowledge, his will, his faith.

On Memorial Day 1956, my battalion, the 178th, was standing at the corner of Wacker Drive and Michigan, getting ready for a parade. I was as sharp as can be: fatigues starched so stiff they could stand alone; creases like Gillette blue blades; combat boots shined to perfection; snow-white undershirt; helmet at just the right angle—low enough to be hip but not low enough to get chewed out about. Later, after marching about a mile, sweat and starch started making the inside of my thighs burn and itch. Sweat was in my eyes, but I couldn't wipe or break my stride. The nine-pound gun on my shoulder was beginning to feel more like ninety pounds. I started thinking, What if I were marching into combat with a full pack in this heat, with my feet and eyes burning and itching, and me scared to scratch? I think that day I fell out of love with the whole idea of war and soldiering.

In July we went on bivouac. It was a real gas, with the police escort through the city by big green trucks, followed by other big green trucks loaded with soldiers, ammo, and guns of every type. Following these were jeeps with commanding officers speaking into walkie-talkies. It reminded me of my childhood, when I used to fashion makeshift walkie-talkies out of wood and broomsticks, tin cans, and string.

Bivouac was held somewhere in Illinois, and it was a real army-style weekend thing, replete with KP duty, guard duty, rifle range—in short, the works. On the range I had to fire one round from a standing position and one from a prone position.

The commanding officer pointed to me. "I want you to disassemble that rifle," he said. "By the time I walk from where you are to the end of this line and back to where you are, I want you to tell me every part in that rifle and have it reassembled."

"Yes, sir!" I bellowed. Under my breath I mumbled, "Asshole."

He must have had rabbit ears. "What's that, soldier?"

"Nothing, sir!"

Somehow I managed the dismantling and reassembling in the specified time. "Okay, soldier, let's see some shooting," he said. "Standing position!" My eye on the target, I squeezed the trigger. He shouted, "Maggie's drawers!" Wait a minute, sucker, this was The Butler shooting. Obviously something I had no control over had gone wrong. I shot again and again. Each time he shouted, "Maggie's drawers!" I hadn't hit the target yet! Damn!

"Would you like to move the target a little bit closer, sonny?" Ashamed and furious, I grunted, "No, sir."

"Well, what if we make the bullet a little bigger?"

"No, sir. I'll get it, sir, I'll get it."

"You'll get your damn head blown off if you don't hold that gun right," he said, continuing to ride me. "Squeeze that trigger, don't jerk it. All right, son, go mark targets."

More than a little pissed off, I managed to say, "Yes, sir." "Keep your head down," he said, fatherly.

We were marking targets and this one guy was lying down behind the target, sleeping or pretending to be asleep. The sergeant came by, saw him, and shouted, "Soldier, get up from there before a bullet ricochets off the pole and kills your ass!"

"Yes, sir," replied the soldier, but as soon as the sergeant left, he went back to his same position. As if the sergeant had had a vision, a bullet ricocheted off the pole and put a hole right through the soldier's helmet. Frightened, the soldier started running in the direction of the lake, near the range, and right into the line of fire. The sergeant tackled him and beat the shit out of him and dragged him back to the barracks.

Wow! Just like a movie! Wait until I tell Mattie and William about this!

✺

Annabelle bought a church and a building in the Lawndale district on Lawndale Boulevard, just south of Roosevelt Road on the West Side of the city. As usual, I was in on the moving and everything. By now, one of Annabelle's grandsons by her son Curtis had joined the group. Like his dad, he was named Curtis, and he was an exceptional talent. But no one was quite sure how exceptional or how talented. All we knew was that one day, while cleaning out a closet, he found this old beat-up guitar, and in a few weeks' time he was playing "Jingle Bells" and other songs by ear. Inside of three or four months he could play every song we knew, plus he had this great tenor voice. When he hooked up with us, the Northern Jubilee Singers took on a new dimension.

Among my fondest memories from the gospel era were the gatherings that were held in a little storefront building, a union hall somewhere around 48th and State Street. The president of the union was a beautiful old man that every-one called Brother Watts. On any Sunday night at the union hall you might hear, depending on who was in town, the Blind Boys; the Soul Stirrers, fea-turing Sam Cooke; the Pilgrim Travelers; the Bells of Joy; or maybe even the newest singing sensation then, a fourteen-year-old contralto who was the lead singer for a family known as the Staple Singers. I never, in my wildest dreams, imagined that these superstar singers and I would someday become the best of friends.

There was one group, however, which was as good as any of them, but for some reason never went much farther than Chicago. They were the Morning Glory Singers, and the lead singer, a man named Rice, had a voice so stirring he could raise you out of your seat by just humming. He was truly a great singer.

Not long after Annabelle moved to the Lawndale area, I became interested in other things and stopped going to church as often. Pretty soon I stopped going altogether.

In fall 1956, I started singing rhythm and blues and took advantage of every opportunity I could to sing.

✺

The first rhythm and blues group I joined was composed of Willie Wright, his brother James "Doolaby" Wright, and Ronald Sherman. We called ourselves the Quails and had as good a sound as any other group, but we always had this problem of finding a good bass singer.

One day, Ronald told us about this guy who lived on the West Side named Earl Smith, who was a dynamite bass singer. So one Saturday we went over to check him out, and sure enough, he was pretty good, and we struck up a pretty good friendship—one, because he was a nice guy, and, two, because he had two fine sisters. Annette, the oldest, was friendly and always tried to make you feel at home. The other sister, Mabel, was nice too, plus she had a great voice.

After the Quails broke up, I tried to get Earl and his two sisters involved in a group. Their dad was all for it, because he was a frustrated musician who played piano and a fair blues guitar. He was very proud of the fact that at one time he had jammed with Nat King Cole and his trio.

For the first couple of weeks, everybody was all for rehearsing, but after a while they were busy, not at home, or something, so I spent a great deal of time talking about music with their dad. He gave me every encouragement and really got mad at his children because they didn't want to rehearse. This whole situation was another lesson. If you really want to blow it with your friends, let your friends' parents start telling them how smart you are and, conversely, how dumb their children are. You can hang it up then. Pretty soon I gave up on them musically, but I would return for social visits because I really liked Annette.

After they fizzled out, the only time I saw them was at the Greater Mt. Sinai Baptist Church on Sunday, and sometimes at choir rehearsal. The choir was known as the Crusaders, and the late James Cleveland was choir director. We also would have occasional visits from Mahalia Jackson, who was a dear friend of the pastor, the Reverend George Washington Jones, and his wife, Willa Saunders Jones. The Crusaders were formed by the Smith family: Annette, Earl, Mabel, and Willie Keys, a member of the church and a very dynamic young singer. The Crusaders also played a very meaningful role in the Passion Plays given by Willa Saunders Jones every Easter under her direction.

One night, after work, I was listening to "Jam with Sam" on WGES Radio, and I heard a song that sounded awfully familiar: "If love is wrong, why was it gave to man?"

I turned the volume up. Yeah, that's the song I wrote with the Quails, and that's Willie Wright singing lead. I'm happy enough to cry as well as sad enough to cry. That's my song, my arrangement, and don't nobody know it but me and those bastards. They stole it. They could have told me! They could have told me! So I cried, not because I was jealous, but because I had been shot down by guys who I believed were friends.

Later, Ronald Sherman and Willie apologized and said that when the opportunity came up, the man with the money said he didn't want to get the whole group back together. He told them, "Just you four guys will do." And that's how it got recorded.

They played the record only a couple of weeks. It wasn't that good a song or a record. But it was my song and they were playing it on the radio, and I knew everybody in Chicago listened to Sam Evans and his old beat-up orange crate—everybody black, that is.

❁

In my senior year the student body was about 65 percent white and 35 percent black. But the black guys were really ripping off the white guys for their lunch money. They had students paying protection dues and all kinds of stuff like that, and it was getting mean. For a while I even got caught up in it. It was easy. The white guys were so scared of getting beat up by now that if you were smiling, you stood a good chance of getting fifty cents.

I was editor of the school paper and vice president of the school student body. So when the rip-off reached crisis proportions, Mr. Portal and Mr. Moehle decided they'd better have a meeting with who they thought to be the black spokespersons. I was called into a meeting along with Howard Toney, Ezekiel Morris, and about six other black students. When I walked into the meeting, I knew that it was a slap in the face, because not one white student had been invited, and in essence what the principal was saying was, "You niggers were messing up, and how can we stop you?"

Always ready to tell my side, I popped right up. "First thing, Mr. Portal," I said, "if we are going to straighten out the school's racial problems, look at it from both sides of the fence. I mean, while you're so concerned about what's happening to the white kids, what about the fact that you've got black kids in a room full of whites singing 'Ol' Black Joe'? You want to solve the problem? Well, I say get some white kids and some teachers like Mr. Hamilton into the meeting, and let's straighten the whole thing out together."

I could tell by the look on Ezekiel Morris's face that he was proud of me, and if he was proud of me, I was really winning, because a few years before that he had popped me in the eye so hard over some chick that I thought I was dying. Yeah, everybody there was with me. Mr. Portal and Mr. Moehle knew I was right, so they postponed the meeting to another time. I graduated before that time ever came.

❁

Jimmy, a friend of mine from the Lawson YMCA, had agreed to chauffeur me and Edy, a girl on the job I was dating, to see Nat King Cole at the Chez

Paree. Limousines were too expensive, and cabs were nearly as expensive as a limo. I didn't drive, and since Jimmy and I were pretty tight, he agreed to pick me up, drive over to pick up Edy, and then drop us at the Chez Paree.

It was nearly time, and I was getting nervous. What will I do if he stands me up? How will I rearrange plans on this short notice? He's already late. I hope he isn't having car trouble. Maybe he forgot. I hadn't talked to him since the night before. I became envious of all the white guys in my graduating class who had their own cars—or their fathers' or uncles' cars—and could arrange to be dropped off or picked up at the prom. I felt helpless, but I kept up a cheerful front.

I could see that Mama was trying to act as though she was not worried, but I knew she was. She couldn't keep cool any longer. "Son, what time did he say he'd be here?" "I don't remember, Mama." But I knew he was late. I just didn't want her to know.

A few seconds later, Jimmy knocked on the door, out of breath and sweating. "Hey, Butler, I'm sorry I'm late, man, but I had a flat tire." "Well, come on, let's go," I said, impatiently. Mama looked relieved. Jimmy acknowledged her and apologized for being late. "That's all right, son," she said. "I understand. Junior, have a good time, son. And you drive careful now, Jimmy, you hear?" And off we went.

We picked up Edy at her house, where she'd been patiently waiting. She looked very relaxed when she opened the door. She was dressed in a pretty pink formal. She looked great.

When we arrived at the Chez Paree, it was like a dream. The lights were low, putting just enough of a glow on the room to make everyone look rich, healthy, and happy. There were waiters dressed in tuxedos, busboys dressed in white jackets, a cigarette girl, and a woman photographer.

Charles, the maitre d', was seating people. I stepped up and gave him my name: "Butler. Party of two."

"Yes, sir, one moment, please," he said, gesturing to one of the waiters. I like this shit. I like it. I like it. "Table 27," Charles instructed the waiter, who we followed to our table on the other side of the room, about four rows back and to the left of the stage. I had been in this room earlier in the spring when our graduating class was invited to meet with comedian Jerry Lewis, who talked to us about the importance of a college education. That meeting had been in the afternoon, and the room had looked naked at the time: no waiters, no colored lights, no orchestra. It looked like a big room in need of repairs, cold and empty. But tonight it was in full bloom and simply beautiful. A chorus line was on the stage as we were being seated. It looked a lot like the kind of thing you would see in one of those musicals starring Fred Astaire and Ginger Rogers. The chorus girls were followed by a comedian who was white funny—Jewish jokes,

Italian jokes, Polish jokes—that kind of funny. He wound up his act with a little song-and-dance routine, took another bow, and left.

The lights went down and drums started rolling. A voice offstage announced, "Ladies and gentlemen, Mr. Nat King Cole." Nat walked on to fanfare and generous, heartfelt applause.

I was awestruck. The man was so sharp, so together. He was neither white nor black. He was universal: a man singing every man's song to every man's woman, the way every man wishes he could sing it.

I couldn't understand how some members of the Birmingham, Alabama, White Citizens Council could have become so enraged at him a year earlier that they beat him up onstage. What had he done except show them that he was suave and intelligent? What emotion had he touched? Was it jealousy? Hate? Ignorance? I just couldn't understand. The more I thought about it, the more I wanted to applaud him.

My night was complete as the audience rose to applaud this magnificent talent. I felt so proud. As we were leaving, I could hear people saying, "Wasn't he great!" "What a singer!"

Outside, Edy and I got in a cab and I took her home. I walked home from her house, reliving every moment of the night. I started singing:

> Sitting by the ocean makes me feel so sad.
> Ain't got the money to take me back to Trinidad.

I did my best Nat Cole imitation, using storefront windows as a mirror to see if I remembered the gestures correctly. It never occurred to me that people might be watching. A couple of people passed me and smiled. They must have thought I was drunk. In a way, I guess I was high—high on one of the most beautiful evenings of my life.

❖

I graduated from Washburne in June 1957, and even though I wasn't number one in my class, I was chosen to give the farewell address. Mama was there, and so was Aunt Pearlie. I wore a gray herringbone tweed suit, a white tab-collared shirt, and a blue tie. I was able to dress so nicely because of Max Bakall, a nice Jewish man who, right after Papa died, extended me credit on my signature alone, even though he knew that I was underage and that if I didn't pay, there was nothing he could do about it. He trusted me. Years later, I thanked him for making me aware of how important it was for people to trust one another. Without the credit he extended me, it would have been impossible to have nice things for Mattie, William, and myself for occasions like Easter and Mother's Day, and, of course, Graduation Day.

After graduation I took another job as a cook's helper at a foundry in Cicero. So now I was working two jobs—from seven in the morning until three in the afternoon at the foundry, and from four until eleven in the evening at Lawson's Y. I had to do it because Edy and I were going to get married—at least that's what I thought.

I don't know what went down. Maybe she never loved me. Or maybe she found out that I was younger than her. Or that Bob was sharp and had a ride and was twenty-three. I don't know. My little partner Sandy, who worked in the dishwashing room and looked up to me, was the one who finally pulled my coat. "Hey, man," he said, "what happened to you and Edy?" "Nothing." "Well, she came to work with Bob, and I think something is going on."

At first I was mad at Sandy, because I thought that if he really was a friend, he'd be minding his own business. Then I realized that he was just doing what he thought was right and probably figured I would do the same if the situations were reversed. I asked Edy about it, and she confessed and gave me my ring back. I was cool about it until I got home. Mama, always there when I needed her, told me, "Son, you've just started to live. There are more girls in the world, some better, some worse, some just as good, and a whole lot of lonely ones, looking for a good man like you." Some years later Mama's words turned into my first certified gold record, "Only the Strong Survive," which in turn became the title of this book.

After a couple of weeks of watching Bob and Edy come to work and leave together, I decided to quit. I acted on that decision one night when I got into it with my supervisor, Margaret, over a customer who bugged the hell out of me. The customer was an old codger who waited every night until just before closing to rush in and order poached eggs. I had long since gotten fed up with this ritual, but it took the Bob and Edy situation for me to finally take action.

✵

Three months after graduation, Ronald Sherman told me about these three guys across the street from him who had recently moved to Chicago from Chattanooga, Tennessee, with the hope of making a record. Two members of the original group had decided at the last minute that it was a fool's errand and chickened out. Ronnie said the remaining members wanted someone to rehearse with them until they could find some permanent replacements. By now I was working one job and had nothing else to do, so I said, "Solid, let's go meet 'em."

When Ronnie took me over to their basement flat on Larrabee Street, I was surprised at the age of these cats. I expected to see teenagers. But these guys, Arthur Brooks and Sam Gooden, had been around, military service and stuff like that. Arthur was stockily built with a light complexion that made him look a lot like that Hawaiian guy on the *Hawaii Five-O* TV series of the seventies. Sam, who was about my height and complexion but thinner, had narrow facial features that enhanced a big, broad smile. Richard, Arthur's brother, was about my age. Much skinnier than Arthur, Richard had distinctive sandy, curly hair that he combed constantly.

Arthur and Richard were dead serious, but I always got the feeling that Sam really didn't give a damn. I remember him saying once that if he didn't make it singing, he could always play baseball. After watching him play one day, I could see why. He could really play. Arthur played a little ragtag piano, but after a couple of rehearsals, I knew we needed help, and the first person to pop into my mind was the little guy from the Northern Jubilee Singers, Curtis Mayfield.

He was living over on Hudson Street, so I went by and spoke with him. I told him these guys had come six hundred miles to do this, and they were serious and could sing pretty good. "If you join us, man," I said, "with the way you play the guitar and the way they sing, we'll come up with a different sound."

Curtis was not easily convinced. He had a group of his own, the Alphatones, and didn't want to drop everything and come with us. I suggested a compromise: "Dig, Curt," I said. "Let's do it like this: You rehearse three nights a week with us and three with your group. Whoever improves first, or seems to have the most potential, will be the group you go with." That sounded pretty hip to Curt, and he started practicing with us.

About a month or so after that, we were sounding pretty good. Curtis had written about five or six songs for us, and Arthur, Richard, and I had put together a tune entitled "For Your Precious Love."

Our name, the Roosters, began to spread. We sang everywhere: house parties, street carnivals, Seward Park, Olivette Institute—all over. My cousin, a drug addict, heard us and convinced me to take $300—my entire savings—and invest it in a show in the Washburne Auditorium. I gave him the $300 to put on the show.

Come the day of the show, we couldn't get in the building because he hadn't paid the deposit and the insurance. People were lined up around the block to see us.

He then conned us into going to the C&C Lounge on South Cottage Grove to do a free show with Gene Ammons and Sonny Stitt. As it turned out, it wasn't quite with them; it was more like singing during the intermission. But we laid them out and laid the drummer out, too. We had this routine where we did the splits. But as I was coming out of my split, my foot caught on a nail and I fell on top of the drums. The drummer was out for the evening.

I don't know how good we were, but the folks sure had fun. Come to think of it, so did we. It still didn't cool out the fact that this man had blown $300 of my hard-earned money on dope, not counting the money we had to give back because he didn't take care of business. It was through this experience that I learned that no matter how good a junkie's intentions are, his first allegiance is to his jones, his addiction. Nothing is sacred to them but the jones.

That experience was a blessing for me because I saw firsthand how a brilliant man could be turned into a hardened criminal, forced to leave his wife and kids and break his parents' pockets and their hearts. He eventually went to prison, killed an inmate, and now is very sick. Dope is death.

☀

"Do you have any songs that you've written?"
"No, but I've got some I made up."

—Vee Jay recording artist Jimmy Reed

By March 1958, things were really looking bad. I wasn't working. I began giving serious thought to going into the Marines with Curtis Cade and Thomas Morgan. We had heard about this buddy system where you sign up and go through basic training together. It sounded cool. Plus, when we got out, we would be real men, because everybody knows the Marine Corps builds men.

Curtis, Thomas, and I went to the recruiting station and talked to this big sergeant who looked like he could beat the hell out of all three of us with one hand; he was the perfect specimen for an induction officer. He gave us some tests, arranged for our physicals, and told us to go back home and wait for the results.

As we waited to hear from the Marines, life started getting back to normal. I continued rehearsing with the group.

One night, like out of nowhere, a guy by the name of Eddie Thomas drove up in this canary yellow and white Cadillac. He looked to be in his mid-twenties, not sharp but clean—no suit and tie but very nice, casual-looking clothes. He said he was a manager, and just to prove it, he packed us all in his car and gave us a whirlwind tour of the clubs on Rush Street and the South Side. With us tagging behind, he went to a bunch of places, speaking with the owner, the maitre d', or anybody who would listen. We were impressed.

A couple of days later, he set up an audition for us with Mercury Records. When we arrived, we were greeted by a man named Don Costa, who took us into a small studio and listened to our stuff. He said he dug the sound but didn't want to sign us right away because his artist roster was so heavy. He then offered us the opportunity to do some background singing with a singer named Eddie Howard. I had never heard of him myself, but for $25 an hour per side, I was willing to do some serious chirping. I found out later that the song was a remake of a song Howard had been successful with earlier, called "My Last Good-bye."

After the Eddie Howard recording, things started to move kind of fast. We started making the rounds to some of Chicago's major record companies: Chess, Vee Jay, Mercury, and some little company out on 55th Street called Savoy Records. Savoy's owner was about the only guy we could catch in. He told us to come back in about a month.

We then went to Chess Records, where Phil Chess gave us a listen. We were wary of singing our songs for Chess because we had heard stories about hidden tape recorders and the like. Phil passed on us, too.

We decided to go to Vee Jay. The first person we met was this little guy with an earring in one ear and a Great Dane at his side. "My name is Abner and our A&R man isn't in today," he said. "Take this number and call back on Wednesday. The A&R man's name is Calvin Carter." It went on like that for a couple of weeks, but by now things were going so fast, I completely forgot about the Marine Corps.

It was around this time that Eddie decided to change our name. The Roosters wasn't cutting it—"too country," he said. Arthur, Sam, and Richard were not too happy about it, because now when they made their record, folks in Chattanooga wouldn't know it was them. "We're gonna lose a lot of sales in Chattanooga," they said, "'cause the Roosters are very popular there."

But Eddie, being the diplomat that he was, showed them that the total picture was much bigger than Chattanooga. "We can always get publicity in Chattanooga that will let the people know that the group was formerly the Roosters."

What's the new name, then? "The Impressions," said Eddie. "Yeah, the Impressions, because we leave a good impression." We were impressed. Wow, what a manager!

A couple of days later, Eddie told us about this white woman from Nashville who had moved to Chicago and wanted to start a record label. "She is rich, got all the money in the world. Her name is Vi Muzynski." Vi was a large woman with platinum blonde hair and a very fluttery way. She talked very fast, squirmed in her seat, and smacked her lips when she talked. She always seemed too heavily made up to me. She was such a nice woman, though, that you tended to overlook everything else.

Vi had these songs she wanted us to sing. We thought they were ridiculous, but we went along because we didn't want to hurt her feelings. We learned the songs and tried to make them as soulful as possible. She seemed very pleased with what we had done and told us she wanted us to go with her to this record company to audition her songs. The record company turned out to be Vee Jay Records, the same place where the little man with the Great Dane had told us to call back and talk to the company's A&R man.

Founded just five years earlier in Gary, Indiana, by Vivian Carter Bracken and her husband, Jimmy, Vee Jay had achieved phenomenal success as a blues and gospel label. Although Vivian's brother, Calvin Carter, was also one of the founders, Vivian and Jimmy used their first initials for the label's name.

A lifelong Gary resident, Vivian got her start in radio by winning a contest created by popular Chicago disc jockey Al Benson seeking to find a "girl and boy" disc jockey team. "There must have been 800 or a thousand people there to get an audition," Vivian told Mike Callahan in a 1981 *Goldmine* magazine article.

"I heard [Benson] announce this contest about 10 minutes before he went off the air," she said, adding that contestants were required to write a one-minute commercial and then present it at a Chicago hotel by seven o' clock that evening.

"It was like ten minutes to six when I heard about it. I hadn't even thought about a commercial, but I listened to his commercial on a clothing store and jotted down notes while he was talking. . . . I wrote my commercial that way."

Vivian and Sid McCoy, the future voice of *Soul Train,* came up winners. The prize: Each was given a fifteen-minute radio show. "That's how we both broke into radio," Vivian recalled.

Vivian quit the show after a few months to return to Gary and devote full time to the Brackens' record shop. It was then that McCoy came up with the idea that they form their own label and gain an edge with distributors by leveraging some of Vivian's unused Chicago airtime. Vivian and Jimmy jumped at the idea and quickly borrowed $500 from a pawnshop to produce their first record: four tunes by the Spaniels, a five-member group that graduated from the same Gary high school, Roosevelt, that Vivian attended.

Vee Jay was launched May 5, 1953, with the Spaniels' "Baby It's You," "Sloppy Drunk," "Since I Fell for You," and "Bounce." Blues singer Jimmy Reed, who left his home in Leland, Mississippi, at the age of fifteen to work in the Gary steel mills, was recorded shortly after the Spaniels.

Vivian soon returned to radio—this time hosting a late-night program in Gary called "Livin' with Vivian" on WWCA-AM.

Vee Jay's audition studio was located on 47th and King Drive. When we returned there with Vi, we learned that the little man with the Great Dane was the company's president, Ewart Abner, and the man we were auditioning for was Calvin Carter.

Calvin Carter

We sang all of Vi's songs first. Calvin was unimpressed. Trying hard to be kind, he asked us to go through the songs again. Still unimpressed, he asked us if we had any material of our own. We said, "Yeah" and went through maybe eight or ten of them. Calvin was more enthusiastic about ours than about Vi's. But he was still not to the point where he wanted to commit himself. He gave us encouragement.

As we were about to leave, he said, "Gee, I really want to record you guys, but I don't really hear that hit song. Do you have any more that you haven't sung? Maybe because they're too old or something? I want to hear everything you've got."

I told the other guys, "Let's do 'Precious Love.'" Everybody shrugged, and

Curtis took his guitar back out and started to play. As we got into the song, Calvin's eyes lit up. He shouted, "That's it! That's it! That's the one! Abner, get me some contracts. Vi, you, Eddie, and Abner better talk."

We don't know what Eddie and Vi and Abner were talking about, but we sure did understand Calvin. He wanted to make a record with us, and that's all that mattered. While we were trying to keep each other cool so that we didn't let on that we were overjoyed, in walked five guys. They were sharp: processed hair, silk suits, and shined shoes. They must be stars, I thought to myself, and before I could think another thought, Calvin said, "This is Pookie Hudson, Gerald, and Dimps, the Spaniels."

We stood there with our mouths open. We had just shaken hands with the Spaniels!—"Good Night Sweetheart," "Baby It's You," "Since I Fell for You"—wow!

Calvin said, "Hey, y'all, sing that 'Precious Love' song again. I want them to hear it." There was a long pause as paranoia set in. Here comes the rip-off. He likes our song and he wants them to record it. That's why they called them and told them to come over right away. This ain't no accident. I'll bet that bastard's got a tape recorder in his desk. Oh, shit, what do we do now? Well, we'll sing it fast and then they can't remember it. But what about the tape recorder in his desk? Well, we'll think of something before we leave.

Our fears were unfounded. The Spaniels had just come back to town off the road and had simply dropped in. Calvin was just genuinely excited, which, I found after working with him, was just his style. As soon as he thought he had a winner, he started promoting it himself and didn't stop until it was a hit.

When we finished the song, the Spaniels began slapping each other's hands and telling jokes and stories about the kinds of changes we would be going through when the record hit. We were very happy and very grateful. Mostly, though, we were very surprised that a group like the Spaniels, with all their successes, would be that decent and down to earth. I made up my mind then and there that, no matter how much success I achieved, I would treat others as Pookie and the Spaniels treated us that day.

As we left the office—rather, the little storefront that served as Vee Jay's office—we sort of floated to the car. Unbelievable. We had been given recording contracts for our parents and attorneys to look over. Attorneys? What attorneys? Shoot, we didn't even know any attorneys, let alone have one. We laughed our asses off.

Mama sat on the bed when I showed her the contract. She looked up at me as if to say, "I'm sorry I can't be of more help. This is over my head. I don't understand any of this." At that moment I finally understood why she and Papa were so insistent on my getting a good education. Now I could see how badly she had wanted one for herself. The next day I took the contract to the lawyer who had gotten Mama a little money when William got hit by a car and broke his arm. He told me it was a fair contract and charged me $12.50.

The Start of Something Big

Eleven o'clock Friday morning. We arrived at Universal Studios on Walton Street between Rush and Michigan Avenues. We were the first ones there, with our bag of lemons and already into the nervous chatter that goes on when everybody is tense but fakes calmness by making fun of the nervousness of others. "I ain't gonna lie," said Arthur, "I'm scared as hell!" We loosened up after that.

"Sweet Was the Wine" was the first song. Four or five takes later, we got into a good groove. But my voice cracked on one note. Calvin had to decide whether to do it all over again or keep it. If we had recorded it a year or two later, no one would have had to sing over again but me. This was before the eight- and sixteen-track machines that allow you to isolate certain instruments or voices on a track. Calvin decided to keep it, explaining that it felt good and that the cracking on the one note was at the end of the record and sounded more like it was affected than a mistake. I later learned that he was afraid my voice was going bad, through either hoarseness or fear; he wanted to get "For Your Precious Love" recorded before I lost it altogether.

He played "Sweet Was the Wine" back a couple of times to convince himself it wasn't too bad. Then he asked us to do "Precious Love." The engineer's voice could be heard in the control booth: "This is 'For Your Precious Love,' take one." Five or six takes later, Calvin still didn't like it. He took the musicians aside and told Curtis to plug in his guitar. He told Lefty and Guitar Red not to play; he wanted only Curtis to play. But Curtis was non-union, so Calvin talked with the musicians and asked them not to report it to the union, because it could cause Vee Jay a lot of trouble.

Two takes later, Calvin wanted to cancel the rest of the session—not because he was unhappy, but because he wanted to get "Precious Love" ready to be sent to the pressing plant. We must have listened to ten playbacks of the song.

We came back the next day and recorded the other two songs, with Curtis playing and singing the lead on "At the County Fair," one of his first compositions.

As we left the studio, Eddie and Vi were all over us, telling us how proud they were and how big we were going to be and all the great things we wanted to hear. It all sounded very hip, but it was unimportant at the time. The only thing we could think of then was how the record sounded in the studio, with real musicians playing and real echo chambers, not the kind of echo you get in the boys' john at Washburne High School, where the sound went all over the place.

After we left the studio, Calvin was so excited that he had Bill Putnam, the engineer, make about seven acetates, or demos, for him. Acetates are not of the same quality as records from a pressing plant.

Calvin took the acetates back to Vee Jay, reserving one for Vivian, who played it once at the beginning of her show, telling her audience it was a new group from Chicago. While she was still on the air, Eddie Thomas called to tell us what was happening. We were all at Arthur's mother's apartment when the call came. We searched around on the radio until we found the station.

"For Your Precious Love," just a thought nine months before and, until eleven o'clock that morning, never having even been played by professional musicians, was being played on a radio station in Gary, Indiana. And we, the five guys whose hopes and dreams and aspirations for a lifetime were tied up in it, stood around an old beat-up radio, listening. Mama Mattie Brooks looked over at us with pride and love. We were on our way.

Part II.
The Vee Jay Years

5.

What's in a Name?

The following Wednesday, exactly one week from the day of the session, Eddie picked us up to go to Vee Jay. It was the day all of us had dreamed about. We were finally going to see a record label with our name on it. Everyone was excited.

While we waited for the records to arrive from the pressing plant, Calvin and Abner regaled us with champagne and jokes and talk about how rich we were going to be, the places we would see, and the women we would meet.

The records arrived just as we were about to leave. We tore at the box they came in, eager to see our name, "The Impressions," written on the label.

Suddenly, everything went quiet. My heart seemingly leapt into my throat. The label read: "For Your Precious Love," by *Jerry Butler and* the Impressions." I didn't know whether to laugh or cry—laugh because I had just been made the featured name in the group, or cry because I knew that Curtis, Sam, Arthur, and Richard didn't like it one bit. Each of their faces was twisted into a half-smile that did nothing to hide their hurt and envy. In that one excruciating moment, it felt as if someone had walked into the room and purposely—cruelly—drawn a shade to temper our gaiety. The silence was deafening.

I finally spoke, addressing my remarks to no one in particular. "You'll have to reprint the label so that it reads 'The Impressions,'" I said. "If you don't, we're going to have dissension in the group before we ever get started." Sam and Arthur mumbled in agreement. Curtis and Richard just kept staring at the record and shaking their heads.

I continued: "We came here as the Impressions, and that's the way we want it." Eddie was nervous. He hadn't known about it, either. Still, he remained silent. He later told us that, at the time, he thought it unwise for us to be raising questions at that meeting, when we were so close to getting things off the ground.

Abner spoke, at first matter-of-factly, then in a tone that bordered on controlled anger. He explained how much it would cost to reprint 50,000 labels and why the company had chosen to feature one guy on the label. It would help us get more airplay, he said, adding that Vee Jay had only our best interest in mind. And besides, they knew more about promotion and publicity than we did; consequently, we should trust them to do what's best for us. Everybody wanted to make as much money as possible. Vee Jay would not do anything to break us up. That wasn't the plan. They simply couldn't reprint the labels, and even if they could, it would take two or three weeks before they could get the record out.

By the time he got through talking, we were feeling sorry for feeling sorry. Abner was like that. He was one of those guys who could sell you the Brooklyn Bridge and then buy it back five minutes later for half the price. Abner's magic worked for the moment. We all left Vee Jay that day with smiles on our faces, but the rift over the phrase "Jerry Butler and the Impressions," and later "The Original Impressions," was irreparable, and would remain so even after forty years.

Promotional Trips

Within a few weeks of its release, "For Your Precious Love" was on every chart in the cities where it played. But when rumors began circulating that Roy Hamilton was planning to "cover" it, Abner felt it was time for a promotional tour. With hits like "You'll Never Walk Alone" and "He" behind him, Hamilton could destroy us before we ever got started. A promotional tour would give us more exposure and thus forestall any talk of coverage.

Covering a record is when a well-known artist records a song almost exactly like the original version. Although Hamilton was black, white acts were the most notorious for covering records. A classic example was Georgia Gibbs's cover of LaVern Baker's recording of "Tweedlee Dee." Gibbs, who is white, literally copied Baker's original rendition note for note. Baker became so incensed by Gibbs's repeated coverings of her records that she asked Congress to intercede. Congress, in turn, refused to give copyright protection to her arrangements.

Cover records of blacks by whites were designed to help allay the fear of white parents who had been led to believe that the so-called "jungle beat" was subversive and immoral. A song like "Long Tall Sally" when performed by clean-cut Pat Boone seemed innocent and tame to white parents. But when a wild-eyed Little Richard had whooped and hollered in an earlier version of the song, it was viewed as just another degenerate "race" record, the term used to describe black recordings.[1]

What some white ministers and parents failed to realize was that white kids were searching for validation, something of their own to identify with—in short, authenticity. They had grown tired of the Moon-June-Spoon type of songs that were holdovers from the thirties and forties. They wanted music that fit their times, that spoke to *their* situations, not their parents'. They wanted in music what they saw on motion picture screens: a rebellious James Dean, an independent Natalie Woods, a leather-clad, sneering Marlon Brando. They had the images but not the music to fit the images, music created by teenagers *for* teenagers. Black music, with its earthy, shoot-from-the-hip sassiness— "Annie had a baby. Can't work no more"—was a perfect fit.

Thus the strategy of playing watered-down versions of black songs backfired. White teenagers, for the most part, ended up buying both versions, and people like Little Richard, LaVern Baker, and Ivory Joe Hunter—rhythm and blues music itself—were able to survive yet another bout with America's hallmark racism.

The rumors of Roy Hamilton covering "For Your Precious Love" were unfounded. In fact, a year later, Hamilton and Clyde Otis wrote "Come Back My Love" for our second recording session at Vee Jay. Also recorded at that session was "The Gift of Love" and "Love Me." It would be the last session we recorded together as the Impressions. (Later, Clyde Otis and Brook Benton would compose "Without You," "The Lights Went Out," and "One by One" for my first solo session.)

Detroit

The promotional tour that Vee Jay planned for us included a two-day jaunt in Detroit, then a return to Chicago to appear on Jim Lounsbury's *Bandstand Matinee,* Chicago's version of *American Bandstand.*

Arthur and Richard's brother, Harrison, had a house in Inkster, a Detroit suburb, and we arranged to stay there. We drove up on a Wednesday and spent the night just having fun and playing cards. The next day we made the rounds to the black radio stations, WCHB in Inkster and WJLB in Detroit. We also appeared on two television shows—*The Soupy Sales Show* in Detroit and a show in Windsor, Ontario.

At the pop radio and the television stations we were treated like a bunch of kids, young kids at that. But that wasn't the problem. Except for Sam and Arthur, we really were no more than kids. We didn't want to be constantly reminded of it. But every insult or putdown that we received at the white stations was more than made up for by the treatment we received in the black community, where, despite our youth, we were treated with respect, like heroes. To black people, young and old alike, we had grasped that elusive thing called success, and, if only for a moment, we symbolized their dreams and aspirations. Black males, for example, saw us as symbols of hope. Black females saw us as suave, worldly guys who had gone places, done things. We were special. What they completely overlooked, however, was that only a few weeks earlier, we had been in the same position as they. We had no complaints with our celebrity; on the contrary, we enjoyed it to the hilt.

Detroit is where I was first introduced to disc jockey exploitation. A disc jockey named Larry Dixon was the first to do it. There would be others. Larry told us so many things, like how big we were going to be, and how Abner was working on getting us on *The Ed Sullivan Show,* and how good we were—all leading up to one thing: the Impressions performing free at a show he promoted every Saturday. If we would stay over and do a song or two at the club, he said, it would really help our sales in the Detroit area. Arthur begged off, saying, "Abner told us we had to be back in Chicago Saturday for Jim Lounsbury's *Bandstand Matinee.*" "Don't worry about it," said Larry, "I'll call Abner on Friday and straighten it out. It's ridiculous to spend the money to come here and not get all the publicity you can out of this town."

All day Friday WCHB played "For Your Precious Love" at least once or twice every hour. Late Friday night Larry called to tell us that he had spoken with Abner and that everything was cool.

On Saturday, Larry spent the whole day talking about Jerry Butler and the Impressions, the "extra added attraction" at his club Saturday night. "That's tonight! Now y'all come on out and meet this super new group."

We prepared for the show, pressing the little uniforms we had bought at Chicago's Maxwell Street Market, a flea market where entire families would come on weekends and hawk their wares, which ranged from old rag dolls to housewares to refurbished radio sets. The Maxwell Street Market also featured cigar-chomping hawkers in ramshackle kiosks, barking "Hot dogs! . . . Polish Sausages! . . . Thirty-five cents!" The musky smell of grilled onions, mustard, and sausages always hung in the air. Then there were the merchants who would literally force you into their dark, dingy shops, insisting that you buy something. In the old days, on any given Sunday, you might find Jimmy Reed, Muddy Waters, or Howlin' Wolf at the market, guitars twanging, harmonicas screeching, singing the blues. This is where we bought our first uniforms: gray silk jackets with black pants, white shirts, and black ties.

When we showed up at the club around seven o'clock, people were lined up, waiting to get inside, where the place was already nearly packed. Larry charged $3 at the door, and no one could get in without purchasing a ticket. Apparently, even if they did buy a ticket, they still couldn't get in.

We didn't have a chance to rehearse with the band because they arrived late and immediately set up and started to play. About nine o'clock the place really started jumping. Larry finally showed up, dressed like some fairytale prince. He walked to the bandstand and declared, "It's showtime!" and then introduced the band, which played a couple more songs. Then he introduced a young guy who sang "Reet Petite" as well as Jackie Wilson ever did. This guy also had Jackie's routine down to every little jerk and riff. His name, I later learned, was Eddie Holland, and he would go on to become the last Holland of the great songwriting-producing team for Motown known as Holland, Dozier, and Holland.

After Eddie finished Jackie Wilsoning the people and had us sufficiently afraid to go on after him, Larry started his rap: "Ladies and gentlemen . . . all the way from Chicago, Illinois . . . five young men who have the hottest record in WCHB land! The creators of that monster hit 'For Your Precious Love.' . . . "

People started applauding and screaming. We broke out in big smiles. We weren't afraid of Eddie anymore.

Larry continued: "Here they are . . . our special guest attraction tonight . . . Jerry Butler and the Impressions!" More screams and more applause. We jogged out on the stage looking confused and anxious. Today, when I see a new group jog out to the microphone and start fumbling and watching each other because they're afraid to look at the audience, trying to compose themselves while standing there waiting for something to happen, hoping that when it does happen it will happen right, I get a flashback to how inept and unprofessional we must have looked that night.

We sang a couple of jukebox favorites, and then Curtis started playing "For Your Precious Love." The place went up in screams. It was strange, but I got the same feeling that night that I had experienced with the Northern Jubilee Singers when the church was with us. It's a feeling of pushing up to your limit and then over, and your spirit lifts your body. It all becomes so real that it's unreal.

We finished, and the audience applauded and screamed: "More! More! More!" We had two encores, singing the same song. After the third time, Larry got us off. Afterwards, there were young, pretty women with pieces of paper wanting autographs; fat ladies with big bosoms and beer and whiskey on their breath, wanting to hug and kiss us; and the boyfriends and husbands of these women wanting to kick our asses.

While all of this mutual love and admiration was being passed between the Impressions and their new fans, Larry Dixon pocketed the $3,000 that these people had paid to see us.

To make matters worse, we had to crawl back into our $400 Chrysler and return to Harrison's house and eat up all the food that this poor working guy had bought to feed his family. Larry didn't even buy us a hamburger. Larry knew that no matter how mad we became, we wouldn't say anything; neither would Abner, Calvin, Eddie Thomas, or anyone else connected with us. This was Larry's town, and if we wanted to sell records here, we needed him, not the other way around. In other words, Larry could pee on us and tell us it was raining—and we had better believe it.

We limped back to Chicago and faced Abner, who, predictably, chewed our asses out royally because we had blown the Jim Lounsbury show. While he was telling us how we had just messed up with the most important white disc jockey in Chicago, I saw Larry's smiling face, telling us through his lying teeth, "I talked with Abner and everything is cool." We got screwed. All that stuff was jive. But the worst of it was the realization that had we had the sense to call Abner ourselves, we wouldn't have gotten burned.

Abner finally cooled down, called Jim Lounsbury, apologized, lied a little, and rescheduled another appearance for us for the following week. Abner was an amazing man.

Eddie Gets Busted

Just as all the good stuff started happening, Eddie Thomas got busted. His dream of being a big-time manager had to be put on hold until he served time

Georgie Woods

in the penitentiary for something having to do with his job as a postal worker —at least that's the way I remember how he ran it down to us. While he would not be with us physically, he told us, his spirit would be with us at all times. It was really a drag for us, and we knew what a drag it had to be for him.

Philadelphia and Georgie Woods

After the Detroit debacle, Vee Jay bought us a green Mercury station wagon and sent us on an East Coast promotional tour that began in Philadelphia, then went to New York for a week at the Apollo Theater before winding up in Miami, the final destination.

In Philadelphia we lived in a little rooming house on North Broad Street called "Mom's." It is where most of the acts lived when they played the Uptown Theater, acts like Mickey and Sylvia, Lee Andrews and the Hearts, Huey Smith and the Clowns, Robert and Johnny—all of whom were on the show with us. We were a replacement act, for one night only, for Ed Townsend.

This was our first time meeting Georgie Woods, the man who would later give me the name I am known by today—Iceman. Georgie—tall, slender, good-looking, and an impeccable dresser—was the undisputed "King of the Disc Jockeys" in Philadelphia. His power was awesome. Record companies, artists, managers, agents, promotion men, and even the politicians wanted to be on his good side because of his influence in the black community.

Born in Georgia and raised in New York, Georgie first tried, but failed, to break into radio in Chicago in 1950. Undaunted, he moved back to New York in 1952, landing a job with radio station WWRL. The job lasted all of three months before he was asked to leave because of his lack of experience. Before he left, his bosses suggested that he find a station outside of New York to hone his skills. The following year, Georgie heard about an opening at station WHAT in Philadelphia and went for an audition. But when management discovered that a New York disc jockey was vying for the job, Georgie was quickly signed. Except for brief stints at WRIL and WLIB in New York and WDAS in Philadelphia, Georgie's entire career was spent at WHAT. We were scared to death the night we performed for Georgie. Sure, we had performed in front of large audiences before, but this was different. This wasn't Detroit, where we virtually were headliners and much closer to home. Philadelphia was more than a thousand miles away, with strange-talking people who called submarine sandwiches "hoagies" and pop "sodas." Also, this was the first show we were on with big stars—stars who had been around for a while and who knew how to mesmerize an audience. Those things, together, had us literally trembling with fear.

As in Detroit, we hadn't had a chance to rehearse with the orchestra, because the show was on when we arrived. Worse still, we didn't have our arrangements yet because we couldn't afford to pay an arranger. Our first payday was nearly a week away.

Before we went on, Georgie gave the first of many rousing introductions to a Philadelphia audience that I and the Impressions would receive over the years:

"We've got a special treat for you tonight," he began. "This group is in town on a special promotion tour, and we asked them to come by tonight because Ed Townsend had to go to New York to do a TV show. But he will be back tomorrow night." The audience started to boo a little bit, but Georgie soon had them back under control. "Wait a minute! Wait a minute!" he said. "When I tell you who's replacing Ed, you'll know you're in for a treat. These guys have a new record called 'For Your Precious Love' . . . " The audience started to applaud

Photo montage by Gordon "Doc" Anderson

amid screams from young girls. Georgie continued, his voice rising, "Here they are, Jerry Butler and the Impressions!"

Doc Bagby's band played a chaser, a show business term for music that accompanies an act's stage entrances and exits. We jogged onstage, bumped into each other, then stood there, looking dumb and helpless, and waited for the music to start. Curtis plugged his guitar into somebody's amplifier and, having told Doc Bagby what key the song was in, he started to play. As soon as he started, the audience again broke into screams and applause. When the applause subsided, we started singing all over again. We finished the song and ran off. The band made a big fanfare chord, signaling the end of our act, but the applause continued. Somebody shouted, "More!" and the whole audience began clapping and stamping their feet to the chant of "More! More! More!"

It was all so great, so exciting. I understood, for the first time, why people said, once you've been bitten by the show biz bug, you never recover. I was so happy, I did the encore with tears in my eyes.

The Apollo

We then moved on to the famed Apollo Theater, where such greats as Billie Holiday, Ella Fitzgerald, Sammy Davis, Jr., Sarah Vaughn, and Mr. Golden Voice himself, Roy Hamilton, had won amateur competitions in previous years. It's often said that if you're successful at the Apollo, you'll be successful anywhere.

The promoter of our show was Jocko Henderson, New York's answer to Philadelphia's Georgie Woods and Chicago's Al Benson. Jocko was number one in Harlem. He had his own television show and everything. He was famous for his so-called "Rocket Ship Show" on the radio and a rap that goes like this:

> Eeeh tiddy yock
> This is the jock.
> Back on the scene
> With my record machine
> Saying, ooh pooh pah doo
> And a how do you do.
> We got good music just for you.
>
> Mommio and Daddio,
> This is Jocko
> With the rocket ship show
> Get up you big bad motor scooter 'n lets go!

He used this rap to open the show at the Apollo and was pretty dramatic about the whole thing. As the audience listened to him, a picture of a rocket ship was projected onto the theater's huge movie screen. When Jocko finished, the movie screen lifted to reveal him standing there in his space suit and helmet.

Appearing with us on the show were the Kodaks, a group of teenagers who amazed everyone with their professionalism. They were really good. They were followed by the Story Sisters, Lee Andrews and the Hearts, Huey Smith and the Clowns, Robert and Johnny, and then us.

We opened with an Elvis Presley hit that got over simply as a matter of courtesy. When we began singing "Young and Warm and Wonderful," a Tony Bennett hit, the audience started to squirm. Some guy hollered out, "Y'all take that white shit someplace else and sing what I came here to hear!" Some people started to laugh; others applauded; the rest remained courteous.

Curtis started playing the intro to "For Your Precious Love," and the same thing that had occurred in Philadelphia happened again, only this time it was louder, and instead of doing one encore, we wound up singing three times before the people let us off.

We were followed by Ed Townsend, the Coasters, and finally the star, fifteen-year-old superstar Frankie Lyman, who had just left the Teenagers and was making his first appearance alone. He was good, classy and sharp. I was so glad to be on the show with him, I went to his dressing room after the show to say hello. He invited me in, but the vibes weren't right. I quickly said hello to him, his mother, his two bodyguards, and some guy who looked like a gangster. I got out of there in a hurry. I started to develop a real dislike for him, which, in retrospect, was silly of me.

Bobby Schiffman and his father, Frank, owners of the Apollo, came back to the dressing room after the first show to greet the acts and to tighten the show wherever possible. They informed us that one of the places in the show that needed tightening was Jerry Butler and the Impressions. We were told that since we were called back three times, we needed to cut our numbers down to two. And try not to waste so much time getting on and off the stage. Honi Coles, Cholly Atkins, Pete Long, and some of the old show business pros gave us some tips that helped us tremendously.

We were well on our way to having a great week at the Apollo when the Name Game monster reared its ugly head again. Whoever was in charge of putting the names on the marquee had inadvertently reopened an old wound. The marquee had "Jerry Butler" in large type and "The Impressions" in small. This affected the rest of the guys so much that they threatened not to perform. Abner eventually had to fly to New York and repeat his Chicago speech before things got back on track.

For a while everything was fine.

In New York, we lived at the Grampion Hotel in Harlem. It was a typical old Harlem hotel: plenty of junkies and rats. The Grampion is the kind of place you live when you're making $1,250 a week and have to pay commissions and expenses and split the rest among five guys. If you expect to have any left for yourself at the end of the week, don't think about living anywhere else but the Grampion.

On our very first night at the Grampion we were a little nervous, because

Calvin had told us about how junkies come up the fire escape through your window and stick you up. He suggested that we leave our money on the dresser. That way, he said, they won't have to wake you up with a pistol to get it. He explained that usually if they see what they want, their attention is not so much on you. This allowed you the option of remaining asleep, faking sleep, or trying to figure out how to catch and surprise them—if you were of the heroic persuasion.

We lived in adjoining rooms. Sam, Richard, and Curtis shared the front room; Arthur and I shared the back room, near the window and fire escape. It always happens: When people are in spooky situations, they tend to talk about spooky things. After we finished shining our shoes and getting ready for the next show, the conversation turned to the telling of ghost stories. These were accompanied by laughter and jokes.

In the middle of all this I somehow fell asleep, only to be awakened abruptly by a noise at the window. I opened my eyes and was startled by a hand in front of my face. I let out a loud scream, which in turn was met with laughter. Curtis had just played another one of his practical jokes at my expense. The noise I had heard was a shoe he had thrown against the wall near the window; the hand turned out to be my own. Curtis, Arthur, Sam, and Richard were rolling on the floor. I had to laugh, too, before falling asleep again.

The second day of our engagement there was a line leading from the Apollo to halfway down Seventh Avenue, and the theater was practically full already. It would be a constant occurrence for the balance of our engagement. The shows ran so close together that it was almost impossible to leave the theater.

An old man, known only as Pops, had a kitchen upstairs and did a very good business selling plate dinners, lunches, and sandwiches. Normally, all you had to do was sign his book for what you had, and he would collect on draw day, payday. Every now and then, some idiot would burn him and skip out without paying. But that meant that that person could not come back to the Apollo without facing Pops, who was there for every show until he died. Most folks were glad to pay up, because despite all the star trappings, such as their names in lights and their records being played on radio and television, many of them didn't have enough money—not even seventy-five cents—to buy one of Pops's famous pork chop sandwiches.

One day Spann, the stage door man at the Apollo, yelled upstairs, "Hey, Jerry Butler, there's somebody down here to see you." I couldn't imagine who it could be. I didn't know anyone in New York except the people on the show. Maybe it's just somebody wanting an autograph, I thought. I checked myself in the mirror because it might be a girl, and she might be fine and my kind. After all, it's one of the fringe benefits that go along with being a recording star. By now I had learned that fine young ladies would do just about anything to share the spotlight with anyone they considered a star. Certain girls liked certain voices. Some liked bass singers; others tenors and leads; and still others simply liked singers and performers, period. Chuck Barksdale and Vern Allison of the Dells were the first to pull my coat to this. The old guys referred to them as "Backstage Annies." Today they are called groupies. I often wondered why these girls were like that. After getting to know some of them, I was impressed that most of them were not after money; they were in search of genuine friendships. Some were faithful to one guy.

I finished primping and dashed downstairs. As I expected, there was this nice-looking girl, not a fox but nice, waiting. I checked her out and quickly noticed that the front of her dress was bulging a bit. It was evident she was pregnant. As I approached, Spann said, "Here he is, baby." She said, "That's not him. That's not Jerry Butler." With this, Spann told her to get out if she didn't know who she wanted to see. She started crying and ran out the door.

Back upstairs in the dressing room, I told Arthur about it. He smiled and explained: "Some nigger tricked that girl into believing he was you and got in her pants. We ain't never been here before, so it was easy to fool her. She probably came over here to tell him she was pregnant, and when you came downstairs, she realized she had been tricked."

Those were the times I wished Arthur were the older brother I never had. I was really amazed at how fast he figured out what went down. It was hard to believe that somebody could be that cruel. But the more I live, the more I find out that whoever made the statement about man's inhumanity to man really said a mouthful. I felt sorry for that girl as I heard Spann holler over the intercom, "It's showtime!"

❖

Monday was draw day, which meant that all the performers who had spent their money over the weekend, or lost it in one of the ever-present card or crap games, could replenish their pockets. We decided we needed about $300 to get our clothes cleaned, pay Pops for his food, and have a little spending change.

After the second show, we got our $300. Every junkie and booster in Harlem had been standing around the corner waiting for the eagle to fly. When it did, they swooped down on the theater with hot suits, hot watches, televisions, radios, rings, socks, underwear, shirts—everything, in your size, shape, and color. You name it, they had it. If they didn't, they promised to have it by the last show, which was payday, the day the eagle flies.

AGVA (the American Guild of Variety Artists) had a local representative who, like the junkies and boosters, showed up when the eagle flew, too. AGVA is the union that is supposed to cover theatrical and circus acts. We were informed that we had to join to perform at places like the Apollo. Abner put up the money while we were on tour. It cost $36 a person, based on how much the act had made the past week, which in our case amounted to $1,250. Whether there were ten people in the act or one, if you made $1,250 a week or worked one week a year, your dues were the same.

This struck me as ridiculous right off the bat. But we were brand-new and needed to belong, so we dealt with it. We decided to pay the dues and make the money.

In the early seventies, right after I recorded "Ain't Understanding Mellow," the issue resurfaced. I was booked at the Michigan State Fair in Detroit. Just before showtime, a big, burly guy who looked like he could have been the model for the character Lucca Brazzi in the first *Godfather* movie came to my dressing room and said, "You Jerry Butler?"

"Yeah."

"You can't perform here until you pay your dues." I wasn't altogether surprised by the statement; I had been expecting it for some time. I had stopped paying AGVA its $36 as a matter of principle. I had grown tired of the strong-arm tactics of union representatives who would show up at places like the Apollo and the Michigan State Fair demanding payment of dues but were nowhere to be found in the Deep South, where promoters routinely skipped out the back door without paying the performers. I told this guy that, but he persisted.

"You can't go on until you pay your dues." Not only that, but my background singers wouldn't be allowed to perform, either, because they weren't in the union.

Finally, I said, "Listen, Mr. Whoever You Are, I am going onstage and perform. If you have a problem with that, go talk to the people who hired me. Tell them I can't go on because I didn't pay AGVA thirty-six dollars in dues."

Maybe the promoter paid it or maybe he didn't. I don't know. What I do know is that we went onstage that evening to a rousing reception.

Some years earlier, the New York AGVA representative had been a kindly but stern old gentleman named John Bunn—Mr. Bunn, as everyone called him. He would come to our dressing room, show his card, and then ask to see ours. If you were behind, he would take it from the box office to be deducted from your salary. If you didn't belong, he would make sure that you were a member in good standing before you left New York. At first Mr. Bunn and I didn't get along, but later on we became very good friends. I learned a lot about AGVA from him.

※

While in New York, we were scheduled to do the Alan Freed show. At the time, Freed was one of the big disc jockeys in New York, the man who had coined the phrase "rock and roll."

We were very excited. We knew that "For Your Precious Love" was a big hit on rhythm and blues stations, but Alan Freed was white, and that meant our record was starting to become popular with white audiences. Calvin told us that we had sold only 20,000 records with Jocko and the other black deejays playing our song. With Freed playing it, we potentially could sell 200,000 copies in New York alone. Dick Clark may have been the biggest TV host with his Philadelphia-based *American Bandstand*, but Freed was in the world's biggest media market, the next best thing to being national. We had already done Jim Lounsbury in Chicago, Soupy Sales in Detroit, and Dick Clark in Philadelphia, and now we were doing Alan Freed in New York.

Alan Freed is another one who made the big time off the creativity of black people. Legend has it that he initially had to be persuaded to play black music while doing a classical music show in Cleveland, Ohio. As the story goes, a local retail record store operator convinced Freed of the potential of rhythm and blues when Freed visited the store and observed white teenagers eagerly snapping up R&B records. Freed began hosting a popular show on WJW called "The Beat Beat," which he soon renamed "The Moon Dog House Rock-'n'-Roll Party," using a phrase popularized by a black disc jockey.

It's been noted before, but I would be remiss if I didn't mention here that the term "rock and roll" had been used by black recording artists long before Freed started using it. Billy Ward, for example, boasted in his 1952 recording "Sixty Minute Man" that he could "rock and roll 'em all night long" because he was a "sixty minute man," meaning he had the staying power to sexually perform for sixty-minute stretches—and do it all night long! As early as 1948, Roy Brown used the suggestive "rockin" term in his "Good Rockin' Tonight" recording. From the time I was a little guy, I knew that rockin' and rollin' was a euphemism for sexual intercourse. Thus I looked on in amusement when the phrase turned up in the American lexicon as something respectable.

A New York street performer using the moniker "Moon Dog" finally brought matters to a head when he sued Freed, after Freed moved to New York, and won. But this was only temporary. Freed eventually won the right to use the "Moon Dog House Rock-'n'-Roll Party" trademark after a court ruled that he indeed had a prior claim. Freed, however, soon dropped the Moon Dog part altogether, leaving only Rock and Roll, which was preferable to station managers anyway.

When we arrived at the TV station, I could feel the excitement. The kids who danced on the show were all white. I wondered how "For Your Precious Love" would go over with them. The white kids I knew weren't really into love songs. They were more into Fats Domino, Little Richard, and Chuck Berry, who, for the most part, made up-tempo R&B records.

But there we were, on TV, performing this strange song that had no sing-along parts, no *doo-bop-shoo-wop*, that mentioned the title only once, and did not repeat any line in the song. "For Your Precious Love" originally was a poem I wrote entitled "They Say." Now it was a hit record.

We signed some release forms and stood around gazing at all these white kids gazing at us, until we were told where we would perform. Curtis had his guitar, and we were dressed in our pink after-six jackets, with black pants, black bowties, white shirts, black pocket scarves, and patent leather shoes. Curtis, Sam, and I worked hard to keep our hair as slick and shiny as our shoes, while Richard and Arthur, with straight hair from birth, hardly did anything at all to their hair.

The music started from the control room. The floor man pointed to us, and we started to lip-sync as the record played. At the end of the record the audience applauded, screamed, and whistled. Alan took a commercial break, and we were whisked down to the limousine, back through Central Park, back to the real thing at the Apollo. I don't think we ever got to meet him. We were just another record that his audience wanted to hear. It caught on in New York, and like most things in America, if it's white, it's right. If it's New York, it's stylish, and if it's promoted, it sells.

We went to the General Artists Corporation offices on Wednesday and met a few of the bookers. Buddy Howe, president of GAC, was tied up in meetings or some such thing. At first, I took it as a slap in the face. If I'm going to pay a company ten percent of my gross, I would like to meet the people who run it. But we were new, and these folks dealt with such big stars I guess they didn't have time to meet all the new acts they signed.

Thursday, closing night on the road, is when everyone says goodbye and expresses how much they enjoyed working with one another. "Are you going to the party at Palm's?" seemed to be the overriding question at the end of an Apollo Show.

Palm's Cafe, just down the street from the theater, started throwing closing night parties for Apollo show people because it made what should have been a slow night a very profitable one. For the price of a drink you could walk in, check out your favorite star close up, maybe even get an autograph or sit and rap for a while.

I remember this one night when Palm's was overrun with stars from the Apollo. It was packed when we arrived. Dakota Staton, the jazz singer, was doing an interview for WLIB radio, which had a remote broadcasting booth set up behind the stage. It was really a fun evening, with all the champagne we could drink and lots of pretty girls. The excitement was enhanced just by the thought of being in a room filled with such great talent. I have always been knocked out by Dakota, but to sit and talk with her, as I did that night, was really thrilling.

Cornelius Cornell Gunther, of the Coasters, was running in and out of the place laughing and having a ball. Cornell acted a little effeminate, but no one ever bothered him because he was always clowning and having fun. He also looked like he could have played football for the New York Giants, with his 18-inch neck, 52-inch chest, and well-proportioned body.

That night was memorable, too, because of Cornell, who was trying to borrow a hundred dollars from Billy Guy, one of the lead singers in the group.

Doug Jones, the bass singer, said, "Don't do it, Billy. He just got paid like the rest of us."

Cornell turned to Doug and said, "Since you've got a big mouth, you lend it to me."

"No," said Doug.

"Please, Doug."

"No."

Cornell tried again, but this time with a different tack. "Pretty please," he said in his softest voice.

Doug was emphatic. "No!"

In a complete turnabout, Cornell said in a hefty voice, "If you don't, Doug, I'll grab you in front of all these people and kiss you." Doug, cursing, gave him the hundred dollars. Cornell laughed and switched out of the cafe. I howled.

Hallandale

The final stop on the tour was a nightclub called, strangely enough, the Palms, located in Hallandale, Florida, a small town outside of Miami. The Palms, an open-air club, was run by a man named Ernie Busker. Outside of the Sir John Hotel, which was about twenty miles away, the Palms was looked upon as the premier black room in the area.

Premier or not, this also was where I ran into major trouble as lead singer of the Impressions. On our arrival at the club, all the signs read "Jerry Butler," without even a mention of the Impressions. The guys were pissed off again, and I didn't know what to say or do to appease them. There was no Abner to cool them off, so I realized right away that I was in for a rough time. The guys knew I didn't have anything to do with what was happening, but it was still a bit much for them to swallow. They became quiet and distant. I felt like a stranger among guys who were my friends.

I began wondering if the little old lady who had blessed us when we were leaving Chicago had instead put a curse on me. We went to her because Curtis's grandmother said we should. Mrs. Washington was a very hip old lady, and we did it more out of respect for her than from the belief that it would do any good.

Anyway, this little old lady said a prayer with us and then blessed some water in the name of God and started to sprinkle it on Arthur, Richard, and Sam. But when she got to Curtis and me, she took the cup and flung the water in our faces, capping the whole thing off by letting the cup slip out of her hand and hitting me in the face with it. We all wanted to laugh, but she was so wrapped up in the whole thing that we started to chuckle. We stopped short of guffaws because we didn't want to insult her.

After we left her house, Curtis said, "She sure did bless the hell out of us, didn't she, man?" We laughed and drove away with three St. Christopher medals she had given us to ward off evil spirits and protect us in our travels. I had the three medals around my neck that day in Hallandale. Yet I felt unprotected and like an outcast.

After the first show, Busker called me into his office. He and another guy, Henry Stone, a distributor, started telling me how bad the show was and suggested improvements and changes to suit their customers. "People down here like blues and a lot of risqué stuff," said Busker. "The dirtier the better." The acts that drew down there, he said, were Hank Ballard and the Midnighters, the Five Royales, and Chuck Willis, ostensibly because they had dirty acts.

As they talked, it became obvious that they thought I owned the Impressions, and that's why they had singled me out. They expected me to go back to the group, jump up and down, and come in there the next night with a better show.

I set them straight. "Mr. Busker," I said, "I don't own this group. I'm just a member, even though my name is out front. I receive the same amount of money from our shows as the other four guys. Anything you have to offer has to be shared with them."

He apologized for assuming I was the boss and sent for the rest of the group. They listened to what he had to say and gave no rebuttal until we were outside. Then they started up with, "Well, he bought it sight unseen, and that's his problem. We ain't changing shit!" I was accused of having gone to Busker and conspired with him so that I could have my way about how the show should go. It got to the point where Sam and Arthur were on the verge of threatening to kick my ass. So, partly out of anger and partly out of not wanting to have to fight these guys, I said, "Hey, man, whatever y'all want to do is fine with me." I went to bed, leaving the four of them to talk it over.

The second night the show was just as bad as the first. Ernie Busker told us that if it wasn't better the next night, he was going to cancel the show.

The following day we made the rounds to the black radio stations in the area, and I met the original Butterball and King Coleman, the guy who created the song and dance called "The Mashed Potatoes." He is now a minister in New York.

After the radio interviews, we went back to the hotel and rehearsed. We learned some new songs and added in a few dirty jokes, and sure enough, that night the show went over better. We didn't like it but the people did, and that was what Ernie Busker was paying for.

The following week we played the Palms in Jacksonville, Florida, which was also operated by Ernie Busker. We did not play the entire engagement. We were supposed to play Friday, Saturday, and Sunday but played only Friday and Saturday. Ernie had sold his Sunday date to a promoter in Atlanta by the name of Henry Wynn.

When we arrived in Atlanta, there were a lot of people at the airport to greet us. It seemed that, without our knowledge, Henry had set up a motorcade to carry us from the airport right to and all over Atlanta's black community. At first I thought it was for our benefit. Later I learned it was for his, not because he wanted to do a good job promoting his show, but because of the rivalry going on between Henry and another black promoter named B.B. Beaman.

Henry's show was at a club called the Casino, over on Auburn Avenue. B.B.'s was at the Magnolia Ballroom, on the other side of town. B.B. had Count Basie and Jackie Wilson. Henry had the Five Keys, Joe Tex, and now the number one song in Atlanta, "For Your Precious Love," sung by Jerry Butler and the Impressions. Henry had a restaurant called Henry's Grill; B.B.'s restaurant was called B.B.'s. The rivalry went on and on, into the early seventies.

If Henry never promoted a show in his life, he promoted that day. The reason for the motorcade was that he had closed the deal with Ernie Busker on such short notice that he had to make sure that people knew we were actually there. So they paraded us all around the city in shiny new cars with "Jerry Butler and the Impressions" in bold red type against sparkling white paper banners taped to the sides.

Young girls, seeing the spectacle and recognizing the name, pointed at the car, screamed, and covered their faces in embarrassment. Prostitutes boldly yelled to us, "Y'all wanna have a good time?" and patted their behinds. We waved back, feeling foolish, and more than likely looking the same way. I have always found it difficult to smile and wave at no one in particular and everybody in general. It's all so phony.

The motorcade wound its way around Peachtree Street, down Auburn Avenue, past the Casino Club, Henry's Grill, and the Royal Peacock to WERD,

Atlanta's and America's first black-owned radio station, where we met popular Atlanta disc jockey Zilla Mayes. From there we went to WAOK and met deejays Piano Red, Alley Pat, and Zena Sears. They all interviewed us and made us feel at home. For the first time, I understood what people meant by southern hospitality. Everyone wanted to feed us, take us wherever we wanted to go, and help in any way they could.

That night the show was well attended but not sold out. B.B.'s show was reporting about the same. Joe Tex was our opening act, and he was doing an Elvis Presley imitation, which immediately told us not to do anything by Presley. He also danced and ended his show by tumbling off the stage, which would have been a good trick even if the stage hadn't been eight feet high. Since it was, it became a great trick. He later told us the reason he could do it without getting hurt was that from time to time he also hired out as a stunt man.

After Joe came the Five Keys, singing the most beautiful harmony you could ever imagine. Their routine was polished to perfection, their appearance par excellence; they indeed were the stars of the show and the act we had to follow.

I wondered if we would ever get our act together and wished that we had been on already, because whatever had happened before or would happen later, these guys would not soon be forgotten.

☀

For the next several months, things went along rather well. There were the occasional flare-ups about the billing, but for the most part we were making more money than any of us had ever made in our lives, and going places that we had only read about or seen pictures of. A place that had once seemed alluring suddenly became just another town that never quite compared to what the pictures and postcards and books had led us to believe.

We returned home about the end of July, and around Cabrini Green we were lightweight celebrities. I mean we were sharp and had a few coins in our pockets, but we still lived in Cabrini Green. All of a sudden, the smells we used to ignore—the pee in the elevators and on the stairs, wine bottles and junkies —suddenly became too much to bear. The old saying about not being able to see the forest for the trees became crystal clear to me. I had been surrounded by this type of filth and dirt most of my life. It had always been there. You work and pray to escape from it, some people by drinking, others by dope, others by hard work and the strength of their convictions. Then there are some who escape it by the grace of God. But no matter what, without something to compare it to, you really can't understand how bad it is. This is why I am annoyed with people who think they know about the problems of the inner cities. You can never know until you have lived there, experienced the inequities, accepted the truth. I am equally annoyed with people living in America's ghettos who think they know how others feel about them. No one can know—or learn— about their fellow men until they walk in their shoes, do what they do, and accept their truth as *they* perceive it.

6.

Coming Apart

The Breakup

We were appearing at the Sam Houston Auditorium in San Antonio, Texas, with Clyde McPhatter, the Coasters, and Syl Austin's band. It was the last of thirty one-nighters. We were tired, and feelings were strained.

I was on the phone with Abner, who was in Chicago presiding over some recording industry convention. I was telling him that the little bit of money we were getting that night wouldn't be enough for plane fare back to Philadelphia. Also, I informed him, the road manager had refused to give us any additional money until he, Abner, had okayed it.

"Okay, baby," Abner said, giving his usual terse response. "I'll call and straighten it out. You'll have the money tomorrow. You guys do well, and I'll see you when you get back home." Click. He hung up.

Just at that moment, Arthur said, "I want to talk to him." "Sorry, man," I said. "He hung up." Arthur pitched a bitch, starting in again with that stuff about me wanting to be the boss and always wanting to do all the talking for the group. "Well, we ain't going on," he finally said, "and you can do all the singing!"

"Who the fuck are 'we'?" I asked, trying to stay calm. But I could feel my anger rising. "Me and my brother," said Arthur. Richard said nothing, but Sam was quick to respond. "I ain't going on, either," he said. All eyes then turned to Curtis.

He spoke in that soft, mellow voice he had used a few months earlier when he explained to his mother why he wanted to drop out of school and go on the road with us. "Mama," he had said, "this is what I want to do, and I know I can make it. This chance may never come again, and I want to take it." She wasn't too happy about his decision but went along with it anyway, thinking, perhaps, that it wouldn't last too long, and Curtis would soon realize that his education was more important. After all, he had just turned sixteen. If he didn't mess around too long, he could always resume his schooling and, with the aid of summer school, still graduate with his class.

"I'm going on, man," said Curtis, "because I want to get paid." "Okay, Curtis," I said. "I guess it's just me and you." Sam had second thoughts. "Well, if that's the way it's gonna be," he said, "I guess I'll go on too." Arthur and Richard were obstinate. "Fuck you, man," they said, mumbling to themselves and walking off from us.

✺

Syl Austin, the emcee, finished his band numbers and said, "Now, ladies and gentlemen, it's showtime!" The people on the dance floor started crowding to the front of the stage. Curtis, Sam, and I stood in the wings, waiting for our cue. "To start things off," Syl continued, "all the way from Chicago, Illinois, ladies and gentlemen, Jerry Butler and the Impressions!"

As I sang our first couple of songs, with Curtis playing guitar and him and Sam adding background voices wherever they could, I kept wondering if Arthur and Richard would cut out all of the bullshit and join us on stage. I didn't realize how stubborn they could be.

It occurred to me, as we went along that night, that Arthur and Richard weren't missed at all. Syl Austin's horn section was playing their part. No one in San Antonio even knew they existed. It was then that I made my decision to leave the group. This is my swan song, I said to myself. I am out of here tonight. I couldn't wait to get back to Philly.

We boarded the plane for Philadelphia the next day. It was my first plane ride. Curtis and I were scared to death; Arthur and Sam were not. They had been in the armed forces—Sam an Army paratrooper and Arthur a Navy seaman—and were not fazed one bit. In fact, they got a big kick out of watching us grab the armrests when the plane took off and when it hit air pockets during the seven- or eight-hour flight to Philadelphia.

✦

Since Eddie Thomas was in prison and couldn't represent us, Abner set it up with Philadelphian Irv Nahan to be our manager. This was worked out during one of our promotional trips to Philadelphia.

Irv looked the part of a manager: long Cadillac convertible, big diamond ring, a wad of money in his pockets, and silk mohair suits. He reminded me a lot of Burt Young, the actor who played Talia Shire's brother in the *Rocky* movies—a big, lovable teddy bear type of a guy. One other distinction: Irv talked so fast at times, you could barely understand him.

Apart from the Impressions, Irv also managed the House of David basketball team, the Philadelphia Shipyard; singer Joe Loco; and comic mime Max Patkin, who performed for several years at Philadelphia Phillies baseball games in the National League. Patkin was the forerunner of team mascots such as the San Diego Chicken and the Phillie Phanatic. Irv also managed the Doc Bagby Orchestra, singer Donny Elbert, and several black acts in the Philadelphia area. In addition, he owned a record label, called Red Top Records, with local Philadelphia promoter Red Schwartz.

We never signed a contract with Irv. We simply had a gentlemen's agreement, calling for Irv to do our bookings and give direction, for which he was paid a straight ten percent. We felt better having him, because if we had a problem, here was someone we could reach in a hurry.

I learned a lot from Irv, including getting receipts for every dime we spent and saving them. "Come April 15th next year," Irv would say, "Uncle Sam will be looking for his percentage." He explained that most black acts wound up behind the eight ball, so to speak, because of incompetent managers and poor accounting. Such managers rarely were able to prove certain expenditures to the IRS at tax time.

When Irv came aboard, he made arrangements for us to get new uniforms and pictures, and he changed our booking agency from General Artists Corporation (GAC) to Shaw Artists, Inc.

When we arrived in Philly, I immediately informed Irv that I was contemplating leaving the group because of all the static. I asked him if it would make

Taking a moment out from touring and making music to attend the 1960 BMI Awards ceremony. *Counterclockwise, from bottom right:* Helen Mayfield; Irv Nahan; an unidentified woman; Annette Butler. *Standing:* Jerry Butler; Eddie Thomas; music publisher Ivan Mogul; Curtis Mayfield. Photo courtesy of Annette Butler.

much of a difference. "Not at all," he said. The only difference, as far as he could tell, was that I wouldn't have four other guys to worry about.

But what about the difference in pricing the act? "People buy an act because of its ability to draw people through the door," he said. "That's what they pay for. Whether it is an act of one or one hundred and one won't mean a thing to them."

But what will happen to the guys? "Abner had planned to split the group anyway, because he saw where he could make two acts out of one." The idea had come to him after Vivian told him how people were coming to her record shop wanting to know who was singing this new song she had been playing. She told them it was the Impressions. "Yeah, we know the name of the group," they said.

"What we want to know is, who's singing the lead voice?" Vivian didn't know; she had never met us. She asked Calvin to find out. After talking with Irv, it soon became clear to me why Calvin wanted to know who was singing what part and what everybody's name was. He had been very diplomatic about it. "I had made a mistake previously with the Spaniels," Calvin explained to an interviewer years later. "If I had given Pookie credit on the records, I could have had two acts when they broke up. I told myself that I would never do that again, that I'd give the lead singer credit on the record. So I put the record out as Jerry Butler and the Impressions." I felt relieved. For the first time since that day in Chicago when the advance record copies arrived in Abner's office, I understood what actually had gone down.

❄

A few weeks later, I settled up with the guys and made my last gig with them. At that point, Curtis and I had been talking, and he agreed to stay with me as my guitarist at a salary of $300 a week. The only hang-up was, Curtis wanted it in writing, a contract. I was crushed. We had been friends all this time, and now he wanted a contract. It seemed so cold and impersonal.

The need for a contract never came to fruition, because after I went to Abner and explained what had happened, including the deal Curtis and I had worked out, Curtis, for some inexplicable reason, changed his mind and decided to stay with the group. I was hurt again.

In any event, we settled up, and I threw in my share of the car and what few dollars were left from our royalties. Abner promised to record both acts and give each the same amount of promotion. Vi Muzynski appeared on the scene again and said to me, "I knew you'd get the big head. Well, that's all right, Jerry, you got everything and we got nothing. But we'll make it somehow."

Her accusations hurt me deeply. Big head? Where was she when I was getting walked on? Who had sent for her, anyway? I guess it was the fellas, because they seemed relieved to have somebody championing their cause, saying the things that they had been saying all along.

But that was all over now. I had to get going. It was almost like starting over: new pictures, new music, new direction. I couldn't wait to begin.

7.

Picking Up the Pieces

Having settled my differences with the Impressions, I returned to Chicago to settle some unresolved matters, including finding a driver, interviewing potential accompanists, recording new material, and doing something I had been thinking about doing for quite some time: visiting the Smiths again and resuming my courtship of Annette, who had been on my mind a lot lately.

But first things first. I hadn't seen any of my friends and family in more than a month. As in the aftermath of Papa's death, I needed familiar surroundings to get my bearings while picking up the pieces I had left behind on the road to fame. I needed the comforts of home to do that. Death had stepped into the path I had been traveling four years earlier, forcing me, at age fourteen, to decide whether or not to be a man. Now, at age eighteen, fame had stepped into my path, forcing me to decide what *kind* of a man I would be. Would I be the big-headed jerk Vi Muzynski had said I was, lording it over my friends that I had become the elusive "somebody" that they themselves had always dreamed about? Would I rub their faces in it, saying, in effect, that I was lucky enough to escape and they weren't? Or would I be as I had always been: loyal to my friends, helpful, down-to-earth, sincere?

I really didn't have a choice in the matter. Fame didn't change me as much as it changed the people around me. People reacted differently toward me after the success of "For Your Precious Love." I began to notice the sense of awe that people developed about me, even the people I had grown up with. All of a sudden I no longer was one of them; I had become a *thing* from another dimension, a "famous person" who merited special treatment. As a consequence, I started to feel awkward around my friends and relations. Georgie Woods had yet to hang the "Iceman" moniker on me, but I was already beginning to feel a coolness toward me among my friends. Perhaps, unconsciously, *I* was the one being aloof and distant, even though outwardly everything was all smiles and handshakes.

The first person I called when I got back to Chicago was my old friend Ronald Sherman.

"How's the fellas?" I inquired.

"Everyone's doing fine," he said, quickly adding that Mrs. Sherman and the rest of the family were very proud of me.

I asked him what he was doing.

"Looking for a job," he said casually. He then informed me that he hadn't worked or done much of anything since graduation.

The timing was perfect. "How about going on the road with me, helping me drive?" I asked. Although at first he was excited and happy about the prospect of finally landing a job, he was hesitant, unsure that he could do it.

"Hey, man, sure you can," I said. "All you have to do is say yeah. I know you can do it."

"Okay," he said with some reluctance.

Problem solved.

Now that I had a driver, I needed something to drive. Abner solved that problem the next day, buying me a '59 Mercury Parklane, a four-door beauty with blue interior. It was my first car, the car I had never dreamed I would have. For that matter, I had learned how to drive only two years prior. Wait 'til Mama, Mattie, and William see this!

I drove all over, visiting people I hadn't seen since I made the record. Aunt Pearlie's restaurant was the first stop. When I walked in, she met me at the door and gave me a big hug. "You want something to eat?" she said. But almost before she could get it out of her mouth, she told everybody in the restaurant, "This is my nephew. He's a singing star, making records and everything." She looked at me with pride as she fought back tears. The little nappy-headed boy she had watched grow up and graduate from high school, who had worked in her kitchen, who she had fussed at, preached at, her brother's son, had made something of himself, and he wasn't even nineteen yet.

Next I drove over to Tom Morgan's house. He, Mr. and Mrs. Morgan, and Tom's sisters and brothers gave me the star treatment, too. I asked Tom about Curtis Cade and James Lowe. None of them had passed the test for the Marines, he said. I cracked up hearing this, because if not for the success of "For Your Precious Love," I probably would have been in the Marines, waving bye-bye to my three buddies standing on the docks as my ship pulled away.

My next stop, although brief, ended up being one of the most long-lasting.

Annette

As I drove to the Smiths, I recalled the last time I'd been there—a few months earlier. What a difference a day makes? What a difference a month or two makes. A few months before, I'd had dreams of going into the Marines, becoming a chef, and settling into the kind of "quiet desperation" existence that Henry David Thoreau wrote about. But "For Your Precious Love" changed all of that—at least for a little while. Now, in place of pursuing a career in the culinary arts, I was pursuing a career in the art of entertainment. In place of walking to work or visiting my girlfriend, I now had a brand new 1959 Parklane automobile to take me places. I even had a new attitude as I rang the bell at the Smiths' house. I was more confident and self-assured than I had been a year earlier. Now I had status and fame and a new Parklane. I had arrived.

I indeed had arrived, though not in the literal sense, of course. I had arrived in terms of my own sense of self-worth. This time, I was on equal footing not only with the Smiths but with everyone else. Don't get me wrong—the Smiths, especially Annette, had never once made me feel uneasy or unwelcome. On the contrary, they were—and are—a wholesome, outgoing, fun-loving family who always try to make every visitor to their home feel comfortable and welcomed, even the late Grandma Pettis, Mrs. Smith's mother, who always said what was on her mind.

My poverty-ridden background was the culprit. I always felt self-conscious about being poor whenever I was around people who I perceived as more well-off than me. I tell this story all the time. We were so poor when I was growing up that my mother would boil chicken feet in water, add a little salt, and that was our meal. Seldom was there meat on the table. One of the things that impressed me about the Smiths was that they actually served chitlins on Wednesday—a weekday! At my house, we were lucky to have chitlins served

Annette

once or twice a year: Thanksgiving and Christmas. Mind you, chitlins—hog entrails—cost only ten or twenty cents a pound back in those days. We, my family and I, couldn't even afford that. Nor could we afford to pay the twenty-cent fare to ride a bus. All of the money I made on my jobs went toward feeding and caring for Mama, William, Mattie, and myself. There was nothing left over for luxuries. Chitlins and bus fare were luxuries.

Standing there on the Smiths' porch, I smiled to myself as I recalled my last visit there. It was nearly midnight, and I had a long way to go. "Well, I guess I'd better be going," I told Annette. "I've got a long walk."

"Walk?" she said incredulously. "Where to?"

"I walked all the way over here, and now I've got to walk all the way back," I said, letting it sink in that I had to walk about ten miles each way *just to see her.*

"Oh, that's a shame!" she said.

"It doesn't seem so far when I walk fast and I have something pleasant on my mind," I said bravely, allowing just a hint of self-pity. We stood there for a moment, silently, in the dark, feeling awkward and tentative.

A voice shattered the silence: "Kiss her, fool!" It was Annette's grandmother, calling from a side bedroom of the Smiths' modest home on Carroll Avenue. I guess I had overstayed my welcome with Grandma, who probably was tired and wanted to sleep. My long, drawn-out goodbye had kept her from doing that. Annette and I looked at each other and laughed, feeling more awkward than before.

There was no awkwardness this time. I felt extremely confident, having resolved to propose to Annette that evening when she got home from her job as a nurse's aide at Presbyterian–St. Luke Hospital.

Annette had been dating some guy for about two years before I came along. He had given her his class ring and asked her to marry him. This put him way ahead of me in the Getting-Annette-to-the-Altar Derby. I had a lot of catching up to do. He had inadvertently made my job easier by joining the Air Force. It gave me an opportunity to lay out my case with deadly preciseness. A few months earlier I would have been nervous, scared, but now, bolstered by my newly acquired celebrity status and a sure-to-please diamond ring, I had no fear at all. It's funny how the smallest bit of success gives you the courage to try bigger and better things. Now that I thought I was big shit and had been around, I felt there was nobody too good for me to rap to. I made up my mind that I would marry either Annette or somebody like her. She was thoughtful and intelligent and had a great sense of humor. And she was fine—yes, my goodness, yes!

When we were alone, I took Annette's hand in mine, dropped down on one knee, and asked her to marry me.

She was surprised at first. But then, with a slight smile, she said, "Yes."

We were married at Greater Mt. Sinai Baptist Church. The Reverend George Washington Jones performed the ceremony. Tom Morgan was my best man; my groomsmen included Harvey Fuqua, lead singer of the Moonglows; Chuck Barksdale, also of the Moonglows; Wade Flemons, who had just recorded "Here I Stand" for Vee Jay; and Earl, Annette's brother. I asked the Impressions—Curtis Mayfield, Sam Gooden, and Fred Cash—to be part of the wedding, but they were unable to attend.

We honeymooned in Philadelphia, which turned out to be a nightmare for Annette but a blessing to me. Georgie Woods offered me $1,200—at the time my biggest payday to date—to perform at the Uptown Theater. I couldn't turn it down. But in hindsight, maybe I should have. Annette has never let me live it down.

The Moonglows. Harvey Fuqua (*top left*) and Chuck Barksdale (*not pictured*) served as groomsmen in my wedding. Other members of the group (*clockwise from left*) are Billy Johnson (with glasses), Peter Graves, Prentiss Barnes, and Bobby Lester.

Had it not been for Ruth Brown and LaVern Baker, Annette's first friends and confidantes on the road, my marriage would have been over before it got started. Ruth, to whom I will always be grateful, took Annette under her wing, gave her the facts of life on the road, shooed away all the Backstage Annies, and made it that much easier for two newlyweds to get their bearings and build a marriage that has lasted more than forty years. LaVern, God rest her soul, was always there when either of us needed a friend, and with a smile that was as big as her heart.

First Time Out

My first time out following the breakup of the Impressions was murderous, frightening, unbelievable. All of a sudden, where there had once been five guys, now there was just one. And I didn't have anybody to blame things on anymore. If things were fucked up, it was because I fucked them up. I knew people liked the Impressions, but I didn't know *how* much they liked them until I left the group.

When I made the decision to leave the Impressions, I had no idea what I was letting myself in for. And since I didn't know what to expect, I therefore wasn't prepared, for example, when a woman in Washington, D.C., got up —right in the middle of my "git-over" song—and said, "I hope a fly flies in your mouth." I was utterly surprised—and hurt—when audiences booed me and threw miniature whiskey bottles onstage. It was a long time before I realized that once people buy into a singing group or an act, they want it to stay that way, just as when they first saw you. They are resistant to change. They didn't like it, either, when David Ruffin and Eddie Kendricks left the Temptations, or when Diana Ross left the Supremes and Cindy Birdsong left Patti LaBelle. People also were hurt when the Shirelles broke up, and when the Beatles, the Doobie Brothers, Martin and Lewis, Sam Cooke and the Soul Stirrers, and Michael Jackson and his brothers went their separate ways. Fans don't want you to do that. They love you *just as you are.*

Episodes from those first horrid months after the breakup are indelibly etched in my psyche, as vivid as the day I first experienced them. I recall, as if it were only yesterday, being onstage and someone saying, "His fingernails are dirty." I still can see the faces of the people who heckled me, although hecklers are a separate breed altogether. They go to shows simply to be pests, to be part of the show. They would go to the Apollo, the Howard, the Uptown, or the Regal, for example, and heckle performers so that their remarks would become part of the show. People would come as much to see the show in the audience as they would to see the show onstage.

When I was with the Impressions, I used to get down on one knee and sing "For Your Precious Love." I remember the time, after I went solo, when this guy came all the way from Baltimore and brought a whole bunch of his friends to see me get down on my knees. But that night I didn't get down on my knees; I just finished the song and walked off the stage. The guy hollered out, "Naw, motherfucker, come back here. I brought all of these people up here to see you get down on your knees. Get down on your knees!" The audience rolled. He wouldn't let the show go on until I got down on my knees. It was hysterical.

The first place I played after leaving the Impressions was a skating rink in Indianapolis. Ronald and I got there late. The musicians—a saxophonist, a trumpet player, a drummer, a piano player who played out of tune, and a bass player—had already set up. They said they knew my music. Basically, these cats were jazz musicians and didn't want to play my stuff in the first place. In the second place, they weren't *good* jazz musicians. I had only two songs, "For Your

Precious Love" and Roscoe Gordon's "I Don't Want Much (Just Want a Little Bit)," a blues song.

Showtime came and we couldn't even get through one song. Everything was all screwed up. I finally had to tell the musicians, "Lay out. Just don't play." I sang a cappella. The song died. I died. I spent six years in one place—in one night. The longest night of my damn life. And then on top of that, the promoter came backstage and said, "We ain't gon' pay you."

Say what! You ain't gon' pay me? I was owed about $350. After what I had just gone through, we definitely were going to boogie up in there *that* night. For one thing, I had already spent the money: for rent back in Chicago, Ron's salary, gas money—you name it. After a lot of cussing, hollering, and screaming, the guy finally paid me, and Ron and I got into our little Parklane and returned to Chicago.

It was clear, after that experience, that I needed an accompanist, someone to perform the role that Curtis had performed when I was with the Impressions. When I returned to Chicago, I quickly put the word out that I was looking for an accompanist. It took a while, and I had to suffer through several more months of horrifying one-nighters in cow barns and skating rinks with out-of-tune pianos—and piano players—before help finally arrived in the person of Phillip Upchurch.

I first heard about Phil through Annette. A friend of her father's from Columbia, Tennessee, casually mentioned one day that his nephew played guitar and was looking for work. A few days later, Phil came to our apartment (303 N. Central Park) with his father, a bus driver. "Jerry, I wouldn't even think about this if it wasn't with you," the elder Upchurch said. I couldn't figure that out, because I was only a few years older than Phillip, who was the same age as Curtis, about sixteen or seventeen. The elder Upchurch was concerned, I learned later, because Phil had been abandoned in Washington, D.C., by the Spaniels a year earlier, when they ran out of money. Later gigs with the Dells and others didn't work out all that well, either.

Until Phil came along, I was out there struggling with no musicians, sort of catch as catch can. Most of what we were doing in those days was touring, and the tours always had a band, such as Syl Austin or Paul (Hucklebuck) Williams. And since guys like me had only a couple of songs to perform, the bands would rehearse the songs and we would perform an hour or so later. But when you left that tour and started playing one-nighters, the whole ballgame changed. Then you were on your own. You had to play with whatever musicians were in town.

Just as things were beginning to settle down, the bottom dropped out. We were working in D.C. on a show with Dee Clark when, just before showtime,

Phil walked up to me in front of the Howard Theater and announced that he was quitting. He had accepted a job with Dee for $25 or $50 more a week—I don't remember which—and that was that.

I managed to muddle through that engagement without too many problems. But I don't know who I was more angry with—Phil or Dee. Phil still argues that he wasn't that cold-blooded. "How does that sound, leaving a good-paying job for $25 more?" he asks rhetorically whenever he's reminded of that day. I have long since buried that episode and moved on. But it hurts whenever I think about it. As for Dee, the two of us had always been rivals, ever since our high school days, when our respective doo-wop groups in Chicago had battled each other for city bragging rights; then, later on, when we both were signed with Vee Jay, Dee enticed my drummer, Leo Morris (Idris Muhammad), to quit and come work for him. On a more personal level, when Dee saw me driving a brand-new white 1959 Parklane, he traded in his brand new black Buick for a white Eldorado. It went on like that for years—all in fun.

As with Phil, I had long since dropped the issue. Dropped but not forgotten. When Dee passed December 6, 1990, in Atlanta, I touched on our rivalry in my eulogy to him. "It wasn't that either of us thought he was better than the other," I said. "I wanted you to succeed and do well so that I might have a standard to follow and do better. I'm sure you felt the same way too."

8.

Learning Experiences

Raymond Tunia

When Curtis left the second time, I obviously was in need of a guitarist. I put in a desperate call to the Shaw Booking Agency.

"We've got just the guy," the agent said. "He just left Ella Fitzgerald and is looking for work. He only charges $200 a week. We'll send him right over."

"Right over" was an outdoor theater called Evan's Bar and Grill in Forrestville, Maryland, just outside Washington, D.C. The club was designed to hold shows both indoors and out. On this particular night it was rainy and messy, so they moved the affair inside. That's where Ron and I eagerly awaited my guitarist.

Around 8:00 P.M. a tall, slender man with horn-rimmed glasses, a black tuxedo, white shirt, and bowtie knocked on the dressing room door and stuck his head inside.

"Good evening," he said. "My name is Raymond Tunia, and I'm supposed to meet Mr. Butler here. I am his pianist, his accompanist." I couldn't quite place the accent, which sounded like a cross between East Coast highbrow and British upper class, but I could tell the guy was well-educated. He looked to be in his late thirties or early forties.

He stepped inside as Ron and I exchanged curious glances. We were looking for a guitar player, but they had sent over a pianist. My concern was that most of the "joints" we played in, especially joints like Evan's Bar and Grill, if they had a piano, it was always out of tune. A guitar player, on the other hand, would simply tune his instrument to the other members in the band.

After I introduced Ron and myself, he immediately got down to business. "Mr. Sands told me I was to receive two hundred dollars a week," he said, adding, "And you pay transportation. Is that right?"

Yes, that's right. He asked if we had any music prepared. We said yes and pulled out the charts for the two songs that constituted my whole show. Raymond studied them for a moment, and I could tell he was disappointed with what he saw. He made some marks on the sheets and then excused himself to go look for the bandleader.

When he left, Ron and I exchanged low fives and danced around like we had just hit the numbers. An accompanist! I could hardly pronounce the word.

By the time we caught up with Raymond, he had found the bandleader and was showing him how he wanted the music played. He had changed some parts for the horn players but focused most of his attention on the drummer and bass player, having the guitarist play chinks and rhythms.

When the rehearsal was over, he said, "I'm going to walk around a little bit and see what's going on."

Ron and I sat in the dressing room and marveled at the professionalism of the man.

Time passed. Raymond had been gone for nearly an hour and a half. The place had started to fill up, and the band began playing. I was due to go on in fifteen minutes. We began worrying about Raymond, wondering where he had gone. I sent Ron to find him as I started to change. My spirits were way up. This was going to be a great show.

Just as I was clipping my bowtie into place, Ronald and Raymond came through the door. I couldn't believe what I was seeing: Raymond's shirt was all fucked up; his tie was twisted around his neck; his nose was red, and so were his eyes. His tuxedo had dust all over it; and he was slobbering. I could smell the whiskey from where I was standing. He just stood there teetering, mumbling that he was ready to play. This man, who had been so beautiful and correct an hour and a half ago was, as my dad used to say, "drunk as a turkey."

I didn't know whether to laugh or cry. But I understood now why a man with all this talent and intellect was playing in a barn like Evan's Bar and Grill. He had not learned how to conquer his passion for the bottle.

At first I was afraid to go on. I didn't know how this guy was going to work out. But my fears were unfounded. Drunk or sober, Raymond Tunia was one of the best musicians I ever met. The show went down as if he had been playing for me as long as Curtis.

As we drove back to Washington, everyone was silent, lost in thought. It was the kind of silence that comes when no one knows quite how to say what's on his mind, although it seemed as if we each could hear what the other was thinking: Raymond was thinking that he had probably messed up another gig. Ronald wondered how I was going to deal with what had happened. And I wondered how a more experienced person in my position would handle a situation like that. In the end, I said nothing; Raymond said nothing; Ronald turned on the radio.

The next morning Raymond was up early and had breakfast before Ron and I awoke. He knocked on my door, once again looking like the dapper gentleman who had come to my dressing room the night before. He apologized and told me that what had happened would never happen again. I thanked him, and he immediately started in telling me what he thought I needed:

"A sheet of music for every musician," he said, "and it should be clean and legible at all times. You should have folders with your name embossed on them.

"I will take the music home with me and rewrite it in my spare time.

"You and I should rehearse so that I know your range, high and low notes, what tempos you feel most comfortable with, what keys you sing best in on ballads and up-tempo tunes."

I listened attentively. My first, real education in music and show business had just begun.

We went and played the Apollo, and all the cats in the Ruben Phillips Band knew Raymond from being with Ella. They were saying, "Aw, shit, Jerry's got him a man now!" It was the same kind of reaction that white musicians would give Phil Moore some years later when we did *The Ed Sullivan Show*. When I walked on the stage, my respect went up, based on who I had playing for me. Raymond Tunia was awesome—and just a wonderful man.

Raymond stayed with me for about a year. It was interesting, because by the time I really wanted—and needed—the kind of musician that Raymond was, he wasn't there. He had come and gone. He was a musician's musician.

Phil Moore

Cannonball Adderly used to say, "If there's something wrong with you musically, go see Phil Moore. He'll straighten you out." Some called him Dr. Phil Moore, and before it was all over, so did I.

I met Phil a year or so after I left the Impressions. Abner and Calvin, recognizing that I needed to develop an onstage act as a solo, called Phil and asked him to work with me. I had never heard of him before.

What I later found out about him was impressive. For example, he had
- studied piano from the age of four;
- attended the Cornish School and the University of Washington in Seattle;
- played with the famous Les Hite band and other dance bands on the West Coast, while working for MGM studios and ghostwriting for film composer Dimitri Tiomkin in the early 1940s;
- moved to New York City to be the musical director for Mildred Bailey's radio show on CBS;
- returned to Hollywood in the late fifties and formed the Phil Moore Four, which included John Levy, the future manager of singer Nancy Wilson;
- appeared in a few B-movie musicals;
- worked as an accompanist and musical director for Lena Horne and Dorothy Dandridge; and
- backed a variety of singers, from Frank Sinatra to Marilyn Monroe.

A tireless writer, arranger, and teacher, Phil founded the Singers Workshop in Hollywood. In between, he recorded four albums bearing his name: *Symphony in Green*, an original composition; *Fantasy for Girl and Orchestra*; *Polynesian Paradise*; and Leda Annest's *Portrait of Leda*.

Under Phil's tutelage, I learned not only the art of getting on and off a stage, but how to hold the attention of an audience. He also taught me about the little things, the subtleties of performing, like playing with my cufflinks and straightening my tie. These were not distractions, he said. On the contrary, they tended to focus the audience's attention on the performer.

Take, for instance, Jack Benny and his patented tilt of the head and folding and unfolding of his arms. He was a master of subtlety. Rodney Dangerfield's periodic tightening of his tie while complaining "I don't get no respect" is not distracting but an expected part of the act.

Phil passed in 1987, but I often think about him, with his calm demeanor, speaking in measured tones, teaching:

"Go and see the great performers," he would say matter-of-factly.

"Why?"

"Because you will learn what to do and what not to do. You'll learn what to do by sitting there *appreciating* what to do. When the show starts getting dull and boring, that's when you'll learn what not to do.

"Never walk onstage cold. Always have something happening. Thirty seconds of dead time on a stage is forever."

He also taught me to be myself by taking pride in being born black. I stopped processing my hair and wearing a do rag after Phil said to me one day, "You weren't born with processed hair, so why destroy what nature gave you?"

"Because that's the style."

"Change the style. Be different. It didn't hurt Belafonte to be different. Why should it hurt you?"

Phil was always recognizable by his double-breasted blue blazer, turtleneck sweater, blue jeans, casual shoes, and trademark Meerschaum pipe, which he would clench tightly between his teeth as words of wisdom fell from his lips.

He had three or four hundred pipes and even got me started collecting them. He educated me about pipe smoking, to the point where I had about fifty or sixty pipes myself, ranging in cost anywhere from $25 to $150.

The last time I worked with Phil was in 1969, when I was booked to do *The Ed Sullivan Show*. I needed a music director, and I called him. We hadn't worked together in about five or six years.

"Aw, Jerry, that's great!" he said. "I'd be delighted. What're you going to sing?" I told him I wanted to do "Brand New Me" and "Where Are You Going," the theme song Bobby Scott had written and I recorded for the movie *Joe*. I wanted to do "Brand New Me" because I was one of the writers and I wanted to get some of that royalty money. But I also wanted to do it because Dusty Springfield had recorded it and it would look like another credit.

"That sounds like a great lineup," he said. "What do you want me to do?"

"I need someone to write charts for a big orchestra."

"Consider it done."

When I went over to the Ed Sullivan Theater with Phil, all the string players and horn players jumped up. "Phil, geez! I haven't seen you in years. What have you been doing?" Amid the handshakes and back slaps, Phil somehow managed to introduce me: "This is my client, Jerry Butler, and we've been working on some things..." "Oh, really? That's fantastic, Phil. It's so good to see you! Where have you been?"

I knew right then that my stuff would be played well because of the respect they had for him. If I had walked in there with someone they didn't know or respect, they would have played the music, but they wouldn't have given it that extra *something*. I have performed on many shows where the musicians were like "Ho-hum, another singer." But with Phil, it was like "You know, Phil, what about this bar sixteen over here, do you really want that? Listen to it; it sounds a little . . . " I loved it! You could just see they were in awe of his musicianship.

It reminds me of a story about Nat Cole. Most people didn't know that Nat Cole was a musician. They thought he was just a singer. As the story goes, he went to do a show on Broadway, and as they were rehearsing the music, a guy hit a bad note in the string section. "Excuse me," Nat said and walked over to the piano and sat down. "You know that note you played, it should've been an A-flat." Right away they said, "Oh, yes sir, Mr. Cole." They were just trying him, trying to find out how much he knew.

That teaches you that if you want to be respected in the industry, you have to know your business. I relearned that lesson some years ago from Quincy Jones as we were taking a stroll down State Street in downtown Chicago. It was during the week of the IBAM (Institute of Black American Music) conference back in the early seventies. Jesse Jackson had asked Quincy, Cannonball Adderly, and a bunch of other entertainers to come to town to help with a fund-raiser at the Amphitheater. I don't know how Quincy and I ended up on State Street. I only recall making a casual comment about young musicians being musical snobs and Quincy turning to me, saying, "Yeah, that may be, but it is important to know what you are doing."

I couldn't argue with that. Those young musicians indeed may have been musical snobs, he explained, but they had a right to be because they had put the time in and mastered their craft. They had reached a certain level of competence that permitted them to speak with authority.

I thought I was paying Quincy a compliment, in that he, the world-famous Quincy Jones, could walk and talk with a Jerry Butler and not put him down, while those young players, some of them just coming out of college, could only talk about jazz and treat everything else as so much bullshit. I was wrong.

That brings to mind another lesson that Phil taught me: "Do what's right when it's right." For example, once he asked me, "What songs do you like?"

I said, "I Did It My Way."

"That's the wrong song for you."

"Why?"

As was his style, Phil lit his pipe, cocked his head to the side, smiled knowingly, and said, "Because you are twenty-three years old and you haven't done shit. You would come off looking arrogant. How does it look, a twenty-three-year-old kid standing on stage talking about 'I did it my way'? Sinatra makes it work because Sinatra has done things. He has lived. He has earned the right to sing that song. He is believable. After you're in the business twenty or thirty years, *then* you will have earned the right to sing a song like that."

Phil drew up a list of performers that he thought I should go see, and on the list was Johnny Mathis. I wanted to see Mathis perform myself—for two reasons. First, he was playing the type of venues I wanted to play: Mister Kelly's and Chez Paree in Chicago, the Copacabana, Carnegie Hall, Basin Street —all of the big clubs. If Mathis was playing those type of clubs, I reasoned, it followed that I should try and do what he does.

Secondly, I wanted to see firsthand what all the fuss was over Johnny Mathis. A few years before, Annette's cousin, Audrey, and I had gotten into this innocuous discussion about great singers, and I made some pretty disparaging remarks about her favorite singer, Johnny Mathis. I don't recall what I said to her, but apparently it was bad enough to make her cry. She was heartless mad at me.

"I was just teasing," I told her. "I don't even know the man! I'm sorry!" But she was terribly upset. Later, Annette said ruefully, "Jerry, you don't know. Audrey idolizes Johnny Mathis." As if to emphasize that, Audrey later moved to California and married a guy that could have passed for Mathis's brother. In fact, I heard she even tried dating Mathis, but when he wouldn't come around, she went out with his brother. Audrey has long since gotten over her crush on Mathis. She has remarried and lives happily in California.

But all that's beside the point. Johnny Mathis was on Phil's list, and I made plans to see him the first chance I got.

That chance came shortly after I wrapped up one of my last albums for Vee Jay. "Make It Easy on Yourself," by Hal David and Burt Bacharach, was one of the tunes on the album, which we did in New York. During the sessions, Burt and I used to unwind by playing basketball at a local gymnasium. One day Burt said, "Come on, Jerry, let's go play some ball. I think Mathis is going to be there." I said, "Okay, I'd like to meet him."

We went and played, and I met Mathis for the first time. I didn't get to see his show that day, but a few weeks later I did. He was performing at the Copacabana. I happened to be in town on some business and stopped in to see him.

The Copa had a policy that you couldn't sit at a table alone, so luckily I ran into some friends and we went in to see the show.

We were sitting there and the lights went down, and the announcer said, "Now, ladies and gentlemen, Mr. Johnny Mathis." The band started playing a fanfare that lasted about three or four minutes. People were applauding the whole time. I said to myself, This is cool.

Mathis finally came onstage, and everybody stood up. He hadn't sung a note yet—they just loved him. He went into his routine, and right away you could see that he was extremely shy and introverted. He didn't say much to the audience. He just sang and sang and sang—until he came to a song called "Maria" from *West Side Story*.

I don't know how to describe it. It wasn't just singing; it was something else. It was that thing Phil always talked about—believability—the ability to deliver a song with such intimacy, such emotion, that the people in the audience forget that they are in a nightclub, forget about going to work in the morning, forget about the kids and babysitters, and *become* Maria—or in my case, the guy who romances Maria. That's what Mathis brought to that song that night. That's what Audrey knew that I didn't know. That's what Phil wanted me to see, to absorb and savor and *use*.

I was the first one out of my seat, applauding my head off, when Mathis finished the song. Years later, when I played the Copa, I remembered the lesson of that night: Don't ever cheat your audience. Do everything with conviction, with style. And most of all, make it believable.

Curtis Mayfield

Looking back on it now, I guess Curtis had always been there when I needed him. For example, he was there when I went looking for a guitarist for the Roosters. He was there when I needed a buffer between me and the brothers Brooks. He was always there with his sense of humor, his pragmatism, his instincts, his great musical sense. When I was left stranded in D.C. without an accompanist, who else could I call but Curtis Mayfield?

"Jerry, man," he said, "I don't know what I would've done if you hadn't called."

The feeling was mutual. I don't know what I would have done had Curtis decided to tough it out rather than perform with me again. After all, we did not part on the best of terms. Two things were in my favor: First, I had heard that the Impressions had disbanded for a while. In fact, Curtis was working at a tobacco shop in Chicago.[1] The second thing was Curtis's own pragmatism. I remembered what he had said back in San Antonio, the day I left the Impressions. "I didn't quit school and come all this way to turn around and go back," he said. "Jerry, I have to make this work."

My reunion with Curt was a lot like the lyrics to "Lost," a song I co-wrote with Kenny Gamble and Leon Huff a few years later:

> I was lost, lost,
> but found in the nick of time . . .

Curtis and I both found each other in the nick of time. My career wasn't going anywhere, and neither was his. The reunion led to one of my first big hits,

Curtis Mayfield

"He Will Break Your Heart," which Curt and I collaborated on. We formed Curtom Publishing during that period, and bought minor interests in Queen Booking. I eventually sold my interests in both.

Curt worked with me for only a few months before he was gone again. I could see it coming, but I didn't know it would come that soon. Curt was anxious to try new ideas and explore different sounds. And so we parted again, this time more amicably. We parted friends and continued as such until his death in 1999.

He was philosophical about the comings and goings of the original Impressions. "Everybody who was part of the Impressions could see that it was God's calling," he said. "It allowed us, as young people, to make the proper decisions that later on helped our careers. I think that has been proven."

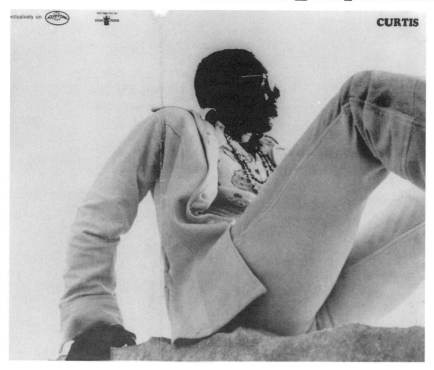

Curtis Mayfield

By the time we parted the second time, both of our careers were on course to reach new heights. I went on to score some major hits for Mercury Records, and Curt, meanwhile, after reuniting with the Impressions, scored big with such hits as "It's All Right," "Keep On Pushing," "People Get Ready," "Amen," and "Choice of Colors." These socially aware songs became, as one writer put it, "the soundtrack to the civil rights movement" and elevated Curt to icon status.

Although we both dabbled in motion pictures around the same time, I came nowhere near the success of Curtis's "Superfly," the theme song for the movie by the same name, and "Freddie's Dead," also in *Superfly*. He released these on his Curtom label, which had another soundtrack hit with "Let's Do It Again" with the Staple Singers, which Curt wrote and produced. He subsequently scored "Claudine" with Gladys Knight and the Pips, and "Sparkle" with

Aretha Franklin. At one point he even turned actor, appearing in a cameo role as an inmate in the prison drama *Short Eyes.*

Meanwhile, I sang the title song to the seventies movie classic *Joe* and also performed one or two more songs on the soundtrack. I also worked on and recorded (with the help of arranger Jerry Peters) the soundtrack to the blaxploitation film *Melinda.* To cap off my rather nondescript film career, I appeared with Ray Milland and Rosey Grier in *The Thing with Two Heads,* a B-movie disaster, in which I played a prison guard. I had only one line in the entire movie. "More power to you, brother," I said to Rosey Grier as he was being strapped into the electric chair. Suffice it to say, it didn't win any Oscars.

But one movie I was indirectly involved with, *Breakfast at Tiffany's,* did win an Oscar—in fact, several Oscars—including one for Best Title Song, "Moon River." I was expected to sing my version of "Moon River" on the Academy Awards telecast because, at the time, I was the one who had done the most to popularize it. Andy Williams, who originally had turned down the song, ended up performing his version (recorded nearly a year after I had made the song a hit) on the awards telecast. My only consolation came from the late Henry Mancini and Johnny Mercer, who took out full-page ads in *Billboard* and other trades thanking me for recording their song.

The point I am trying to make here, in contrasting my career with Curtis's, is that survivors like Curtis Mayfield seem to have an extra measure of resiliency—perhaps it's that "sterner stuff" that Shakespeare talks about—that allows them to overcome adversity better than others, often coming back stronger than before. Maybe Darwin had it right with his "survival of the fittest" theory. Some people, or species, may indeed be more fit than others to withstand the worst calamities. Perhaps there is a gene or something that comes into play whenever disaster strikes that causes some human beings to cope with tragedy better than others, especially those of us who simply wilt in the face of disaster. I am reminded of Coretta Scott King and Jacqueline Kennedy, who endured their respective tragedies with such grace and fortitude.

9.

Making My Mark

The summer of 1959 had been truly one of the happiest, best times of my life. As that summer all too quickly faded away, my life path encountered a major fork in the road. As I was soon to learn, so had the path of rock and roll. It was the end to the decade I loved best, the 50's—and it was the end of innocence. My life, the music I loved, and society would soon be changed forever.

—Harry Turner, *This Magic Moment:*
Musical Reflections of a Generation

"The End of Innocence"

As I struggled through my first full year as a solo performer and recording artist, America struggled with some centuries-old problems of its own. In 1960, the American people attempted to address some of those problems by choosing as their president a young senator from Massachusetts to lead them through the social malaise of the sixties. Building on the momentum of the civil rights movement, President John F. Kennedy came into office with a new plan for America which he called the "New Frontier." He promised, among other things, to place more emphasis on social welfare programs and civil rights. It wasn't until the last year of his assassination-shortened presidency, however, that Kennedy actually sent a civil rights bill to Congress—and then only because he literally was forced to.[1]

By most accounts, three major events forced the president's hand: the 1960 sit-ins by black college students at lunch counters in the South; the 1961 Freedom Rides, in which an interracial group of college students from the North traveled by bus to the South to test the effectiveness of a 1960 Supreme Court decision prohibiting racial segregation in public areas; and the 1963 protests in Birmingham, Alabama, against the infamous chief of police Bull Connor, who unleashed fire hoses, billy clubs, and attack dogs on peaceful protesters.

Sensing the changing mood in America, performers such as Bob Dylan and Sam Cooke began to admonish the nation in song. Dylan's "Blowin' in the Wind," for example, prophesied the upheavals of the sixties and seventies, while Cooke's "A Change Is Gonna Come," strangely reminiscent of the Civil War song "Wake Nicodemus" by black composer Henry Clay, held out hope for better times. Clay wrote:

> There's a great time coming
> And it's not far off,
> Been long, long, long on the way.

A century later, Sam Cooke wrote:

> It's been too hard living,
> But I'm afraid to die
> 'Cause I don't know what's out there
> Beyond the sky.
> It's been a long, a long time coming
> But I know a change is gonna come.

As Dylan and Cooke wove their prophecies, Curtis Mayfield waited patiently in the wings, observant, cautious, preparing to introduce his haunting composition "People Get Ready."

At the beginning of the fifties, however, there was no hint of the trouble ahead. The mood of post–World War II America was reflected in the innocent, inoffensive, "feel-good" tunes of artists like Pat Boone, Rosemary Clooney, and Perry Como. Hula hoops were the rage; an affable conservative war hero, Dwight D. Eisenhower, occupied the White House; and the country was enjoying one of the highest standards of living in its history—for that matter, one of the highest standards of living in the history of the world. There was reason for optimism.

Midway through the decade, however, changes began creeping into American society—at first imperceptible, later stark and revealing.
• In 1953, Senator Joseph McCarthy of Wisconsin began conducting hearings on Communist subversion in America and Communist infiltration of the

Armed Forces. Following the hearings, paranoia swept the land as Americans became less trustful of one another.

• In 1954, a band from Chester, Pennsylvania, Bill Haley and the Comets, recorded "Rock around the Clock," which was used as the theme for the movie *The Blackboard Jungle*. The movie's soundtrack marked the first union of black rhythm and blues with southern rockabilly. The Age of Rock and Roll was born. Blues musician Muddy Waters would later remark, "Rhythm and blues had a baby and they named it rock and roll."

• On May 17, 1954, the Supreme Court ruled in its landmark *Brown vs. Topeka Board of Education* decision that segregated schools are "inherently unequal."

• On December 5, 1955, a boycott of city buses led by Martin Luther King Jr. began in Montgomery, Alabama. The boycott would last fifty-four weeks.

• In September 1957, federal troops were sent to Little Rock, Arkansas, to enforce integration of Little Rock High School.

• On October 4, 1957, the Soviet Union launched the first earth satellite, *Sputnik,* into orbit, which led to fears that America's education system was not competitive with the Soviets'.

• In 1958, the controversial African-American singer Paul Robeson finally had his passport reinstated by the U.S. government, which had revoked it in 1950 because of his outspoken, unpopular views on racism and Communism.

As the walls of segregation began to crumble, the complacency that had marked a strong and optimistic America at the beginning of the decade gradually gave way to an America that had become increasingly introspective and unsure of itself.[2]

Meanwhile, on the international front, America's hegemony as the moral and military leader of the so-called "free world" was at once being usurped by countries like France, which increasingly was becoming the refuge of choice for dissident American expatriates and intellectuals; and by the Soviets, whose one-million-strong army and dazzling space exploits had given pause to even the most adventuresome of America's vaunted "military-industrial complex."

The decade finally came to a close, but not before tragedy struck. On a cold winter night in 1959, three of rock and roll's most promising performers— Buddy Holly, Ritchie Valens, and J. P. (Big Bopper) Richardson—died in a small-plane crash along with their pilot. (I had performed on the same show with them several weeks prior at the Brooklyn Fox Theater. Clyde McPhatter, the Solitaires, and others also were in the show.) Like a macabre metaphor, the crash, as well as the careers of these promising performers, summed up 1950s America: What had begun so innocently and optimistically at the beginning of the decade suddenly came crashing down at the end. In his 1970 classic "American Pie," Don McLean characterized the tragedy as "the day the music died."

But for people like Harry Turner, who grew up in Greenville, South Carolina, the music he had grown to love—rhythm and blues—had died much earlier, trampled in the onslaught of rock and roll. Turner, a white southerner whose lifelong passion for rhythm and blues had led to close friendships with hundreds of artists, wrote a book about the demise of his beloved music, *This Magic Moment: Musical Reflections of a Generation.* Nelson George, who is black, wrote a similar book, *The Death of Rhythm & Blues.*

Since the early seventies, Turner has been heard on more than seventy radio stations, paying homage to what he calls the "original American art form" and crusading for its creators to be remembered.

"While rhythm and blues was forming itself in the late forties and early fifties, white kids picked up on it big time," said Turner, recalling the first time he heard "this danceable, bouncy rhythm and blues music."

Only a few radio stations in the South were willing to play what was then called "race music." Prominent among these was Nashville's WLAC, whose signal beamed throughout the Southeast. "From around eight or nine in the evening just right on up to the wee hours in the morning, they played solid rhythm and blues music. We kids would listen to that music, sometimes against our parents' wishes."[3]

The greatest influence, however, came from the playing of "beach music." Said Turner, "Every summer kids from all over the South, especially the Carolinas, would go to the Grand Strand area surrounding Myrtle Beach, where there were pavilions or open-air clubs for them to dance.

"The reason the beach was special was that the kids from Greenville, Charlotte, Atlanta, Winston-Salem and Columbia would come and find out that they were basically listening to the same things in their cities.

"Also in the area was Atlantic Beach, which was for blacks only. It was adjacent to the white beach. White kids could hear the jukeboxes blaring this great black music. On many occasions those songs you would hear on the Atlantic Beach jukeboxes would be the ones that in a week or two the white kids were playing.

"It was fantastic. It started in the late forties, in the jitterbug and big band era, with such acts as Louis Jordan and his Tympany Five, the Ravens, the Orioles, the Five Royales, Fletcher Henderson and his orchestra; then came Ruth Brown, Fats Domino, Big Joe Turner and groups like the Clovers, Drifters, and Dominoes.

"The white kids totally dug black rhythm and blues. It was a phenomenon in what you would consider the racist South that the favorite music of white kids was black music. It basically was more the middle-class and upper-class white kids because the lower class could not afford to go to the beach to have this mixture of stuff that was danceable.

Performing at Kimball's club near Oakland, California, in 1994. My sister Mattie (*left*) and Terisa Griffin provide background vocals. Photo by Charles McMillan.

"It was a special love affair. Nothing has ever brought blacks and whites together better than this music did. They not only loved the music but loved the artists who performed it. Racism totally vanished when it came to that. Rhythm and blues was at the forefront of real harmony."

To illustrate, Harry tells this story:

"A friend of mine owns a restaurant in Charleston. We were putting on a festival, and when he found out that Jerry Butler was coming, he said, 'Man, I can't believe it, my all-time favorite, Jerry Butler!' He said, 'Let me tell you about Jerry Butler and what Jerry Butler meant to me in my overall view of life.'"

Harry's friend worked at a radio station in Mississippi where they played rhythm and blues music part of the time, and they had black deejays as well as white. "When these shows would come through in the early days in the South," he said, "quite often you would have shows for all-white crowds or all-black crowds. Or, you would have blacks in the balcony and whites on the main floor, something of that nature. It was the same show but separated.

"This particular show was two shows: one for whites, one for blacks. He was told that the show he should go to was the one for blacks, so he was only one of two white deejays in this entirely black audience. He was just loving it. He loved the other acts on the show, but Jerry Butler was the one he really came to see. This was in the early sixties.

"You gotta keep in mind," he said, "that I came from what would be considered a redneck, racist background. My parents thought blacks were not equal to whites, and that's what I was taught.

"Suddenly, here comes Jerry Butler out onstage. They announce him. He comes out and the spotlight hits him. He's in this shiny blue silk suit. He starts singing his big hit 'He Will Break Your Heart.'

"Right then and there," he said, "It just busted wide open this stereotype my parents tried to present to me of blacks being different from whites, because here I was watching and listening to the classiest individual I had ever seen or heard in my life. It forever changed my view on race relations. I became a different person because of Jerry Butler."

Harry says his friend beams when he tells that story. I can see why. It is a good story, and not because I am featured in it. What's good about it is that there are tens of thousands of magical moment stories all over America just like it, where cherished values are reexamined and individuals come face to face with their own humanity. It is especially heartening to me that rhythm and blues music so often is the catalyst.

Helping Each Other's Growth

As the decade of the sixties unfolded, young whites in the industrial North, like their cousins down south, began to take a closer look at the America they had inherited from their parents. Many of them were appalled at what they saw: deception, double standards, dishonesty. Some—especially those inspired by beatnik writers Jack Kerouac, William S. Burroughs, and Allen Ginsberg—started "turning on" to drugs and alcohol and "dropping out" of society. They immediately began setting about to define their own moral and ethical standards. But by the mid-sixties they had succeeded only in creating a counterculture of hedonists who reveled in doing their own thing while flaunting their contempt for authority. They became known as "hippies," "flower children," and "peaceniks." War, racism, and capitalism were antithetical to the lifestyles of these free-spirited teenage anarchists, who trusted no one over thirty. "Make love, not war!" they chanted on college campuses and street corners across the nation. For some, even long-held religious beliefs were no longer venerated. Instead, they embraced the newer—at least for them—transcendental Eastern philosophies, such as Buddhism and Krishna Consciousness.

The people who made up the hippie culture of the sixties and seventies are not to be confused with the self-indulgent, self-aggrandizing "Baby Boomers" who grew up to be the fiftysomething movers and shakers of the nineties. No, they are another breed altogether. Just recently, as the following excerpt from a 1995 *Time* magazine article by Stewart Brand suggests, the world owes much to hippies.

> Newcomers to the Internet are often startled to discover themselves not so much in some soulless colony of technocrats as in a kind of cultural Brigadoon—a flowering remnant of the sixties, when hippie communalism and libertarian politics formed the roots of the modern cyberrevolution. At the time, it all seemed dangerously anarchic (and still does to many), but the counterculture's scorn for centralized authority provided the philosophical foundations of not only the leaderless Internet but also the entire personal-computer revolution.

We owe much more to yet another group of whites from the sixties: those who identified with the plight of black Americans by joining in their struggle. While not as committed to the struggle as Andrew Goodman and Michael Schwerner—two young white men from the North who, along with James Chaney, a black civil rights worker, gave their lives to the cause—these young whites were no less sincere in their efforts to right centuries-old wrongs. Murry Swartz was one of these.

I met Murry in 1959 when, at the urging of my manager Irv Nahan, he drove to Washington, D.C., from his native Philadelphia to see me perform. Irv had recently hired Murry, who had just been kicked out of college, to help with road managing duties for some of his acts. At the time, I was headlining a show at the Howard Theater, and Irv asked me to show Murry around. I was about twenty years old, and Murry was twenty-two or twenty-three.

Murry was bitten by the show biz bug the moment he stepped inside the theater. "Right away I knew this is what I wanted to do," he said, recalling that day. "I wanted to be a part of this. I wanted to get down and be loved by the brothers and make my presence known."

We hit it off from the very first day. "It was some kind of chemistry," he said. "We were two young boys out there. It was family, from Annette to the driver to all of the musicians."

It was obvious from the start that Murry desperately wanted to fit in, going so far as to try out every little piece of humorous racial material he could think of, and making a fool of himself in the process, to show that he belonged.

I decided to have a little fun with him, while teaching him a valuable lesson.

Murry Swartz (*right*) backstage at the Taj Mahal in Atlantic City with Richard Pryor in 1993. It was one of Richard's last performances before he was afflicted with multiple sclerosis. Photo courtesy of Murry Swartz.

About the second or third day at the theater, I informed Murry that if he really wanted to be one of the brothers, he had to get himself a do rag.

"A do rag?" he said quizzically.

"Yeah, one of these," I said, unraveling the scarf I wore around my head to hold my process in place. Except for Sam Cooke, all the black acts in those days processed their hair with a greasy lye-based solution designed to straighten kinky hair. We called the process a "do," as in "hairdo." We wore do rags to keep moisture from getting to our hair and spoiling the do. Murry agreed to have a do and to wear a do rag.

"But first let's go buy some boots," I told him. "You gotta have boots to be a brother." So we went over to the shoe store and bought some black boots with zippers up the side.

"Now you need a blade to go in the boots," I said, and we went down a couple more blocks and bought a switchblade, which Murry immediately tucked inside his new boots.

The moment of truth finally arrived. Murry bought his first do rag. Right there in the store I taught him how to drape it over his head and tie it like the brothers.

Murry recalled, "I'm walking around all week backstage with my do rag and boots, gettin' down with the brothers. I'm sleeping with my do rag at night, and during the day I'm walking in these cheap-ass boots that are actually giving me a corn—I never had a corn in my life—and the damn blade is rubbing up and down my leg, cutting me. But I'm not taking any of it off. I have to go on with the program because I wanted to be down. I wanted to be accepted.

"I came home from this eight- or nine-day adventure and walked into my parents' home. My mother, being born in 1907 and coming from a generation of Jewish immigrant families and everything, she looks at me and says, 'What are you doing? What kind of a business are you in? I want you out of this business right away!'

"'No, Mom,' I said, 'My friend got me this. . . .' Well, she was fit to be tied when she looked at her little rosy-cheeked son with this head rag on and a blade in his shoes."

After a while, I wasn't exactly sure who was kidding who. Were we both just putting each other on, poking fun at the silliness of maintaining racial stereotypes?

In any event, I wasn't quite finished with Murry, not just yet. About six months later, I talked him into actually getting a process. Recalling the day I took him to get his first do at a barber shop up on Pennsylvania Avenue in Baltimore, Murry said, "I was not going to have curly hair anymore. I was going to have straight hair and swing it around some kind of way.

"I thought my brains were boiling! My scalp was so burnt, my hair turned orange-colored by whatever chemicals were in there."

We spent a lot of time in Baltimore, which was somewhat segregated at the time, even though it was above the Mason-Dixon Line. It was a segregated city in a lot of ways. But there were a couple of places where we could stay together. I would get a suite, which cost about $100 or $150 a week, and Murry would get a room next to me. We would come back after the shows, get a bottle of champagne, drink it together, and then we would start wrestling—mostly, I think, just to relieve tension.

"We would fight until we were bloody," Murry recalled. "It was just wonderful. I never had a brother; I had all sisters. I guess that is what it would be like if I had had a brother. It was just the two of us having these wonderful, wonderful times together."

The good times were tempered by the bad. As I noted before, black artists could not stay in any of the hotels in the South. We had to stay in black rooming houses and black motels. I remember this one gig we had in Columbia, South Carolina. We got rooms in this little motel called the Pines, which was a bunch of little cabins with an open piece of ground in the middle. When we went to check in, Murry, who always wanted to stay where the artists stayed, said to me, "I'm staying here, too." But the man who owned the motel was afraid for him to register. He was afraid that if there was a white guy on the registration, it could cause problems for him. But Murry persisted and stayed at the motel.

The next day was an off-day, and some of the guys decided to play a game of softball. Murry, who loved softball, came running out to play. Remembering the scene the day before, we all said in unison, "Oh, no!" Although there was no written rule about whites playing softball with blacks, we didn't want to risk it. We sent Murry back to his room.

It was only April or May, but it was already hot in the South. On top of that, there was no air conditioning in the cabins. Recalled Murry, "You could've died in this little room. They were all out there picnicking, playing ball, drinking cold pop and everything, and I had to stay in my room." He always thought I enjoyed seeing him suffer like that, but I didn't.

As for racism itself, Murry was more frustrated than he was disgusted by the extreme bigotry. As a young Jew growing up in a predominantly Irish Catholic neighborhood in Philadelphia, he was well-acquainted with bigotry, having encountered a lot of anti-Semitism on his way to and from school. By the time he met me, Murry had a pretty good feel for what I and other black acts were experiencing in the South and elsewhere.

As time passed, I could see that Murry was becoming very protective of me, as well as some of the other artists he worked with. "I became extremely sensitive to what was happening in the political and social world prior to Kennedy getting into office," he said. "I became one of those staunch young liberals who got caught up in what was happening in the United States. The whole social, cultural thing was changing. Aretha was having her first big hit at the time ["Respect"], and because of her tremendous success and visibility on a national basis, all the young reverends that were around, especially out of Atlanta with SCLC (Southern Christian Leadership Council), called the office all the time. They were trying to get Aretha and other artists to perform and raise funds that were desperately needed to achieve what they were trying to do."

By that time, Murry was making quite a name for himself, especially among black promoters. He was responsible for getting not only my contractual guarantees but also my percentage of the door. I don't think Irv had that kind of an arrangement with his other artists—that is, a single artist owning the whole package (in partnership with Irv) including the other acts on the show. Murry was responsible for making sure that all of the acts got paid, and that Irv and I got our percentage.

That wasn't as easy as it sounds. To begin with, they didn't have sophisticated ticket systems then like they have today. It was just a roll of tickets. Here's how it worked: Let's say you had a red roll of tickets and your original starting number was 1,000. If you took the count at the end of the evening and it was 2,212, then you had sold 1,212 tickets. That's how you figured your gross.

Recalled Murry, "Some of these guys were like the early fight promoters. They were slick old guys. One of the most memorable was James Dudley, who promoted dances at the Capitol Arena in Washington, D.C. Dudley used to loosen up the roll with red tickets. He would put ten or twelve tickets inside the roll. I was lucky enough to grab one of those tickets at the door and see that it was not a corresponding ticket number. He was slick all the time like that. It was a game with him.

"But he loved working with us. He would always put on the pots for us. He was known for cooking fabulous gumbo. He was one of those guys who had that chuckling, rumbling sort of laugh, and if you caught him at something, it was hard to get angry with him.

"Sometimes I would stand at the front door and say, 'All right, Dudley, I'm checking everything that comes through here.' What he would do then was send his boys to the side door and sell tickets there. I didn't have but so many eyes. It was always a game going on with this man.

"Sometimes Dudley would sit in the box office himself and sell tickets. I saw him work this a few times:

"Somebody would come with a ten dollar bill, and the advance ticket price may have been five dollars, six dollars the day of the show. They would give him ten dollars. He would keep talking to the person, and the next thing I know, he would give the person two dollars' change. The guy would come back and say, 'Mr. Dudley, my money ain't right.' And Dudley would say, 'How do I know it ain't right? You needed to count it in front of me.' He would just flimflam everybody.

"Dudley would also have a boldly painted sign in the box office showing the price of a ticket as $2.50; however, if a customer inquired directly about the price, he would say $3.50. If the customer protested, saying, 'But the sign says $2.50,' Dudley would laugh, give the dollar back and say, 'Oh, I thought you couldn't read.'

"We just loved the guy," said Murry. "Maybe there are just as many hustlers out there today—white, black, or indifferent—but it was done with a different spirit, and you accepted it differently. We loved working for these people. Not only working for them, but they also brought you into their homes after the shows and fed you. You got to meet their families. It was just a day that will never be the same in the music industry—ever."

One would think that Murry, being Jewish, would shy away from eating soul food, with its predilection toward pork dishes such as pig feet, chitlins, ham hocks, bacon, and pork sausages. But that's not the case. "I didn't come up in a kosher home," he explains. "We were raised in a conservative synagogue. We maintained all of the religious holidays and so forth, but not in the way of keeping kosher."

Murry, who now resides in Charleston, South Carolina, says there is not a week that goes by that he doesn't go to Miss Martha Lou's, a black-owned restaurant in Charleston. "I still have to have my collards," he says. "I still have to have my ham hocks, my smothered chicken."

Murry's taste for soul food came with the territory. We ate near or where we performed, and that usually was deep inside America's urban ghettos. Despite our successes, rhythm and blues artists never quite made it uptown to enjoy gourmet meals of escargot and escarole. Expedience dictated that we settle for a simpler cuisine, featuring as its centerpiece a hog's carcass.

"Every city had its special little place where you could eat," Murry recalls. "If we were in Washington, it was the Key or Cecilia's Lounge. Mom's [in Baltimore] was right across from the Royal Theater. Mom was one of the best cooks in the country. She was just fabulous. I would go in there and she would say, 'Lord, I've never seen a white boy eat like that in my life!' She just loved fixing food for me, and I had an incredible appetite.

"I remember one day Arthur Prysock's brother, Red, was getting married. We were playing at the Royal Theater. He pulled up in a bus, and they were doing the wedding reception at this little shack, at Mom's, across from the Royal Theater. Everybody came out on the avenue. It was like a celebration. It was just great, great times."

All of this was going on while I was signed with the Shaw booking agency, a white-owned agency based in New York. It soon became apparent, though, that Shaw couldn't meet the needs of black artists such as Curtis Mayfield, Gene Chandler, and me. As if on cue, black artists started invoking Stokely Carmichael's "Black Power!" mantra, taking their fortunes and their destinies out of the hands of the Shaws, the William Morrisses, and the General Artists Corporations and placing them in more trusted hands—their own.

The founding of Queen Booking Agency, named after the self-styled "Queen of the Blues," Dinah Washington, was a direct result of that kind of push for self-determination among black artists. When Dinah passed in 1963, Curtis, Chicago record producer Carl Davis, Irv Nahan, and I took over the agency. It soon grew to become the world's largest booking agent of black talent, with such entertainment giants as Aretha Franklin, Sammy Davis, Jr., Richard Pryor, and Curtis Mayfield listed as clients.

Black artists, although they enjoyed working the chitlin circuit, longed to work in the big rooms in New York and Hollywood, in casinos in Las Vegas and Reno, and overseas in Paris and London. Agencies such as William Morris and GAC couldn't, or wouldn't, book them in those venues. Whatever the reason, black rhythm and blues artists saw in those oversights an opportunity to escape the clutches of unscrupulous managers and booking agents. Increasingly, they began taking matters into their own hands, becoming their own bosses, packaging their own shows, forming publishing and recording companies, hiring their own promotion people, and some, like James Brown, buying interests in radio stations. They were in complete rebellion against the kind of "plantation" atmosphere that permeated the entertainment industry during those years.

I could see it coming as early as 1961, when, after I had achieved a bona fide hit on Vee Jay with my recording of "Moon River," Andy Williams ended up getting all the recognition for his version of the song on the Grammy and Academy Awards shows. At first I was bitter about the whole affair. But it got me thinking: Why blame Columbia Records for promoting its own artist, Andy Williams, on award shows that were telecast on CBS, the parent of Columbia Records? The thing for me to do, it suddenly dawned on me, was to own as much of my talent as possible, essentially adopting the mercantile theory of business for myself—that is, sell more than I bought. That's what all artists should have been doing, parceling themselves out on a piecemeal basis. In other words, instead of buying into managers' schemes about *your* future, plot out your future yourself and offer percentages for various aspects of your talent. For example, if you write songs and perform, offer a record company a percentage of the publishing rights to that song in return for a percentage of the mechanical, or reproduction, rights owned by the company—quid pro quo.

In the case of "Moon River," had I owned any or all of the rights to the song, I would have been in a much better bargaining position as to who would perform it on award shows. The task, then, on the next go-around, was to set up a publishing company to control the songs I write and perform. I think Sam Cooke had something like that in mind when he formed KAGS publishing company, which grew into SAR Records.

It was that kind of thinking that finally pushed Curtis Mayfield and me to buy into Queen Booking and to form Curtom Publishing with Eddie Thomas.

Irv Nahan and Murry also bought shares in the agency and essentially ran the operation.

As the agency grew and an increasing number of managers and artists became associated with Queen, Murry's responsibilities increased, resulting in his spending more time with booking matters than with management.

As time wore on, however, I became more and more disturbed by some of the things I was witnessing. For example, known mob figures were muscling their way into ownership of record companies and distributorships; my friends were being intimidated into signing contracts with personal managers and agencies that openly cheated them; and black newcomers were being channeled onto the same chitlin circuit treadmill that the older artists had fought so hard to either expand or upgrade.

As much as I hated the thought of giving up on a good idea, I decided to cash in my Queen Booking shares. This bothered Murry, who said of my decision, "It really broke my heart, because if there was one person in the business that I had this really close relationship with, it was Jerry. It bothered me not only for Irv Nahan's sake, but for my own. I didn't want to lose a friend."

Murry stayed on with the agency, which had almost totally come under the control of Gaetano "Big Guy" Vastola.[4] Queen also was becoming more selective. "We were able to turn down artists if we didn't like the management or the recording company that they were with," said Murry. "We had Gladys Knight, the O'Jays, and all the acts from Philadelphia International. Kool and the Gang were beginning to happen, and of course we had the Queen, Aretha."

It was around this time that Murry started taking more interest in Richard Pryor. "I had always loved Richard Pryor," he said. "He was kind of starving to death at that time. But he was this brilliant talent that I just adored. He had just recorded *That Nigger's Crazy,* and I flew out to Los Angeles, found out who his manager was, and sat and talked with Richard. He was scared, paranoid. It was Richard—who he is today—this sensitive guy who was insecure and so forth. And I just knew, not only that the album was fantastic, but that Richard had this incredible potential.

"He trusted me for some reason, whereas a lot of people didn't. If someone says they're honest, watch out. I didn't necessarily tell people I was honest, but they knew where I was coming from. It just so happened that the chemistry was there with Richard and me. He believed in what I told him, what I thought could happen in a very short period of time. Almost as if I had written a script, it happened for him in the next six months, above and beyond anything he ever thought could happen, particularly the dollars.

"I am very proud of what Richard and I accomplished together. To me, it was like winning the heavyweight championship of the world."

What they accomplished was to make Richard into a superstar. Murry performed a similar function as manager of Patti LaBelle.

Murry has, of course, come a long way from the time he simply wanted to be one of the brothers. He credits me with helping him to see himself from the perspective of a friend. Over the years he has learned that, in his words, "You live off of what you do yourself. No one can give you a stamp of approval. People can share information with each other and help each other's growth, but everything else we do, such as being accepted as one's own person, has to be earned."

☀

Red Schwartz and the Rise and Fall of Vee Jay Records

Bringing a record to market is like waging a war: your guys against theirs. Radio station against radio station. Artist against artist. Group against group. Promotion people against promotion people—all jockeying (no pun intended) to be number one, whether it's the number one record, number one station, or number one talent.

There are several parallels between a record war and a shooting war. For one, they both produce lots of casualties; for another, to the victor goes the spoils. In record wars, as in shooting wars, you're only as good as your foot soldiers, the people who fight in the trenches. In the record wars we waged at Vee Jay and elsewhere during the late fifties and early sixties, there was no finer foot soldier than Red Schwartz.

Red (no relation to Murry Swartz) was, like Murry, there at the beginning of my career and almost single-handedly won the many wars Vee Jay fought on my behalf. In fact, had it not been for Red, there probably never would have been Jerry Butler the singer, or even Curtis Mayfield and the Impressions. He was our Sergeant York, our Audie Murphy, our Colin Powell and Norman Schwartzkopf all rolled into one. Red went into battle as the national promotion man for Vee Jay Records, armed only with his love of the blues and an openness that was—and still is—infectious.

Then again, it didn't hurt to be a friend of Dick Clark, a fellow Philadelphian who just happened to be the emcee for the nation's number one dance show for teenagers, *American Bandstand.*

Clark recalled the day Red brought a demo of "For Your Precious Love" to his office:

> Our doors were always open to representatives from the record labels who wanted to convince us to play their latest releases or book their newest artists.

Most of these people were honest, hard-working and fun to be with. One who has remained a friend to this day is Red Schwartz. . . .

Red was working for Vee Jay Records in Chicago when he dropped by our office. He picked up the music playlist of songs we had set for *Bandstand* that day, and without asking anyone, crossed off a song and added the record he was pushing. "Hey, what are you doing?" I yelled at him. I told him he should at least let me hear the record first. "If you hear it, so what?" Red replied. "You'll say it stinks. Just play it on the show." I listened to it first anyway, and it sounded like a funeral dirge.[5]

But Red persisted. "You've gotta play it, Dick. Believe me, this is a hit," he said, echoing his own words of a week earlier when he had tried to convince Ewart Abner, then president of Vee Jay, that "For Your Precious Love" had merit. "I love this!" he told Abner, who had invited him to Chicago hoping to interest him in becoming Vee Jay's man in Philadelphia. At the time, Red was a blues jockey—the only white person with that title—at radio station WDAS. "You're the reason we've been selling so many records in Philly," Abner told Red, an avid fan of one of Vee Jay's top acts, Mississippi-born blues singer Jimmy Reed. Jimmy's "sweet" style of traditional Delta blues had left its mark on Red, as well as on the Rolling Stones, Bob Dylan, and others. Jimmy sold more records in the 1950s and early 1960s than any other blues artist except B.B. King.

During the interview in Chicago, Abner asked Red to listen to several records and give his opinion of each. Red listened attentively, but, according to Red, it wasn't until he heard "For Your Precious Love" that he found something that he liked.

"I love it," he told Abner.

"It's too slow," Abner responded. "We'll never put it out."

"Give me three demos," said Red. "One for me, one for Georgie Woods [the top disc jockey in Philly], and one for Dick Clark."

The following week, back in Philadelphia, Clark finally relented, saying, "OK, Red, I'll preview it for the kids. If they like it, we'll put it on the air."

The kids loved it.

Red grabbed Clark's phone and called Abner in Chicago. "Turn on *American Bandstand*," he shouted into the phone.

"Why?" said Abner.

"They're gonna play 'For Your Precious Love,' that's why!"

"What!" Abner nearly dropped the phone. "Somebody go across the street and get a TV!" he yelled, partly into the phone and partly to his staff in the adjoining room. "Dick Clark is playing our record."

Later that evening, Georgie Woods followed Clark's lead and played the record, not once but twice. "This is so nice, we've got to play it twice," he told his radio audience. Red played it three times on his show.

"For Your Precious Love" would later go to number 11 on the *Billboard* chart.

Abner, obviously impressed, called Red in Philly and told him, "Any white man who can pick a hit just like that has got to be my national promotion man." Red accepted Abner's offer and quickly rose from foot soldier to battlefield general for Vee Jay, directing the promotion of such records as Gene Chandler's "Duke of Earl" and Betty Everett's "Shoop Shoop Song." He even had a hand in the career of a then unheard-of group in England called the Beatles.

The story of the role that Vee Jay played in launching the Beatles' recording career is grossly underplayed here in the United States and elsewhere. Capitol Records takes most of the credit for bringing the Beatles to America, but it was a different story back in the fall of 1962 when EMI, a British company with ties to Capitol, asked Vee Jay to sign the Beatles. EMI had gone to Capitol first, but Capitol, exercising its right of first refusal, turned them down. Vee Jay accepted the EMI offer and bought the rights to three Beatles recordings: "Please Please Me," "From Me to You," and "Love Me Do."

The Beatles were actually a throw-in from EMI affiliate Trans-Global. The original offer was for Vee Jay to pick up the contract of Frank Ifield, whose "I Remember You" was the number 1 hit in Britain. The Beatles were simply a sweetener for the five-year deal.

A few weeks after the signing, in September 1962, Vee Jay released "Love Me Do" in England. But the record didn't do much, hovering around the twenties on British charts. When the Beatles' next single, "Please Please Me," went to number 2 on the charts, Vee Jay released it in the United States. "Please Please Me" stayed on the Top 40 charts at Chicago's WLS for two weeks, making it the first Top 40 appearance for the Beatles in the U.S. Red was instrumental in getting them there.

"The Beatles weren't the only white group we had," said Red. "We also released records on the Four Seasons," including their September 1962 hit "Sherry." The Four Seasons went on to have ten Top 40 hits for Vee Jay.

The following year, however, things started coming apart. Rumors started flying that Vee Jay was in financial trouble and wasn't paying the Four Seasons all of their royalties. Suspicions grew around the way Abner ran the company. His critics said he was operating as if the company was still a small business. He boasted that he kept many of Vee Jay's financial records in his head.

In a surprise shake-up, however, Vee Jay announced on August 3, 1963, that Abner, public relations chief Barbara Gardner, and Bill Sheppard, the head of promotion and A&R, had left the company.

Less than a week later, Trans-Global, acting for EMI, asked Vee Jay to release Frank Ifield from his contract. Vee Jay complied, releasing Ifield on or about August 8, 1963.

Confusion soon followed. When the new management team, headed by Randy Wood, came in, it was under the impression that Vee Jay had also released the Beatles. But they hadn't. According to Calvin Carter, "EMI claimed they sent us some kind of mysterious telegram, but they never could find the telegram."

The Four Seasons situation finally came to a head on August 13. The group, which technically wasn't under contract to Vee Jay, filed suit against Genius, Inc., which was. The Four Seasons wanted out of the contract because of Vee Jay's alleged nonpayment of royalties.

Meanwhile, Capitol, which had been spending a small fortune promoting the Beatles, was not amused when Vee Jay, realizing that it still held the masters for "Please Please Me" and "From Me To You," released them as a single. Capitol immediately had an injunction placed against Vee Jay, barring it from manufacturing, distributing, advertising, or otherwise disposing of records by the Beatles. Capitol contended in its suit that since the contract between the Beatles and Vee Jay had been canceled on August 8, 1963, Vee Jay no longer had rights to the group.

Amid the chaos, Randy Wood, who had been with Vee Jay since 1960, was named president of the label, Jay Lasker was named executive vice-president, and Calvin Carter vice president in charge of A&R and Publishing. To make matters worse—at least for Calvin and Red—in the midst of all the confusion, Vee Jay packed up and moved to Santa Monica, California. It was a smart move for Wood and Lasker and the rest of the new executive staff, because they lived in California. But for Easterners like Red and Calvin, who had developed a rapport with certain disc jockeys and production people, the move was a disaster.

Indeed it was a devastating blow for Red, who over the years had fought gallantly and well in the trenches for Vee Jay, taking everything the opposition threw at him. At one point he was able to lob a few salvos of his own into the fray. For instance, when he first started with Vee Jay, Red would walk into Top 40 radio stations and white disc jockeys would say, "'Oh yeah, you're that guy with that little nigger record company in Chicago.'" After Vee Jay's success with the Beatles and others, Red was able to counter, "No, I'm the guy with that big nigger record company in Chicago, and I don't want to hear that anymore. If you call people niggers, then you're going to call me a kike, a Spanish guy a spic, a Japanese guy a jap. I don't want to hear that. Just call it the way it is. If you don't like somebody, you don't like him for what kind of person he is, not for

From left: Randall Wood, president of Vee Jay Records; Vivian Carter Bracken, owner of Vee Jay Records; football great Rosie Grier (New York Giants, Los Angeles Rams); singer/songwriter Jerry "Iceman" Butler.

how he was born." From then on we had their respect. We had gotten our foot in the door and were in a position to say things like that.

After the move to the West Coast, Vee Jay started a new label, Tollie (Calvin's middle name), because radio stations had started to complain that Vee Jay had too much product on the air. At one point, the company had 14 of the Top 100 on Vee Jay or one of its subsidiaries.

Vee Jay introduced the Tollie label with the Beatles' single "Twist and Shout," which reached number 2 in *Billboard,* and number 1 in *Record World* and *Cashbox.*

But even though the company had sold millions of records by the Beatles and had gotten a ten-year moratorium from its creditors on outstanding bills, Vee Jay still had problems. The Brackens did not like the way Wood and Betty Chiappetta, a future owner of the company, conducted business. They rehired Abner and, in 1965, moved the company back to Chicago.

But it was too late. Vee Jay's financial problems were overwhelming. In 1966, after only thirteen years of operation, the company closed its doors. The company responsible for bringing the first Beatles records to the United States and the nation's largest African-American-owned record company was bankrupt. "It was tragic," Red later said of the bankruptcy.

After the company closed its doors, Red took a promotion job at Roulette Records, working for the infamous Morris Levy. The job lasted only a year or two before Red was on the move again, making stops at United Artists and MGM Records.

A few years after Red's departure from Vee Jay, the music industry underwent some drastic changes. For one thing, small, independent record companies became nearly extinct. Gone were the days when a small record company like Vee Jay could launch the Four Seasons with independent distribution. By the late eighties, only Levy's Roulette Records and a few others were able to compete with the majors: CBS, Warner, RCA, Capitol-EMI, PolyGram, and MCA.[6]

By the late seventies, even the remaining independents—big and small—were swallowed up by the majors. Capitol-EMI bought Liberty Records and United Artists Records; MCA bought ABC-Dunhill. They also began to distribute labels. MCA distributes Motown; Virgin is distributed by WEA, Def Jam by CBS.

As the majors bought more labels and involved themselves in more and more distribution deals, they soon came to the realization that they needed more market share to justify the expense of having their own distribution outlets. This translated to hiring more promotion people—people like Red Schwartz. But when they looked around, they discovered that the Red Schwartzes were already working for them. In fact, they were being overworked. There were too many records and too few people to work the records.

Enter Joseph Isgro, Fred DiSipio, and a group of independent promoters known as the Network.

> Though the term "Network" conjured images of a powerful, secret society, it referred to the tendency of the promoters to work as a loosely knit team. Each member had a "territory," a group of stations over which he claimed influence.[7]

"I know Joe Isgro and I knew Freddie DiSipio," said Red of the most wellknown of the Network men. "I knew them all." But he quickly distanced himself from the payola scandal that erupted following the disclosure of the Network in a 1980 *Billboard* article.

"Not me!" he says emphatically when asked about the Network and payola.

Dionne Warwick (*second from right*) with (*from left*) Chuck Jackson; Caldin Street of the Velvelettes; Jerry Butler; and Martha Reeves, of Martha and the Vandellas. Photo by Charles McMillan.

"I was never caught up in that." He does admit, however, that while he was at Vee Jay, Abner would "give me orders to take this money to Detroit or whatever and distribute it. But it was under his orders. It was never money I earned for myself. I was too honorable, I guess."

In March 1977, Red quit the music business to take a job as a salesman for a Los Angeles car-leasing company, where he remains today. At age seventy-three, he enjoys an occasional dinner with Dick Clark, his old friend from Philadelphia. But there are times when he becomes reflective, looking back with nostalgia at a bygone era when, after a long, hard-fought battle, the warriors would go home, relax, and wait for the next battle.

Making It Easier on Myself

In 1962, a group called the Gospelaires was adding background vocals to the Drifters' "Mexican Divorce" when Burt Bacharach took notice of one of the session singers, twenty-one-year-old Dionne Warrick. "She had pigtails and dirty white sneakers . . . and she just shone," recalled Bacharach, adding that the group, which included Dionne's sister Dee Dee Warrick and their aunt Cissy Houston, "was dynamite . . . but there was something about the way [Dionne] carried herself that made me want to hear her sing by herself. After I did, she started to do all our demos."[8]

Thus began the long collaboration of Dionne Warwick and the writing team of Bacharach and Hal David. It also was my introduction to Bacharach and David, who wrote "Make It Easy on Yourself," a song that figured prominently not only in my career but in Dionne's as well.

Over the years, there have been different versions of how I came to record "Make It Easy on Yourself," depending on who tells the story. The most popular version goes like this:

When Florence Greenberg, the owner of Scepter Records, heard a demo by Dionne called "It's Love That Really Counts," it absolutely floored her, and she quickly signed Dionne to a recording contract. Dionne chose as her first single "Make It Easy on Yourself," for which she had done the demo. But to her dismay, Bacharach and David told her that I had already recorded it. Feeling betrayed—and this is where things get a little murky—Dionne shouted at them: "Don't make me over, man!" In other words, "Don't try to con me." A few days later, after she had calmed down, they played another tune they thought might make a great first single for her. They called it "Don't Make Me Over." When the record was pressed, a printing error made Dionne Warrick over into Dionne Warwick.

True, Burt and Hal did offer me the song, but not until Florence Greenberg had turned it down. The way I remember it, Calvin called me into his office one day and said, "Jerry, listen to this," and he played a demo record. I listened. When it finished playing, I said, "Man, it's a great song, and the girl who's singing it, the arrangement and all, is a hit."

"Well," said Calvin, "they're not going to put it out. The lady who owns the record company doesn't like the song. We like the song and think it will be a major song for your career."

I was ecstatic and shortly thereafter we flew to New York. We wanted the same arranger who had recorded the demo to arrange and conduct on my session. That turned out to be Burt Bacharach.

On the day of the session, Burt showed up at the studio with this knock-yourself-in-the-eye-gorgeous woman. And I mean gorgeous. She had on this orange dress and was sporting one of those I-am-definitely-rich suntans. She looked absolutely fabulous.

So there I was, trying to sing this song; Burt was trying to conduct the orchestra; and Calvin, in the control booth, was chewing on his pipe, trying to make believe that he was paying attention to nothing but the sounds coming through the speakers.

Midway through the session, Calvin said, "Hey, Jerry." I said, "What?" "Keep your mind on the song, man." Everybody in the studio cracked up. I hadn't realized that I was staring at the woman, who Burt later introduced as Angie Dickinson, his soon-to-be wife.

As Calvin predicted, "Make It Easy on Yourself" went on to become one of my biggest hits, reaching number 20 on the *Billboard* pop chart and number 18 on R&B following its release in August 1962. In that same year, "Don't Make Me Over" hit the pop charts, launching Dionne into the outer stratosphere of stardom.

Recently, a writer commented on my rendition of "Make It Easy on Yourself," saying that it was "the first Bacharach song to *sound* vaguely like a Bacharach song. . . . All these years later what's remarkable about the song is how grown-up it sounds—as much a reflection of Bacharach's elegant melodic line as of the stoicism conveyed by Butler's vocal and David's lyrics."[9]

10.

A Little Help from My Friends

Little Willie John

My first year on the road after leaving the Impressions was a tremendous learning experience for me. But I was fortunate to have people like Little Willie John, Sam Cooke, and others—guys who had been performing on their own for a while—to help me get over some of the rough spots.

Like so many rhythm and blues pioneers, Little Willie John has never received the recognition he deserves. Rhythm and blues song stylists such as Sam Cooke, Jackie Wilson, and James Brown, although deserving of the accolades they received for their artistry, owed much to this 5'2" dynamo from Detroit. So did other artists, including John Lennon and the Beatles, whose recording of "Leave My Kitten Alone" was modeled after Willie's 1959 hit. Willie's version of "Fever," copied note for note by Peggy Lee and Elvis Pres-

Little Willie John looks on as his sister, Mable John, signs an autograph for Bill Doggett.

ley, remains the standard for the song, even though Lee and Presley had bigger hits with it. His material has been recorded by scores of artists from the Beatles to Fleetwood Mac to the Blasters.[1]

William Edward John, named after his grandfathers, got his start in church with a group called the United Five, consisting of Willie and his older siblings Mertis, Jr., Haywood, Mildred, and Mable. Mertis, Sr., a "stickler for family unity," formed the group to keep his children from fighting and to do "something tangible" with their time. Mertis abhorred the thought of girls and boys fighting, especially his own. His children would never do that, he said. If he heard them arguing, he would yell, "Cut out that arguing and strike up a song!"

The United Five performed for several years, mainly in the Detroit area and often with well-known groups like the Mighty Clouds of Joy. "Willie would always steal the show," said Mable. "He had all of the antics and did a lot of crazy things."

When they weren't singing in church, they sang at home, where he also was the attention-getter. While the others sang from inside the house, Willie always stood in the doorway so that anyone passing by would hear him singing "just a little bit louder than the rest," said Mable. And because he was so small, people would say, "Look at that sweet little boy."

Shortly after graduating from high school, Willie started getting restless. Singing with the family wasn't enough for him. He craved the excitement of night life, of living on the edge. With Mable's help, Willie began sneaking out of the house at night to compete in amateur shows at the Paradise Theater. He promised to "get back before midnight"—before Mertis returned home from his job on the assembly line at Chrysler-Dodge Motors. A neighborhood kid named Levi Stubbs, who later would sing lead for the legendary group the Four Tops, often joined Willie on these late-night escapades.

One night Levi's mother went to the theater to see him perform. But that night Little Willie, also known as Edward, took first prize. The next day, Mrs. Stubbs inadvertently brought Willie's late-night adventures to an end when she stopped by the John household and blurted out, "That Edward really did good last night, didn't he?" Willie's amateur days were over.

In 1955, Willie finally "broke rank" with the family and went on the road with bandleader Paul (Hucklebuck) Williams. Before leaving, Willie told Mable that he was going to be a star. "I'm going as far as I can go," he said. He was only eighteen.

He indeed went far—and fast. His 1955 debut recording for Syd Nathan's King label, "All around the World," set the pattern for a remarkable string of hits: "Need Your Love So Bad," "Suffering with the Blues," "Fever," "Let Them Talk," and his last, "Sleep." One critic called "Need Your Love So Bad" "one of the most intimate, moving vocals ever recorded."

The competition between Willie and Levi for first prize in the amateur shows foreshadowed the later competition between Willie and Jackie Wilson over which of them would close a show. These battles with Jackie were "brutal" at times, said Mable. "We were all booked by Universal Attractions. Ben Bart and Dick Allard put these shows together and would book Willie and Jackie. Both wanted to do it because they were from Detroit, knew each other well, and both enjoyed their craft. Willie would say, 'Put me on first.' Then Jackie would say, 'Well, I don't know, I'll go first on the first show and you close. You go first the second show and I'll close.'"

I was an eyewitness to one of those battles. It was 1959 and we were playing the Rockland Palace in Harlem with Jackie Wilson, Little Willie John and his band the Upsetters, the Drifters, and some other acts. An argument started about who was going to close. The promoter—I think it was Teddy Powell—couldn't solve it. So finally Little Willie said, "Don't worry about it. I'll go on first, and Jackie can get on if he can."

The Drifters opened the show; I was next; and Little Willie sent the Upsetters on ahead of him. They were a show in themselves. Formed in Macon, Georgia, in 1952, the Upsetters first gained prominence as Little Richard's band, performing on recordings such as "Tutti Frutti" and "Good Golly Miss Molly." When Richard went into the ministry, Little Willie took over the band. The *name* "Upsetters" reflected their style of play—that is, they played with such fervor that they not only rocked the houses they played in, they "upset," or uprooted, them from their foundations. Popular band names from that era were the House Rockers, the Temper Toppers, and the Bushwhackers.

Just before Willie went on, the Upsetters started playing one of his songs, "Heartache": "Heartache, it's killing me . . . " The way they played it, it *was* absolutely killing. The groove was so tight. When Willie finally came on, all the wide-bottom sisters got to doing their thing, dancing and carrying on. When he got around to "Talk to Me" and fell down on his knees, the sisters started throwing their underwear, purses, stockings, and everything else up on the stage.

Willie just stayed out there. It wasn't like he intended to do his little time and come off. He really went out there to milk the crowd until they didn't have any more applause to give to anybody. He had drained them dry. By the time he came off, the place was turned out. There was nobody left for Jackie to sing to. I discovered over the years that Jackie won a battle or two himself. But that night it was all Willie.

Dee Clark and I had a similar rivalry, which I recalled when I spoke at Dee's 1990 funeral: "We all wanted you to do well," I said, "but I just wanted to do better."

Things turned tragic for Little Willie in 1965. He was arrested, tried, and convicted of manslaughter following an altercation in a Seattle nightclub. He was sent to Washington State Prison.

"What happened should not have happened because there was no reason for it to happen," said Mable, recalling the events leading up to Willie's imprisonment. "What happened was, after the show was over, people were having an after-party—you know, where you go to another little club and the whole show goes over there, and you eat and drink until daylight. Willie was good for that, because he loved to drink.

"He went to this after-hours bar, sat down, and ordered a drink. A lady came over to the table and asked, 'Are you Little Willie John?' He stood up and said, 'Yes I am.' He offered her a seat and she sat down. Right after she sat down, this man came over. His name was Roundtree. He was pretty close to 300 pounds. Willie was about 135 pounds—wet.

"The man told her, 'Get up! Get on away from there!' At the time, Willie thought this man worked at the place and was thinking that the young lady was imposing on him, and that's why he was asking her to get up. Willie said to the man, 'It's okay. She's with me.' He told her again, 'I said get up!' But she didn't move. So he hit her, knocking her to the floor. Willie said, 'The lady is with me. Don't hit her.' At that point, the man proceeded to hit Willie. He knocked Willie out of his chair. He hit the floor. When he got up, he hit him again. He knocked Willie down about three times.

"The last time he hit Willie, Willie said he remembered hearing the bartender behind the bar pushing a knife down toward the end of the bar. He said, 'Willie, defend yourself. He's going to kill you!'"

Willie, an epileptic, told Mable that he could feel a seizure coming on. He went into an epileptic seizure. "When he came to himself, there was nobody in the club but Willie and the dead man. The knife they say killed this man was a tiny paring knife.

"Everybody who came forward to talk on Willie's behalf ended up dead, or something happened and nobody could find them. Even the promoter was found dead just before he was due to testify. He had $3,000 in his pockets, so it was not robbery.

"Willie went to trial and was accused of manslaughter. We spent a lot of money getting it to that. At one point, I received phone calls from people I did not know who said I should back off. So a lot of things that happened went unpunished."

On several occasions, Mable got Willie out of prison to do performances. He used the money he earned for court and attorney fees. Mable also arranged for Willie to fly to Detroit to record for Capitol Records, for which he received a $10,000 advance.

Meanwhile, Willie's contract with King Records had expired, and he was "between negotiations" with both Capitol and King. When King learned that Willie wanted to go to Capitol, they tried to stop him by telling Capitol that Willie owed King some sides.

"In the process of all of that," said Mable, "Willie died. He had pneumonia. He had a seizure and died in his sleep. He died in the prison hospital."

During his incarceration, Willie sent several letters to Annette and me, through another inmate, complaining about his treatment in prison. He wrote to us, he said, because of all the people he had met in show business, he trusted us the most. We felt honored. Annette forwarded the letters to Darlynn,

Willie's wife. We were crushed when he died. Not only had we lost a friend, but the world had lost a great talent.

A Family Affair

I always tried to discourage my siblings, especially my brother Billy, from going into the music business, mainly because I didn't think it was all that it was cracked up to be. It's a dirty game, I told Billy, and no place for someone with the kind of analytical mind that he has. I believe he has the makings of a brilliant engineer or lawyer.

But what do older brothers know? Both Billy and my sister Mattie got into the business anyway, and both have done quite well, especially Billy, who, as a co-writer with me on "I Stand Accused" (a reworked version of his "I'm Just a Man"), has had his work recorded by such notables as Bobby Blue Bland, Eddie Floyd, Al Green, and Isaac Hayes. A tremendous songwriter in his own right, William, as the family calls him, scored a huge hit in 1966 with "Right Track," a recording that Los Angeles music critic Nancy Yahiro recently referred to as a "classic." Music historian Robert Pruter called Billy and the Enchanters, the group he formed in high school, "one of the most compelling acts to come out of Chicago in the mid-1960s."

"Music *is* a dirty game," William admits, but he adds, "I have no regrets about getting involved in it."

While he credits Curtis and me with teaching him a lot about songwriting, Billy reminded me recently of how he, Mattie, and I learned how to structure a song by reading *Hit Parade,* a magazine based on the popular fifties TV show by the same name. The magazine printed out the sheet music of the hits performed on the show. It helped us learn how not only to sight read but how to structure songs as well.

Since Mama wouldn't let us listen to stations that played the blues, stations she often referred to as "devil stations," we had to either watch *Hit Parade* on television or listen to programs like *The Shadow,* comedy shows, or soap operas on radio. We often chose *Hit Parade.*

The three of us would gather in our one-bedroom apartment, mostly around the potbellied stove in the middle of the living room on a Saturday or Sunday night, and watch or listen to our favorite shows. When the radio wasn't on, however, we entertained ourselves by singing the church or kiddie songs Mama had taught us. We were always in a musical environment.

Billy got interested in music around the age of twelve, about the time the Impressions started rehearsing in our basement apartment. "When I first heard Curtis playing the guitar," said Billy, "I wanted to play just like that."

He received his first guitar, a box guitar, from my oldest sister Dorothy, who bought it from a pawn shop. Curtis tuned it for him, and I sent him to Chicago's Cosmopolitan School of Music at Lyon and Healy to learn how to play.

"I was in the process of mastering my trade when I got bored with it," said Billy. "What they were teaching me was not what I wanted to play. They were teaching me classical guitar. I can still play some of the classics, but what I wanted to play was rhythm and blues.

"Rhythm and blues came to me through a process of osmosis. I had been exposed to it and was surrounded by it all of my life."

Even though I was against it initially, I did all I could to help Billy when he and the Enchanters asked me to help them set up an audition with a record company. I sent them to Curtis, who at that time was working with Carl Davis at Okeh Records.

Carl and Curtis had the group do a demo session of several songs, including Billy's "Found True Love," which was released in the summer of 1963. It sold well in Chicago and established the group's name but didn't do much nationally, although it reached "Bubbling Under" status on *Billboard*'s Top 100 chart.

But as with the Impressions, the group's early taste of success caused some dissension within the ranks, and two members of the original Billy Butler and the Four Enchanters group dropped out. The group then changed its name to Billy Butler and the Enchanters, which is how it appeared on their next record, "Gotta Get Away," written by Curtis and recorded in February 1964. The record lasted three consecutive weeks on *Cashbox*'s national rhythm and blues chart.

Another Curtis Mayfield song, "I Can't Work No Longer," was the group's biggest and last hit before it broke up in 1965 and Billy went solo.

In the summer of 1966, Billy had a national hit with "Right Track," which lasted twelve weeks on *Billboard*'s R&B chart. He later formed a group called Billy Butler and the Infinity, but did not have much success. Sometime around the mid-eighties, he started working with me as my guitarist, while continuing to write.

My sister Mattie is a different story. Although for the past twenty-five or thirty years she has been working as a background singer for me whenever I go on the road, she is more of a homebody, preferring to spend her time administering WECAN, the community organization she founded after witnessing an "arson for profit" fire that took the lives of thirteen children. "The mother of one set of children was ill and could not get out of the house," said Mattie. "When they brought her out, she was charred beyond recognition. I had nightmares for months behind that. But it started me talking to my neighbors and asking what the hell was going on."

The Iceman Band rhythm section during the eighties consisted largely of (*from left*) Charles Matthews (piano), my brother Billy (guitar), John Howard (bass), and Ira Gates (drums).

She eventually turned to the world-renowned community organization TWO (The Woodlawn Organization) for answers. "But all they would say was, 'It's a political matter.' 'Killing a mother and thirteen children isn't about politics,' I told them. 'It's about murder!'"

WECAN was started in 1979, a year after the fatal fire. Since then, Mattie and her organization have won several awards, including the prestigious Petra Award, named in honor of an Italian woman immigrant who fought for the rights of the poor in America. In 1995, Mattie received a master's degree in business and community development from Manchester College in Manchester, New Hampshire.

"I don't like people who take advantage of people who can't help themselves," she says, explaining the motivation behind many of her actions. "I was taught that you don't stomp on people when they are down.

"I also don't like being pushed around, which is something I got from my father. I think I inherited his mouth, too, because both of us were known to curse people out from time to time. But Papa was a great man. He would not take welfare. As a matter of fact, he once ran a caseworker out of the house when she said, 'Mr. Butler, we're gonna put you on welfare.' He said, 'I don't want your damn welfare. I want you to find me a job, even if it ain't nothing but sweeping the streets. I want to be a man and work and raise my family myself. I don't need your charity.' Mama was the same way. We all have a lot of pride."

Like me—and a lot of other people—Mattie wears several hats: running WECAN, being a mother to her three children, and singing background for me. I wonder where she gets the energy.

"WECAN is like shock therapy," she says. "It keeps me sane, gives me balance in my life. I always feel a sense of refreshment when I return to one or the other of my dual careers."

I had gone through about three groups of female backup singers, including Patti LaBelle and Nona Hendryx, before Mattie came aboard. She stepped in when Patti and Nona left for Europe and later returned as the highly successful LaBelle vocal group. While they were in Europe, I picked up another group and toured with them for a while, but things didn't work out. I started auditioning backup singers around the mid-seventies, and Mattie, who was helping out at the Songwriters Workshop, started touring with me. She has been with me ever since.

Sam Cooke

> *It's been too hard living, but I'm afraid to die*
> *'Cause I don't know what's out there beyond the sky*
> *It's been a long, a long time coming*
> *But I know a change is gonna come, oh yes it will*
>
> —"A Change Is Gonna Come," by Sam Cooke

Sam Cooke, like Little Willie John, was a phenomenal performer and one of the people I looked up to and sought out for advice during my "formative" years in the music business—the Vee Jay Years, as I refer to them now, 1958–1966. As with Little Willie John, Sam's untimely death not only took away a personal friend, but left a tremendous void in the entertainment world.

Sam was shot dead December 11, 1964, by Bertha Franklin, the manager of a $3-a-night Los Angeles motel. Franklin claimed that Sam had attempted to rape Lisa Boyer, a young woman who had checked in with him, and that he had also tried to assault the fifty-five-year-old Franklin when the younger woman fled to phone the police. In a still controversial decision, the coroner's office ruled Sam's death justifiable homicide.

From the beginning, as details about the shooting and the people involved became known, skeptical fans, including me, began to have doubts about the

Sam Cooke

official version of Sam's death. Why, for example, would someone as popular, rich, and handsome as Sam risk being caught in a cheap motel with a woman like Boyer? (The initial police report described Boyer as a prostitute with an extensive record. The police later retracted the report, saying they had confused Boyer with another Asian woman named Lisa.) Why would Sam sign his own name in the motel register if he had abducted Boyer and was planning to rape her? What happened to Sam's money? Why was the inquest done in such haste? If the official version was true, why wasn't it proven in court?

Fueling the controversy and lending credence to several conspiracy theories is that Sam's death came during a reign of terror in the South: four young black girls were murdered in a Birmingham, Alabama, church bombing in

1963. In the same year, Medgar Evers and John F. Kennedy were assassinated; and three months before Sam's death, Malcolm X was assassinated.

Something else was strange, too. Three years earlier, Jackie Wilson, Little Willie John, Arthur Prysock, and Jesse Belvin had been ordered out of Little Rock, Arkansas, at gunpoint after they refused to perform before a segregated audience only days after four Negro freshmen at A&T College in Greensboro, North Carolina, had tried to integrate a local lunch counter. All except Little Willie John headed south, to Dallas, for their next gig. When they passed Hope, Arkansas, they discovered that their tires had been slashed. Jackie and Arthur were lucky; Jesse wasn't. Daniel Wolff recounted Jesse's demise in *You Send Me:*

> Five miles south of Hope, on Highway 67, his car went out into the passing lane, going eighty-five, and hit another vehicle head on. Belvin, his wife, and the driver were all killed. No one ever proved that Jesse's tires had been cut, but the accident was a sign of the times. The rock & roll road was dangerous enough all on its own; add sudden national attention to a civil rights movement, and the singers became actors in a larger drama.[2]

Were all of these killings tied into some kind of white supremacist movement? What role did the FBI play in all of this? Sam was enormously popular and no doubt attracted the attention of then FBI director J. Edgar Hoover, who allegedly launched a covert operation in late 1961 aimed at getting rid of potential "black messiahs." A few months before his death, Sam was proclaimed "the world's greatest rock and roll singer" by then world heavyweight boxing champion Cassius Clay. A friend of both Malcolm X and Sam Cooke, Clay (who later converted to Islam and took the name Muhammad Ali) eventually was stripped of his boxing title—and his means of support—for refusing to fight in Vietnam. Sam, Malcolm X, and Muhammad Ali most certainly would have qualified as black messiah candidates, if indeed there were such people to begin with.

Sam was the first major black artist to cross over to popular music. True, Chuck Berry, Fats Domino, and Little Richard crossed over before him, but they did not have the charisma or the boyish good looks of Sam Cooke, whose fans included tens of thousands of young, impressionable white girls.

Four years after Sam's death, Martin Luther King Jr. and Robert F. Kennedy were assassinated.

Coincidences? Conspiracies? Who knows? All I know about Sam from the few times that we worked together is that he was an amazing performer, a good friend, and a great guy. He was a music pioneer and a civil rights activist who, like so many artists of our time, preferred to work behind the scenes. He also was a smart businessman whose SAR Records set an example for many of us in the business to follow.

In my own dealings with Sam, what stands out in my mind is the show we did for promoter Henry Wynn in Charlotte, North Carolina, in 1960. The show was part of a southern tour that included Dee Clark, the Crystals, the Drifters, Solomon Burke, Little Esther, Dionne Warwick, and the Upsetters Band. Daniel Wolff wrote about it in *You Send Me:*

> [T]he audience was supposed to be kept segregated by a rope down the middle of the theater. The local fire department came backstage and—their Southern accents strained into politeness—said, "Mr. Cooke, we'd appreciate it if you wouldn't jump down into the audience, 'cause we're not sure we can control the crowd if you do." By then, says Butler, "we were all feeling our oats and well into the militancy kind of thing." So Sam said, "They can't tell me how to sing!" and, midway through the show, jumped off the stage.

> Security knew it was coming, caught him, and threw him back, and Sam was furious—for a day. Then he and Butler got to laughing so hard about it they couldn't stop. "Man," Cooke told his friend, "they threw my ass back up onstage!"[3]

Stephen J. Whitfield, in *A Death in the Delta: The Story of Emmett Till,* offered the following explanation for why the South went to such lengths to combat miscegenation:

> In the immediate aftermath of *Brown v. Board of Education,* the Deep South exhibited the paranoia of a closed society that could not distinguish the defense of a "few essential social areas" from the entire structure of white supremacy. The preservation of white patriarchy seemed to require the suppression of even the most insignificant challenges to its authority. In Gunnar Myrdal's view, sex was "the principle around which the whole structure of segregation of the Negroes . . . [was] organized." And it was because of sex that racial segregation, which seems in retrospect so unintelligible and so kooky (if not insane), was intended to permeate every aspect of society—and generally did.[4]

All that aside, there are several parallels between Sam and me. We both were born in Mississippi, "by the river in a little tent"—Sam on the Sunflower River in Clarksdale and me on the Yellow Dog River near Clarksdale. Our sharecropper parents migrated from Mississippi to Chicago with their families when we were still relative toddlers. Sam's parents and mine were devout members of the Holiness faith. We both got our start in entertainment by singing with gospel groups—Sam with the Soul Stirrers and me with the Northern Jubilee Gospel Singers—before crossing over to "soul" music. Sam went solo in 1957; I followed a year later. Although we both formed our own record labels and publishing companies, this is where the parallels end. I came nowhere near the heights that Sam reached in his brief but productive career.

Neither did I reach the depths of suffering that Sam reached. Although he was long divorced from his first wife, Dolores, Sam suffered deeply when she was killed in what many called an "intentional" automobile accident. Following that tragedy, Sam's eighteen-month-old son Vincent by his second wife, Barbara, drowned in Sam's swimming pool. Sam never got over it.

As the lead singer of the Soul Stirrers, Sam established himself as one of gospel music's biggest stars. So when he crossed over in 1957 and his recording of "You Send Me" climbed to number 1 on the pop charts, Sam had already had a taste of stardom. I say "taste" because by selling 1.7 million records, appearing on national television shows such as *American Bandstand* and *The Ed Sullivan Show*, and performing at top nightclubs like the Copacabana, Sam rose to another level of stardom.

Considered by many as "The Man Who Invented Soul Music," Sam struggled mightily for artistic self-determination after the initial success of "You Send Me." Consequently, after becoming fed up with producers who wanted him to sing witless teen songs like "Teenage Sonata," he decided, in 1959, to form his own label, SAR, an acronym for Sam, Alexander (J.W. Alexander, his manager), and Roy (Crain).

SAR Records was primarily an outlet for Sam's talents as songwriter and record producer. SAR was launched with a single by his old gospel group, the Soul Stirrers. Shortly after, however, SAR began releasing R&B recordings by Johnnie Morisette, the Simms Twins, and the Valentinos. Although the Simms Twins reached number 42 on the charts with "Soothe Me" in 1962, and Morisette number 63 with "Meet Me at the Twisting Place," the SAR singles never scored any big hits. The Valentinos, meanwhile, had three modest chart records.[5]

My friend Johnnie Taylor, another former gospel singer who crossed over to soul music, scored a modest hit on SAR with Sam's "Rome (Wasn't Built in a Day)." So did Mel Carter with Sam's "When a Boy Falls in Love." Billy Preston, then a sixteen-year-old organist and sideman at SAR, launched his R&B career with "Greazee" on SAR's subsidiary, Derby. Preston later gained fame as a sideman, background singer, and featured performer with some of Britain's greatest recording stars.

Sam also had a great influence on the style of the new-generation Jamaican artists such as Bob Marley and Jimmy Cliff, especially after his first West Indies tour in 1960.

Otis Redding

One of the people I most admired during my Vee Jay years was Otis Redding, who appeared with me on several shows. As with Sam Cooke, Little Willie John, Jesse Belvin, and others, I struck up an instant friendship. It was

hard not to like a guy like Otis. He was one of those good old country boys—
a big old country boy—who charmed everyone he met with his down-home
openness and broad, country boy smile.

The thing you marveled at about Otis was that he could take a two-syllable
word like "longing" and turn it into eight syllables:

> Lawd, these arms of my-eye-eye-yine
> Are long-ong-ong-ong-ing-ing-ing-ing
> For yoo-woo-ooo-ooo-ooo.

He begged better than anybody I ever heard. As one writer put it, "Otis
Redding knew how to beg, plead, cry, and crawl for love like no other self-
respecting man this side of paradise.

"Nothing in his career, as documented numerous times in the many splen-
did reissues that have appeared over the years, explains where the Big O, as he
was affectionately known, learned to vocalize the pure ache of a man caught up
in unrequited love, driven and distraught in his desire—a brother who would
seemingly give up everything for someone to answer his plea for love, tender-
ness, and affection."[6]

I have often wondered about that myself. Where did Otis get such passion,
such anguish, at such a young age?

The day we wrote "I've Been Loving You Too Long" was a fluke. I was
changing planes in Atlanta and happened to stop by the Delta first-class
lounge. Otis was sitting in there.

"What are you doing here?" I asked.

"I'm going to Buffalo."

"I am too."

"What are you going there for?"

"I'm doing a show."

"I am too."

"Where are you playing?"

"Someplace called Kleindinst Music Hall."

"I am too."

We had a big laugh about the whole thing, then flew up to Buffalo together,
shared a cab to the hotel—that was in the days before people sent a limousine
for you—and checked into the Buffalo Sheraton.

After the show, we went back to the hotel, opened up a bottle of J&B,
and sat up in his room and talked stuff. Otis pulled out his guitar and said,
"Man, let's write some songs." I said okay. "Here's a song I've been working on
for a long time," he said. "I ain't been able to finish it."

He played it. It wasn't much of a song.

I said, "Here's one I've been working on, and all I really have is a title and a verse."

"What's the title?"

"It's called 'I've Been Loving You Too Long.'"

A guy had come backstage at the Regal Theater in Chicago one night and told me, "Jerry, write a song about this." I started writing the song and got to this part:

> I've been loving you too long to stop now.
> I've been loving you too long to stop now.
> You've grown tired and you want to be free,
> But you've become a habit to me.
> I've been loving you too long to stop now.

We started messing around with it—bang, bang, bang—and Otis said, "Man, I love this thing. Gawd damn, that's good!"

We got drunk and went to bed. The next morning he called me. "Hey, Jerry, I'm gonna take the song home with me and finish it." I said, "All right, go ahead."

About two weeks later, I was in Detroit and someone asked me if I had heard Otis Redding's new song. I said no. Later that evening, Otis called.

"Man, it's a smash," he said.

"It can't be a smash. You just learned it two weeks ago."

"Man, I went right home and recorded the song. The song is on the street, and I'm telling you, it's a smash. Let me play it for you":

> Oh, I've been lovin' you a little too long-wong-wong-wong . . .

I said, "Yeah, you're right. It's a smash. It's a smash because of the way you are singing it."

Since then, Joe Cocker has done it; Aretha Franklin has done it; a whole bunch of people have recorded it; but nobody touches Otis:

> You've grown tye-eye-eye-eye-ed
> And want to be free.
> Oh, good gawd,
> I've been lovin' you a little too long-wong-wong-wong . . .

I tell you, boy, if you don't believe that, you don't believe fat meat is greasy.

One music critic called "I've Been Loving You" "one of the most soulful recordings ever made." If you measure songs by royalty checks, I'm inclined to agree. I receive more royalties from Otis's one recording of that song than I get from everything I ever recorded.

Otis, whose sound was deeply rooted in gospel and country blues, epitomized rhythm and blues singing. But if you listen closely, you can tell he was greatly influenced by the pop sounds of Sam Cooke. Otis was a great admirer of Sam. He was one of the few artists who recorded a tribute album to Sam after Sam's death in 1964. Coincidentally, I was working with Otis in Jackson, Tennessee, the night Sam was killed. I remember it well because I drove from Jackson to Houston, Texas, to see Annette, who was undergoing exploratory surgery. Then I drove back to Jackson. I don't remember what Otis said about Sam's passing, but I do know he was pretty broken up about it.

On December 10, 1967, almost three years to the day after Sam's death, the twin-engine Beechcraft plane that Otis was flying in plunged into the icy waters of Lake Monona, killing seven of its passengers, including Otis, who, along with his band, the Bar-Kays, and pilot Richard Fraser, was en route from Cleveland's Hopkins Field to Madison, Wisconsin, where he was scheduled to play two shows at the Factory.

I first heard about the plane crash when Dionne Warwick, appearing at Mister Kelly's in Chicago, returned to the stage after a break and announced that the plane Otis was in had gone down.

Otis died less than a week after completing "(Sittin' on) The Dock of the Bay," which he wrote while living in a boathouse near San Francisco. It was his only number 1 pop record. He was twenty-six years old when he died.

Don Taylor

*I know I was born with a price on my head, and I know that my music will
go on forever. Maybe it's a fool say that, but when me know facts, me can say
facts. My music will go on forever.*

—Bob Marley, quoted from *Marley and Me*

I was working at Sir John's Night Beat Club in Miami in late 1964 when Jamo Thomas, then my valet, bongo player, driver, and all-around everything else, came to my hotel room and said, "Buck, there's a young guy outside with no shoes and no shirt, and he says he knows you. He's also looking for work. Is there anything we can do for him?"

"Maybe there is something we can find for him to do," I said. "Tell him to come on in." I knew exactly what Jamo was up to. He had been trying for weeks to get me to reduce his work load, and this presented a great opportunity to do just that. "What about giving him the valet job?" Jamo said. "Okay, let's see if he's interested." Jamo left and in a few moments returned with Don Taylor.

I immediately recognized Don as the energetic, ambitious young Jamaican I had met a year or so earlier when I performed in the Bahamas. At that time he was running a valet service as well as doing odd jobs for several of the acts that came to the Bahamas during the late fifties and early sixties. Don wound up in Miami after Jackie Wilson, who was so pleased with Don's valet service, gave him $60 to buy an airplane ticket to Miami. The plan was for Don to meet up with Jackie and eventually become his exclusive valet. In the interim, however, Don read that I was performing in Miami, and he came by the hotel to say hello and to see if I needed anything done while he waited for Jackie. It was Don's first trip to the States.

I hired Don as my valet at a salary of $40 a week plus room and board. In his book *Marley and Me,* Don described the outcome of that meeting: "Little did I realize at the time that this would be the beginning of my entry into show business and the tremendous success which I have achieved up to today."

Little did *I* realize at the time that Don would work only a few months as my valet before getting involved in an argument with Jamo, which eventually led to Don's dismissal. Years later, neither Don nor I could recall what the argument was about. But it must have been serious for me to fire him.[7]

In the years that followed, Don became a naturalized citizen of the United States, joined the Army, moved to Los Angeles, and eventually managed the careers of some of the biggest stars of the day, including Anthony and the Imperials ("Tears on My Pillow," "I Think I'm Going Out of My Head"), Martha Reeves of the Vandellas, and Don's greatest success story, fellow Jamaican Bob Marley.

Marley and Don were made for each other, each complementing the other at every turn. Marley's laid-back style of ganja smoking and the Rastafarian religious practice contrasted sharply with Don's high energy, American-style deal making, and fast-paced living. Where Marley was creative and spontaneous, Don was calculating and deliberate. Marley disliked America; Don loved it. Marley felt uneasy in the company of the likes of Chris Blackwell, owner of Island Records; Don, on the other hand, relished the opportunity, matching his business acumen against Blackwell's—and enjoying it.

Both men came from similar backgrounds, although Don, who grew up in the quieter East Side of Kingston, Jamaica, had fared much better as a youngster than Marley, who was raised in the hills of Nine Miles in St. Ann and later in West Kingston, the poorer side of the city. Both had white fathers and black mothers who abandoned them at a young age. Both were tenacious in their dedication to their respective pursuits: Marley seeking to raise the quality of life for his Jamaican countrymen, and Don reaching for the heights of the entertainment world. Both succeeded, but at a dear price.

In December 1976, during a meeting with Marley in Marley's Jamaican home, Don was shot several times in an apparent assassination attempt. Marley

Hanging out with Don Taylor. Photo by Charles McMillan.

and his wife Rita were also shot. All three survived, but Don, who mistakenly was pronounced dead by a nurse, took the worst of it with a bullet in his spine and would have been paralyzed for life had he not been flown to Miami for surgery.

In *Marley and Me,* Don claims that America's CIA was behind the assassination attempt. Why? According to him, Marley's desire to put on a free Christmas concert for the people of Jamaica was seen by the CIA as an endorsement of former Jamaican prime minister Michael Manley and his socialist policies. After Don's return from New York, where he had gone to hire a film crew for the concert, Don said Marley told him, "Don Taylor, when you were not here, the other day a white boy came here and told me that if I do not tone down my blood claat lyrics and if me no stop tek weh the white people from America them a go tek weh me visa and me can't go to America again." Don, who also alludes to the CIA's being behind Marley's untimely death from melanoma, said he later found out that one of the crew members he hired was "the son of the CIA Director, William Colby. . . . When I learnt of this it left very little doubt in my mind that there had been a CIA plot and that its one intention was to kill Bob Marley."

After Marley's death, Don got into a serious legal squabble with Bob's widow, Rita, over Marley's estate. Although their differences were eventually resolved, Don is still bitter about the whole experience.

The last time I saw Don was in 1996 in Kingston. I was sitting with my manager, Charles (Mack) McMillan, at an outdoor cafe when Don drove up in a stretch limousine. Don, who briefly lived with Mack and his mom in Chester, Pennsylvania, after I fired him, greeted us warmly. As he talked about his book *Marley and Me* and all that had gone on in the intervening years since last I saw him, the germ of an idea popped into my head: What if I were to write a book myself—a book about survival and the inexorable human spirit?

Bill Matheson

One day in late 1965, the owner of my newly hired interior decorating firm paid an unexpected visit to my home. Accompanying him was a tall, bespectacled man with dark hair and a warm smile. The man, who looked to be in his early thirties, was introduced as Bill Matheson.

Although he was introduced as a relative of the owner, it wasn't until a later meeting that I learned that Bill also was the owner's lawyer, and that neither he nor I knew that we were being used in a ruse to collect payment for a defective piece of furniture, for which I had refused to pay the firm.

I'm a great believer in the old adage that things always work out for the better, because that's exactly what happened in this case. Bill Matheson ended up becoming not only my lawyer but my manager as well—and one of my most trusted friends and advisors.

Bill recalled how he felt when he left my home that day: "I was so pissed off," he said, adding that he told the decorator, "Don't you ever take me to somebody's house where you're trying to collect money from them and tell them I'm your lawyer and bullshit like that! I don't sit down and eat food at people's houses and then go after them as your lawyer. If you want me to write them a letter, that's fine, but don't ever use me that way. It made us both look like a couple of pigs."

Bill Matheson is like that. In all the years that I have known him, I have never had occasion to question his integrity or his loyalty, whether to me, a relative, or a client. He is one of the most open, honest—sometimes brutally honest—people I have ever known.

About a month or so after I met Bill, and unbeknownst to me, Annette called him and asked if he would represent her in a dispute with a dry cleaners that had ruined one of her dresses. "It wasn't the sort of thing I did, actually," said Bill. "At the time, I was a labor lawyer handling union problems for a law firm that did almost exclusively labor and corporate work. But I felt so embarrassed over the way my client behaved, I decided to take her case. I don't recall if I was successful or not. I know I didn't charge her for it."

He was indeed successful—that is, he at least made a believer out of Annette, who began a lobbying campaign for Bill to handle my contract problems with Vee Jay, where I was beginning to feel betrayed and abandoned. During that time, Abner had left Vee Jay and then returned. When he did, it seemed that all we had built up until then was beginning to fall apart. I had been consistently turning out records and albums, making hit after hit, touring, television appearances—everything—then all of a sudden, nothing. On top of all that, I believed that Vee Jay wasn't giving me a correct accounting of my royalties. I was feeling hemmed in, trapped.

I talked with several lawyers, and all of them said there was nothing they could do about it. Finally, at Annette's urging, I agreed to call Bill.

When I went to see him in his office, one of the first things he asked me was how I got into the business. I told him about going to Washburne Trade School, studying to be a cook, forming the Impressions, marrying young, signing with Vee Jay, and so forth. I added that I really thought I was going to be a cook. I had no idea I was going to hit it big as a singer. But to answer his question, I got into show business quite by accident—being in the right place at the right time with Curtis, Eddie Thomas, the Impressions, Calvin Carter, et al. Of course, having at least a modicum of talent had a lot to do with it, too. But in retrospect, it all came down to a combination of happenstance and talent.

Then it was Bill's turn to talk. I learned that he had graduated from the University of Michigan, had earned his law degree from Yale, had recently married, and was currently employed as an associate in the law firm of Stickler and Lederer. In addition to working as labor lawyers for Sears, Allstate, and a number of the major insurance companies in the United States, Stickler and Lederer was the general counsel for Solo Cup, which manufactured paper and plastic cups.

"The wife of the major shareholder of Solo Cup was a lady named Dorothy Hulzman," said Bill, "and she wanted to sing. She had been a singer before she married her husband, and now she was in her fifties or sixties and she still wanted to sing. So every now and then, they would get together, four guys, and she and the four guys would do a record. She sang under the name Dora Hall and the Solo Cups.

"And it was always a big joke. Being labor lawyers and corporate lawyers, we didn't want any part of it, or of her. So we farmed it out to a lawyer named Dick Shelton."

At the time, Dick Shelton was working for Curtis Mayfield, as well as for a number of other entertainers. He was probably the best-known music lawyer in Chicago, considerably older than Bill. The only other entertainment lawyer was Sidney Korschak. Bill gave Dick Shelton a call.

"Dick, I have a problem here," said Bill. "A young man came to see me, and I want to help him if I can, but it sounds a little complex. I don't know anything about rhythm and blues music, and I want to know more about it.

"Dick said, 'Well, what's the guy's name?' I said, 'His name is Jerry Butler.' Dick said, 'Well, you know he's hot.' I said, 'I didn't know he's hot.' 'You didn't know he's hot?' I said, 'I listen to opera. You got any opera singers?' I listen to opera in my spare time. I have season tickets to the Lyric Opera.

"I explained to him what the problem was over at Vee Jay, and Dick said, 'Yeah, if he doesn't have a record out in another six months, he's dead. He needs a record on the street fast.'"

Bill and I started to meet regularly so that Bill could get a better handle on things. He said to me, "You know, I know nothing about music. I didn't even take the course on copyright when I was in law school." This, again, is what I really liked about Bill. From the moment I walked into his office, I knew I could always count on him to be up front with me. He wouldn't lie. Many of the lawyers I engaged before meeting Bill pretended to know a lot about the music business. They would make a superficial, cursory examination of my situation, throw up their hands, then take my money and run. Bill wasn't like that. He wanted to know everything he could about a situation, looking for every advantage, absorbing enormous amounts of information in the process, and then he would take action.

I told him that I actually knew a lot about the music business, and if he knew something about the law, then maybe we could work something out. We decided to have lunch a few times to see what we could come up with. In our second or third conversation, I think, I told Bill that I wrote many of the songs that I recorded for Vee Jay and that I also was a lyricist.

Meanwhile, Bill started going to the newsstand, buying *Billboard, Cashbox,* and *Variety.* "I'm reading them on the commuter train," he said, "going back and forth to the suburbs every day. Most of what I'm reading I don't understand at all—but I'm reading it. And I'm doing a lot of research.

"I find out that a songwriter has to sign a contract, too, with the publishing company. The Vee Jay recording contract gave Vee Jay, or its publishing affiliate, first call or exclusive rights to anything that Jerry wrote, which struck me as one of the really great inequities of the deal. But there was still such a thing as a songwriter's contract for every song—and copyrights."

Bill decided that it was time to visit Abner at Vee Jay.

Describing that first meeting, Bill said, "Abner greets me—this little man in a sweatshirt with a toy mouse on it—a strange little guy, weighed about ninety-five pounds soaking wet. Fast-talking. Different from anybody I had ever met before in my life. Abner was the smartest guy I ever met in the record business, period. No one came close. In fact, he was overqualified to be in the record business. He never reached his full potential. This guy should've been teaching philosophy in college.

"He apparently was a voracious reader. He could remember everything he read. He had something close to total recall. He was just a genius, not because he read a lot. Calvin Carter read a lot. Calvin Carter was a bright guy who read a lot, but Calvin read authors like Langston Hughes; he was somewhat limited in his reading by his own complexion, whereas Abner would read anything. He'd read something translated from the Chinese just to find out what they were thinking, although he didn't relate to or identify with them. He was a brilliant, Renaissance guy, although I didn't see all of that when I first met him. But I saw something. I realized I was dealing with an extremely clever guy.

"He was trying very hard to be nice to me. I could read people pretty well. I had a number of years sitting across the table from Jimmy Hoffa and a bunch of tough Teamsters. I negotiated with unions so long I used to laugh and tell my wife that whenever I negotiated with a union, I could tell which members of the bargaining committee had done time. They're different from anything you've seen anywhere else.

"I read Abner pretty well. He was being nicer to me than he should've. He was being nicer to me than I would've been to me had I received me in the office the way he did. I thought he was a nice man, but I didn't think that was the reason, because there were times when I was saying things that were so dumb that Abner obviously was visibly trying to maintain control of himself not to just throw something at me.

"I kept going back, and he never said no to me. He would tell me he was busy, but he would see me. I said, This guy is stroking me. There's something going on here that I can't get hold of. But he definitely is weak.

"So I asked to see all of the writers' contracts. I wanted to see everything they had in their files on Jerry Butler. And we find out that they forgot to have Jerry sign about twenty-five contracts. He just wrote the songs in the studio; they went out and got the publishing; and they never got the contracts signed. They had blank contracts with no signatures on them in the files."

In one of our sessions I had mentioned to Bill that we would often work well into the night at the studio, and there was just no time to sign a contract.

"It was supposed to be done the next day," said Bill. "Maybe Abner took care of it. But during the period that Betty Chiappetta and Randy Wood ran the company, they were so busy having fun, a lot of the contracts didn't get signed. The thing was, I represented a guy who was a songwriter on practically everything he recorded, and they didn't get contracts signed!

"So I throw this up to Abner and he says, 'Yes, that's true, and I'd like to get them signed.' And he pulls out this huge bunch of contracts, and he wants Jerry to sign them. He says, 'Help us out. We're kind of in real trouble. We really need this.'"

When Bill told me that, I thought, What nerve! After we laughed about it, I said, "Well, what do you think?"

"First of all," he said, "I smell a bankruptcy coming. I don't think this guy can pull it out. I'm not a specialist in that, but I do know that a bankrupt company sells its assets. Any asset it sells within six months prior to the time it files bankruptcy, the trustee can set those sales aside." Therefore, if Vee Jay was planning to file bankruptcy, Bill figured, it had sixty days to sell the assets, because six months before the bankruptcy, anything after that could be set aside. If they had assets that they wanted to sell, they had to do it right away.

Bill and I were having lunch pretty regularly then, brainstorming back and forth. I would tell him about the music business, and together we would try to figure out what was going on.

Meanwhile, Bill was still reading *Cashbox, Billboard,* and *Variety,* but getting nothing out of *Variety,* "a really bullshit magazine," according to Bill. One day he ran across an article in either *Cashbox* or *Billboard* announcing that Benny Goodman's brothers, Gene and Harry, were buying the catalog of Conrad, Tollie, and Gladstone, Vee Jay's publishing company.

Bill recalled, "When I read the article, I called Chess. Leonard Chess thinks he's going to sign Jerry, and I must say I'm holding that out to him, because in what appears to be a friendless world, it's possible that Jerry's manager has been negligent or bought off, whichever. It's obvious we needed some allies.

"So Chess says to me, 'Hey, listen, I own Arc Music. Goodman's my partner. That's me who's buying those catalogs. I'm putting up a quarter of a million dollars.'

"I said, well, I've got news for you. You're not buying the songs written by Jerry Butler because I'm not going to let him sign the contracts.

"Leonard Chess—God rest his soul—got us out of the contract. He said, 'Hey, you send a wire to Gene Goodman and tell him what you've got in mind. Let him know, because we're supposed to meet tomorrow and give him a quarter of a million dollars out of escrow at [Chicago's] LaSalle National Bank.'

"I suddenly realized why Abner's been stroking me: He wants to keep cool so that he can get a quarter of a million out of escrow.

"I sent the telegram, and now everyone's screaming at me. I get an invitation to come down to the LaSalle National Bank. I'm going to meet them all there: Chess, his brother Phil, Abner, Goodman, who I never met, but I know of his brother, Benny.

"My boss walks into my office. He says, 'You're working on the Sears brief?' I said, 'No, I can't, Phil. I've got something I've got to do this afternoon.' He said, 'Is it something you're doing for Sears and Roebuck?' 'No.' 'Something you're doing for Allstate?' 'No.' 'Something for Solo Cup?' 'No.' He said, 'What is this?'

"I said, 'It's my new client, Jerry Butler.'

"'The singer you keep going to lunch with? You're putting this guy that nobody's ever heard of . . . ?'

"'Actually, people have heard of him, Phil; it's just that *you* haven't.'

"'You're putting this in front of Sears?'

"I said, 'Look, there's a quarter of a million dollars in the LaSalle National Bank, and I've got to go down there and sign the releases.'

"Phil says, 'If you think your private clients are more important than the firm's clients, then you ought to be somewhere else.'

"I said, 'Phil, we can do this two ways. I can be out of here tomorrow, or I can stay thirty days and clean up my files. But I think you're right. I don't belong in this firm.'"

Bill was determined to go to LaSalle National Bank. He quit the law firm that afternoon.

When he arrived at the bank, Bill said, "Abner looked like his dog had just died. He was really upset. 'Why isn't Jerry here?' he said. 'It's because he can't face me, right?'

"I said, 'Jerry isn't here because he doesn't want to call you names. He's still loyal to you. You haven't played straight with him. You haven't had a record on the streets in six months. He needs to go somewhere and have records out. He's got a wife; he's got a family. He can't wait for you guys to sit another six months, going into bankruptcy.'

"So Abner signs the release. The Brackens are there—Vivian and Jimmy—and they sign. I also had a notary there."

I was on the road somewhere with Irv Nahan while all of this was going on. Bill called me later and said, "Guess what? You're not under contract with Vee Jay anymore. You're free."

That was it. After eight years, I was no longer a Vee Jay recording artist. Up until that moment, I thought I would feel elated. I didn't. I felt cold and alone.

"Breaking up is so hard to do . . . "

Booking It

As soon as I severed my relationship with Vee Jay, I started getting calls from other record companies and booking agents. So did Bill. Dick Shelton was right—I *was* hot. Still, I didn't want to be out openly soliciting a new contract for myself, so I asked Bill to serve as my manager. Although Irv Nahan was my manager, according to Bill, "there was a bunch of stuff that he should have been on that had slipped by." Bill, who seldom missed an opportunity to utter one of his favorite phrases, added, "Most managers are practicing law without a license, anyway." I agreed. By having him work in the dual role of attorney and manager, I avoided paying legal fees. It was a great arrangement. As with Irv, Bill and I never had a written management agreement. I believed, like Bill, that "if your word is no good, a piece of paper will not make it any better."

When my bookings started to fall off, I blamed Irv. Since I had once owned a piece of Queen Booking and had recently re-signed with the agency, I felt I was owed something, out of either friendship or loyalty. Bill was worried—and so was I—that maybe Irv was being taken care of on the side by Abner, who was also tight with Ruth Bowen at Queen Booking.

By then, Bill and I had decided on a non-defensive strategy in an effort to take charge of my own career. This meant not only demanding and getting what was due me from Vee Jay, including my eventual release, but getting the kind of bookings that other top-selling recording artists were enjoying, even those who had not achieved what I had in my brief career. It also meant that if I had to change booking agencies, then so be it.

Bill flew to New York to give the word to the current heads of Queen, Ruth Bowen and her husband Billy, a former member of the Ink Spots.

When he confronted the Bowens, Bill apparently was unaware that one of Queen's partners, Gaetano "Big Guy" Vastola, was a reputed member of the Genovese crime family and had the reputation of being able to "tear a human being apart with his hands." But that probably wouldn't have fazed Bill anyway, because, as he puts it, "I had the advantage of being so dumb, I wasn't smart enough to be scared of these thugs."

When he met with the Bowens and told them how I felt, either Billy Bowen or someone else remarked, "Hey, I taught Jerry Butler how to dress."

Bill said, "I find that hard to believe."

"Why?"

"Because Jerry Butler is one of the best-dressed guys I've ever met, and you look like a pile of dirty laundry."

Bill said they wanted to throw him out of the window. No one talked to them that way. "I was so stupid," said Bill. "I was walking in places by myself and meeting people. Anybody with any brains would say, 'Hey, you're twelve stories up, you moron. They're going to throw you out the window!'"

It amazed me, after hearing stories like that, that Bill was still walking around on two legs. It was serious, scary stuff, but we always managed to find some humor in it.

❁

After I left Queen, I signed with Associated Booking, headed by Joe Glaser, the loud, profane New York talent agent credited with turning around the careers of such greats as Dinah Washington, Billie Holiday, Lionel Hampton, Lou Rawls, and Louis "Satchmo" Armstrong. Leonard Feather once said of Glaser, "Meeting the irascible Glaser for the first time was an experience some found terrifying. His barking voice was tough, his manner abrupt; his language could turn telephones blue. Yet in moments of repose he could be as amiable as a clergyman and as generous as Santa Claus."[8]

Glaser is primarily identified with Satchmo Armstrong, who had deep respect for him. Legend has it that Armstrong trusted Glaser so much that he never read his contract or questioned any moves Glaser made for him, including paying Armstrong's income tax, looking after his insurance, protecting him from lawsuits, and even paying his band members. Until his death at the age of seventy-one, Armstrong continued to call his longtime manager "Mister" Glaser.

For his part, Glaser once told a *Times* magazine reporter, "I'm Louis and Louis is me. There's nothing I wouldn't do for him." And there wasn't. I remember him telling Bill and me how he literally went door to door trying to get someone to listen to Armstrong's demo of "Hello, Dolly!" No one was interested—that is, until he took it to Kapp Records, owned by Jack Kapp, the founder and president of Decca Records. In February 1964, "Hello, Dolly!" shot to number 1 on the charts, and eventually it went gold. At year's end, it was named "Song of the Year" and "Best Vocal Performance, Male" by *Billboard*. It also became Armstrong's signature song.

"I tried to tell the sonofabitches!" said Glaser. "They wouldn't listen. They can eat their fucking hearts out!"

But not all of Glaser's acts revered him or displayed the kind of loyalty toward him that Armstrong did. Dinah Washington started rival Queen Booking because she felt that Glaser had been dragging his feet in getting her suitable dates. Billie Holiday, whose first record deal was obtained by Glaser, argued with him over the direction of her career; other top-name acts simply didn't like him.

I remember the time when Glaser, an ex–fight manager, gave Bill and me some tickets to a light heavyweight title fight at New York's Madison Square Garden between Dick Tiger, an aggressive counterpunching Nigerian, the challenger, and the champ, Puerto Rican José Torres. The Puerto Ricans were out in big numbers that night, rooting for their guy—but to no avail. Tiger beat the shit out of him.

But the partisan Puerto Rican crowd didn't see it that way. When the decision was announced, all hell broke loose. Bottles, tables, and all kinds of shit started flying by. The Puerto Ricans were sitting in the balcony, and we were on the main floor. Bill yelled, "Oh shit!" and grabbed a folding chair, held it over his head, and started crawling out of the arena. I followed.

The next day we went to Glaser's office. "How'd ya enjoy the fight?" he asked enthusiastically.

"We damn near got killed!" said Bill.

"Where did you sit?"

"Ringside."

"You dumb sonofabitch!" he said. "You shoulda got the hell outta there! You saw the guy was losing. Those Puerto Ricans woulda killed ya!"

He was something.

He called Earl Wilson one day: "Earl, come up here. Got a guy. He's a singer. Recorded 'Moon River.' Wonderful, wonderful version of it. You oughtta do something for the motherfucker. You know, write about him or something."

The next day, there was indeed an item about me in Wilson's famous and well-read *New York Post* column. That was the kind of guy Glaser was. Despite his abrasiveness, some people just loved him; some didn't.

Bill and I were at Joe's office one day and Bill said to him, "Joe, we want you to do for Jerry what you did for Lou Rawls."

"What the fuck! Lou's got these fucking gold albums," Joe shot at Bill. "I can't do that for the sonofabitch." He pointed at me. "He's got to get his own gold albums. What the hell do you think I am? I'm busting my balls trying to get him work. What the fuck do you want?" I couldn't answer that; nor could Bill.

Then there was the time he sent Annette some macadamia nuts. I sent him a letter thanking him. So he sent a letter back, thanking me. I sent him another letter. He finally wrote, "Will you quit writing these fucking letters?"

Part III.
The Mercury Years

11.

The Producers

Jerry Ross

My first producer at Mercury was Luchi DeJesus, whose main claim to fame was co-writing with Brook Benton and Clyde Otis "A Rockin' Good Way (to Mess Around and Fall in Love)." Benton and Dinah Washington had a huge hit with the song, which reached number 7 on Billboard's pop chart and number 1 on R&B. Later, in the seventies, Luchi made some noise writing and arranging the theme song for the blaxploitation movie *Black Belt Jones*. The arrangement incorporated a unique blend of Latin jazz and rhythm and blues funk. Luchi used this mix of styles in some of the things he produced on me, in particular "Alfie" from the movie by the same name. "Wait'll Burt hears this!" he gushed after the session.

Knowing Burt Bacharach and the way he approaches his music, I don't think he was the least bit pleased with what Luchi had done to his song. I wasn't. Neither was I pleased with some of the other material Luchi selected for my first album. I'm not trying to badmouth Luchi. If I do come off that way, then I hope he forgives me; it's not personal or intentional. It's just that I wanted my first time out of the chute at Mercury to be dynamite. Stupendous! Something that would more than justify the kind of money Mercury had invested in me. The album Luchi produced on me fell far short of my expectations. As I recall, I told him just that. Thus, we worked only one album together.

Next up was Philadelphia songwriter and producer Jerry Ross, who had two big hits for Mercury in 1966, his first year with the label: "Sunny" by Bobby Hebb, which went to number 1 worldwide, and "98.6" by Keith. Both were million sellers.

The following year Ross scored big again, this time with Chicago group Spanky and Our Gang, whose "Sunday Will Never Be the Same" went over the million mark; and another million seller: "Apples, Peaches, Pumpkin Pie" by Jay and the Techniques for Mercury's subsidiary, Smash. I definitely felt I was in good hands this time.

Ross, who calls himself a "musicologist," spent some time with Armed Forces Radio. That experience provided him a jump start for one of his earlier careers in broadcasting: record promotion. As a promoter he met many recording artists, including Bobby Darin, Chubby Checker, the Four Aces, Vic Damone, Tony Bennett, and a group from Chicago called the Impressions. "I became a great admirer of the group, he said."

As a teenager he had studied trumpet and voice, but he soon realized that "there were so many other people out there who were so much better than me. That's when I decided to get behind the scene, and started writing."

Working with local disc jockeys Georgie Woods, Jocko, Fat Man, and Bill Curtis gave Ross a leg up on the competition when he started looking for airplay for his own material. Dick Clark and producer Tony Mamirella would insist that Ross get additional exposure before introducing a record on *American Bandstand*. "They would always say to me, 'Go get me some activity. Break it somewhere else.'

"So I would go to Allentown, Baltimore, Pittsburgh, or wherever my contacts were good, and get some exposure and airplay. Then I'd come back and say, 'Look, we're number 10 in Pittsburgh with this particular record.' Dick, of course, played or introduced just about every hit record I was involved with—fortunately, there were many of them—but he didn't play them until they were hits somewhere else.

"I was very fortunate in the early days in exploring my instincts and ideas and the feel that I had from the street. The very first record that I produced, by the Dream Lovers, called 'When We Get Married,' went Top 10. That convinced me I was doing something right. The Dream Lovers were the background doo-woppers behind Chubby Checker, Dee Dee Sharpe, the Dovells, and all those hits on Cameo-Parkway. But they never got any credits. I think what they got was a hoagy and a cheese steak, and that was it."

Between 1961 and 1965, Ross wrote for and produced local acts, including a young, mixed group called the Saffires that had a big hit called "Who Do You Love," which went Top 30. He followed that with another female group called Candy and the Kisses, who had a big dance hit called "The Eighty-One." His musicians on those sessions were Bobby Martin, on vibes; Bobby Eli, guitar; Joe Macko, bass (all of whom became part of the Philadelphia MFSB scene); and Leon Huff and Tommy Bell, pianos.

Around that time, Ross came across a seventeen-year-old by the name of Kenny Gamble. "Basically, I took him under my umbrella, worked with him, recognized his God-given talent, and really taught him how to write that three-minute record. You couldn't get a record on the air unless it was under three minutes. I believed in him as a recording artist. He sang like Brook Benton, had a wonderful voice. I signed him with Columbia Records as an artist.

"We worked together for several years, collaborated, wrote a lot of hit songs together. I cut a record with Tommy and Kenny called 'Kenny and Tommy' on my Heritage label, which is now a collector's item.

"Then, as our careers started going different ways, I was called up to New York by Mercury because of the activity that I was creating in the Philadelphia market. My mentor at Mercury was Shelby Singleton, who brought me into the company, gave me the opportunity to use all of my promotional and marketing tools and my creative instincts to really put it all together.

"We went to New York and moved lock, stock, and barrel to Mercury Records. It was a wonderful tenure there for me."

Indeed it was. The first artist he produced, Bobby Hebb, went to number 1 with "Sunny." Then he found a group in Allentown, Pennsylvania, called Jay and the Techniques, who scored million sellers with "Apples, Peaches, Pumpkin Pie" and "Keep the Ball Rollin'."

"It just went on and on," said Ross, referring to Keith, another artist from Philadelphia, who had the huge hit "98.6."

After those successes, Ross was invited to Chicago to see a group called Spanky and Our Gang. "I saw them in a club on the North Side called Mother Blues, and I just flipped out over them. We cut a couple of big hits with Spanky called 'Sunday Will Never Be the Same' and 'Lazy Day.'"

Then I entered the picture. Mercury had informed Ross that I was looking for a fresh direction and some new motivation. They asked him if he would be interested. He said yes. He flew to Chicago, met with me, and played some of his songs. I liked them and told him I thought that it would be a good collaboration. That was the beginning of our relationship.

We did an album or two together, cut some great songs. One of the songs we recorded was "Mr. Dream Merchant," a song which Ross said I "breathed life into."

Shortly after that, I met Kenny Gamble and Leon Huff, although Ross thinks he is the one who introduced us. He is partly right. One of the songs Kenny and Leon played for me when I first met them was "I'm Gonna Make You Love Me," which Gamble, Huff, and Ross wrote and first recorded with Dee Dee Warrick. When I heard it, I knew right away that they would be great. In addition to me, Bobby Hebb, Jay and the Techniques, and Bill Deal and the Rondells also recorded it.

The background singers that Ross used on all of his Mercury hits were Ashford and Simpson and Melba Moore. They also worked with me on all of my recordings in New York. "I was fortunate enough to surround myself with a lot of talented people who eventually went on to create their own mark in the industry," said Ross. "That was the nucleus of it. We had a great rhythm section, some wonderful arrangers in Jimmy Wisner and Joe Ranzetti, who worked with us on a lot of the dates."

When Ross decided to leave and do his own thing again, he took some of his artists with him. I had a fixed contract with Mercury and stayed on. When my contract was up, however, I joined Kenny and Leon in Philadelphia.

Ross revived Heritage, stayed in New York, and signed a number of new acts, including Bill Deal and the Rondells, with whom he had at least three chart successes: "May I," "I've Been Hurt," and "What Kind of Fool."

Ross's early influences while studying music were jazz and pop stars like Frank Sinatra, Stan Kenton, Stan Getz, Jazz at the Philharmonic, Johnny Smith, and one of his all-time favorite jazz singers, Johnny Hartmann. Over the years, Ross has been trying to get me to do an album called *If Johnny Were Here,* featuring the songs of Sondheim, Bacharach, and people that Hartmann never got a chance to work with. "That's still on the back burner," he said. "I'd still love to do that." I think it's a good idea.

When music changed in the eighties and went into the Pearl Jams, the Bon Jovis, hip hop, and rap, it lost its appeal to Ross. "So what I did, basically, was take all of the experience and training and instincts that kept me in the music business and I directed it into another area. I have been licensing music into film and television for the last ten or fifteen years, and into compilation, reissue albums, getting some of the great songs from the fifties and sixties into advertising and commercials.

"I represent a lot of wonderful writers and record companies. As a matter of fact, up until recently, I had almost a thirty-five-year relationship with Philly International and Gamble and Huff. They were one of my major clients. I've licensed the Philly International catalog to now be sold and marketed through EMD-Capital. I also just licensed their entire catalog into Europe, to a company over there called MCI—not the phone company, but Music Collection International.

"Before I got involved in it, you couldn't find a CD on Teddy or Lou Rawls. You can now walk into a store in Johannesburg, South Africa, and find a Teddy Pendergrass CD or MFSB or Billy Paul. So their product is now all over the world, and they are once again millionaires."

Ross also represents the Four Seasons; Larry Brown, who wrote "Tie a Yellow Ribbon"; the Chi-Lites; the Artistics; Jackie Wilson; and Larry Weiss, who collaborated with Ross on "Dream Merchant." Weiss also wrote "Rhinestone Cowboy."

"Last year we did the Eddie Murphy movie *The Nutty Professor.* Teddy Pendergrass did 'Close the Door' in that particular film. In *Boogie Nights,* the recent Burt Reynolds film, I licensed 'Ain't No Stopping Us Now' by McFadden and Whitehead, because they used a lot of disco music in that film. It's also being used in the UK for a commercial for Budweiser. That's the commercial with the anteaters going down into the ground. If it's successful there, they may roll it out over here.

"We did a lot of commercials with Ameritech out of Chicago. Burger King, of course, uses a lot of it. It's a lot of fun. I solicit literally hundreds of advertising agencies, music supervisors at all the studios, independents, Warner Brothers, and Columbia. If I find a movie that's in pre-production, what year it's in, we solicit a dozen or two pieces of material that we think would fit the genre. Sometimes we hit the nail right on the head. They get back to us and say, 'Yeah, we'd love to use this particular piece of music.' That's always good news."

Gamble and Huff and the Sound of Philadelphia

In any discussion about regional "sounds," such as the Motown and Memphis sounds, you simply must include the sound of Philadelphia, one of the most recognizable sounds of the sixties and seventies.

And when you mention the sound of Philadelphia, invariably, almost in the same breath, you must pay homage to Kenny Gamble and Leon Huff, the chief

Kenneth Gamble
(*standing*) and
Leon Huff

architects of that sound. Kenny's lyricism and Huff's musicianship are the bedrock on which this unique blend of music genres rests.

"First and foremost, the Philadelphia sound is a combination of great songs and great artists," said Kenny, pointing to the main components of the sound: a guitar player who plays in octaves like Wes Montgomery; vibes and piano à la the George Shearing Quintet; Huff, "who is probably the funkiest piano player you can find"; funky drums; and great arrangements. "Mix all that with gospel and classical music, and you have the sound of Philadelphia."

Also add to that the availability of some retired classical musicians from the Philadelphia Orchestra, who, according to Kenny, "had a ball playing with us."

"We also had Bobby Martin, Tommy Bell, and Jack Faith. These guys, very accomplished musicians, were the arrangers. Tommy Bell was just learning at that time, and he was able to experiment with a lot of the product we were doing."

Kenny includes me among the "great artists" who helped develop the sound of Philadelphia. I'm not being modest, but "great" is stretching it a bit, although the music we created together while I was signed with Mercury Records was imbued with that great Philadelphia sound.

I first met Kenny and Leon in 1968 at Pep's, a little show bar in Philadelphia owned by Kenny's godmother, Loretta Adams. Kenny, who worked at a record shop around the corner, heard that I was in the bar, and he and Huff dropped in and asked me if I would listen to some of their material. I learned later that Jerry Ross had invited them to write songs for me, but they never got the opportunity. One of the songs they played for me that afternoon was "Lost," which I liked a lot.

"That was the beginning of it," said Kenny. "We sat down and talked a little bit. I think we instantly jelled together. In fact, after that we went to New York and recorded 'Lost' and two other songs. The record did fairly well, not a real big hit. But as a writing team, we went on to do other sessions, including an album called *The Iceman Cometh*. This was the first time we worked as a writing team."

After that, we would work the same way: sitting in Kenny and Leon's office—Kenny, Huff, and me. Huff would be on the piano, while Kenny and I would come up with the lyrics. Huff and Kenny would come up with some concepts and play some chords, and I started singing. That's how we came up with "Never Gonna Give You Up," which is considered a classic today.

"The way we wrote together was so easy," said Kenny. "It was like magic—a magic moment for us. We laughed a lot. We had a lot of fun. We would talk about different situations that people would get themselves into in their love life and whatever, and we would write about it. We would look at it from every angle we could think of.

"We were going to do three songs that day, but if my memory serves me correctly, we only did that one song, because we wanted the track, the music, to be perfect. We must have cut that song fifteen or twenty times—just the track—so that it would have the right feel. We finally got it. What you hear is what we were able to get.

"All three of us were perfectionists. We wouldn't allow one note to be wrong. If there was a bad note, we would do it all over again.

"The equipment was not like what it is today, where you would punch in and do things like that. When we started recording, we were on four-track. It was just starting to go to eight-track. Our engineer, Joe Tarsia, who also was a tremendous part of our team, was with us from the beginning."

I wholeheartedly agree. Joe Tarsia is as much a part of the Philadelphia International success story as Gamble and Huff. They could have done very well without me and other writers and artists, as they have proven so often, but I doubt if they could have done as well without Joe. He was the glue that held everything together. The "magic" in the writing of such songs as "Only the Strong Survive" and "Hey Western Union Man" might still have been there, but it would not have been as bright, or as dazzling, I think, without Joe's magical Midas touch. He has a gift; he is an acoustical engineering genius, as far as I'm concerned.

I was surprised when Joe asked me in 1995 to be his presenter at Philadelphia's prestigious Walk of Fame ceremonies, where he was one of ninety-five Philadelphians being honored for their work in the music business. Of all the people he could have chosen for that honor, he chose me. I felt honored.

"I was lucky enough to get a plaque," said Joe, "and they asked me who I wanted as a presenter. I thought back to somebody who was very important to me and I said Jerry Butler."

After Joe opened his Sigma Sound studio, located in central Philadelphia, the hits followed in rapid succession. "What really kicked it off in the beginning," he said, "were the Intruders' 'Cowboys to Girls' and 'Expressway to Your Heart' by the Soul Survivors, a white group with an urban sound." This was followed by Thom Bell and the Delfonics' "Didn't I Blow Your Mind."[1]

When I came along, "it was like a hand in a glove, like magic," according to Joe, sounding an all too familiar theme. Kenny and Leon introduced me to Joe in 1967, while he was working for Cameo-Parkway Records, which at that time was the largest independent label in the country. "Never Gonna Give You Up" was recut at Cameo-Parkway.

Shortly after that, Kenny and Leon signed the O'Jays, then signed a deal with CBS Records and had a string of hits with CBS: Billy Paul, the O'Jays, Harold Melvin and the Blue Notes, Lou Rawls, the Three Degrees, and Teddy Pendergrass. Tommy Bell was cutting the Delfonics, the Stylistics, the Spinners, and Johnny Mathis, among others.

"That period was very productive," said Joe. "People came from all over the country—people like Stevie Wonder, B.B. King, Johnny Mathis, and David Bowie. Hits beget hits. People in our business tend to follow where the hits are. For instance, when Prince was in Minneapolis, everybody went to Minneapolis to make records; when Nirvana was in Seattle, everybody went to Seattle to make records. We benefited from that like Motown did and like Muscle Shoals and Memphis did when they were making hit records."

Joe's electronics career got started in the late fifties, in the research department at Phillips Electronics. He had recently married and begun fixing TV sets at night, "trying to pick up some extra money.

"One day a guy said to me, 'Can you fix a tape recorder?' I said, 'Sure.' It just so happened the tape recorder was in a studio, and I never left. I started working there for nothing.

"At Cameo-Parkway I worked as an assistant under a guy named Dave Appel. That's where I sort of got my background. But my first job in a studio was fixing equipment. I used to build it and fix it."

One of the most productive and inspiring writing sessions I ever had with Kenny and Leon was the one when we wrote "Only the Strong Survive." Here's how Kenny remembers it:

"I had been talking to a guy on the phone one night—the night before we wrote 'Only the Strong Survive,' he said, "and at the end of the conversation we both agreed that, in order to make it in this world, *only the strong survive*. I wrote the title down, and when we got back together, I said, 'Man, this is a great title,' and—boom—right then we started writing the song."

I came up with the story line, while Kenny and Huff embellished it with what Kenny calls "the hooks and good sing-a-longs." The whole experience was, in Kenny's words, "something that you really can't describe, something that happens maybe once in a lifetime, people getting together and harmonizing so well."

We wrote and recorded several other songs during my tenure with Mercury, among them "Are You Happy," "Hey Western Union Man," and "Moody Woman."

I am proud to be listed among the "unique voices" that Kenny and Huff sought out to record. "There is nobody else who sounds like a Jerry Butler," Kenny would later say. "That's what we were really looking for—people who were individuals—people like Eddie Levert. The only person who sounds like Eddie is his son, Gerald." Others included in Kenny's unique voices category are Patti LaBelle, Lou Rawls, Teddy Pendergrass, and Harold Melvin.

"Today, I don't think it is the same level of artistry that it was back then. It's different; however, I think this is good for this generation. Some of the grooves that they are creating today are fantastic. The best part about it is that they are taking a lot of our old stuff and recycling it and bringing it back in different forms. They can take four chords off of one of our songs and write a whole new song to it.

"I respect the young people today in their ability to use the technology that's available to them and come up with their own music and expressions of the world.

"But just as we wrote about the world as we saw it in our day, that's what the kids are doing today. They are writing songs about how they see the world.

Take a song like 'Love Train.' We felt that. We felt that people all over the world should be at peace with each other. That was the message we were trying to relate.

"'Only the Strong Survive' was a message song, too. That song was so important that someone like Elvis Presley recorded it. It is a great song, with a lot of meanings to it. It could be a love song, which we made it, but it also relates to life: You can't let something get you down, no matter what it is, no matter how much it hurts.

12.

"Kill or Be Killed"

He would cup his hands over his ears and nervously walk the floor, trying as best he could to drive out the demons that stalked him with their maddening sound. It was always "the sound, the sound" that prompted his bizarre behavior, including getting up in the middle of the night and working feverishly to pitch a tent on the living room floor, where he would spend the rest of the night rocking from side to side, holding his head, and crying. He would go days without sleep, walking back alleys in whatever town we were in, talking to himself. He tried everything he could in a desperate effort to kill the sound. But nothing seemed to work.

One day, in one of his more lucid moments, he described the sound to Annette. "It was a funny sound, a loud rumbling sound, sort of like an earthquake," she said. It would start with a low hum and soon build to a loud drone that became increasingly louder. Over the years, he became convinced that the sound that stalked him, that invaded his sleep and raped his mind, was the sound of a train roaring down a faraway track. "Can't you hear it?" he would say, sometimes screaming the question.

He first heard the sound in a rice field in Vietnam—just before he emptied his M-16 rifle into the bodies of some terrified, screaming Vietnamese women. "Bam-bam-bam-bam-bam," he said, mimicking the rapid-fire report of his M-16. He spoke matter-of-factly: "Our orders were to destroy the enemy. If we didn't kill them, our own people would kill us. It was kill or be killed." He was eighteen at the time.

He said his bullets tore with such force into the bodies of the women— young women as well as old—that they lifted them off their feet. It took only a few seconds, but those seconds seemed suspended in time. Everything seemed in slow motion, as an eerie silence hung over the field. Then, as the bodies fell, it seemed as if the earth moved beneath his feet with a thundering roar, as in an earthquake, or like a train roaring past; it was the same sound he had heard before the shooting, but much louder.

When he looked at the grotesque, twisted bodies of the women, he wanted to retch. "That's something I never want to see again," he told Annette. But he never could escape the sight, nor the sound. *The Sound.* They were part of his madness, an apocalyptic view of his own future, his journey into the heart of darkness.

One day he casually announced that he was going out "to kiss a train." We all thought he meant he was going to catch a train. We thought nothing of it because he had said it so often.

But it all came together that day: the bizarre behavior, the madness. Bernard Williams, my quiet, gentle bongo player, stepped in front of a fast-moving train and finally, irrevocably, killed the sound. *The Sound.*

"In the Name of Freedom"

Nineteen-sixty-six was a landmark year in more ways than one: It was the year I parted company with Vee Jay Records and signed a five-year contract with Mercury Records. Most important, it was the year that Anthony and Randall Butler, my twin sons, were born. It also was the year that I became more politically aware.

I think a lot of Americans were becoming more politically aware around that time. The war in Vietnam was raising alarms, even though the Tet Offensive was still two years away. In previous years, Tet—the Vietnamese New Year —had been a time for truce. But on the night of January 30, 1968, the United States Embassy in Saigon was attacked and overrun by Viet Cong guerrillas.

My sons, Tony (*left*) and Randy, preparing to go on a fishing trip in the mid-1970s.

Part of the attack was filmed for television. When the raw, unedited footage was shown to the nation the following evening, it marked the turning point in how Americans viewed the war and its political leaders.

I had reached that point two years earlier, when Randy and Tony were born, December 7, 1966. Nothing is more sobering than the realization that one's sons might one day have to risk their lives in a war with no meaning. I also had concerns about the Vietnam War because, despite the fact that I was never called for the draft, I was still draft age and classified 1-A.

Other Americans had different concerns. On January 6, 1966, John Lewis, then an official of the Student Nonviolent Coordinating Committee (SNCC), issued a statement condemning both American participation in the Vietnam

War and the draft. In his statement, Lewis said SNCC was "in sympathy with and supports" those who did not respond to a military draft that compelled them to "contribute their lives to United States aggression in Vietnam . . . in the name of the 'freedom' we find so false in this country."[1]

Lewis's and SNCC's opinions were not shared by a majority of African Americans. A Gallup poll conducted for *Newsweek* that year found that three out of every four black Americans supported the draft and believed that the Selective Service System was fair.

In the weeks following Lewis's statement, however, SNCC's stance on the draft had the support of other black leaders, notably Georgia state representative-elect Julian Bond and Black Panther leader Eldridge Cleaver. Dr. Martin Luther King Jr., who did not endorse SNCC's antidraft policy, encouraged all those who opposed the draft to seek conscientious objector status. He expressed the hope that the Selective Service System would consider civil rights work an acceptable alternative to military service. Also in 1966, Representatives Adam Clayton Powell and John Conyers both questioned the fairness of the draft in regard to African Americans. They took their cues from Malcolm X, who had said in a 1964 New Year's Eve speech in McComb, Mississippi, that the U.S. government was the most "hypocritical since the world began," because it "was supposed to be a Democracy, supposed to be for freedom, but they want to draft you . . . and send you to Saigon to fight for them, while blacks still had to worry about getting a right to register and vote without being murdered."[2]

In early 1966, the vast majority of African Americans apparently did not share these beliefs. But as the Vietnam War escalated and increasing numbers of young African Americans were drafted, sent to Southeast Asia, and killed, black opposition to both the war and the draft grew. In June 1969, another *Newsweek* survey found that "almost half of all African Americans thought the draft was racially biased." Some blacks went so far as to call the draft genocide, a way of systematically exterminating young African American males.

Most whites, meanwhile, opposed the draft on philosophical, legal, and moral grounds, arguing that it was wrong to force anyone to participate in a war against his will.

Here again we see the dichotomy in the American system that Earl touched on in his introduction. While African Americans opposed the draft because they thought it imposed a disproportionate burden on *them,* whites opposed it on legal and philosophical grounds. This is in line with the 1968 Kerner Commission Report on Civil Disorders, which concluded, "Our nation is moving toward two societies, one black, one white, separate and unequal."

What the commission overlooked, or ignored, in its report was that two separate and unequal American societies had been in existence for hundreds of years, beginning with the institution of slavery. There is ample evidence to support my contention. For example, in housing, restrictive covenants permitted whites to move into clean, spacious suburbs, while blacks had to settle for overcrowded, crime-ridden ghettos. In music, separate and unequal airplay of white and black recording artists saw the rise of white-dominated rock and roll and the downward spiral of black rhythm and blues, the source of it all.

Even on the battlefield things were different.

> Most black guys, I think, didn't know what we were fighting for. Some thought there was a war going on back home in the streets. It was tough enough back there, so why did we have to come over here and fight?[3]

Recently I learned that whites and blacks in Vietnam listened to different music, too. At my June 1998 commencement exercise, a fortyish-looking African-American gentleman named Eugene Goodman came up to me, shook my hand, and said, "I've always wanted to meet you. Did you know that your music got me, and a whole lot of other guys, through Vietnam? Your songs kept us going."

I was amazed. I had heard similar comments from veterans before, particularly about "A Lonely Soldier," which I recorded for Vee Jay in 1960, but never anything about the stuff I recorded during the Vietnam era.

Curious, I asked Goodman to be more specific. Without hesitation he listed "Never Gonna Give You Up," "Lost," "Are You Happy?" and "Only the Strong Survive." "I knew all of them by heart," he said. "A lot of us did." By *us* he meant African Americans.

Shortly after that, I did some research on songs from the Vietnam War and came up with the following:

> To most of us, the Vietnam War has a rock and roll soundtrack. All the songs of the sixties were part of life in the combat zone; troops listened to music in the bush and in the bunkers. They had their own top forty, of songs about going home, like "Five Hundred Miles," or "Leaving on a Jet Plane," or of darker or more cynical album cuts which reflected their experiences: "Run Through the Jungle," "Bad Moon," "Paint It Black," or "The Night They Drove Old Dixie Down."[4]

But nothing about "Only the Strong Survive" or any Motown, Stax, or Chess recording artist, even though Goodman, who served with the 1st Battalion, 3rd Marine Field Operations Unit, said black infantrymen would listen to my music and the "Supremes and the Temps for hours" in Vietnam. But like most things American, the airways and clubs in Vietnam were segregated. More disturbing was something else that Goodman said:

"A race riot jumped off in Vietnam in '69. A brother had gotten killed. It was so bad they had brothers coming from Phu Bah and Chu La. What happened was, some white guys jumped a brother called Muscles, shot him point-blank, and killed him. The word traveled through the jungle just like the drums in Africa. The brothers just vamped on the place. They refused to go back to their units until they were assured that justice would be done. No amount of threats or anything could sway them. This went on for about two or three days. I was shipped out before it was resolved, so I don't know if anybody was court-martialed or not."

I don't believe for one minute that the U.S. government used the draft to systematically exterminate young African American males. But the facts are these:

• Between 1965 and 1970, the height of American involvement in Vietnam, blacks constituted slightly more than 11 percent of the draft-eligible population, aged nineteen to twenty-six, but were 14.3 percent of all draftees.

• During the 382,000-man draft of 1966, more than 47,500, or 13.4 percent, of the inductees were African-American.

• The following year, 37,000 blacks were drafted, representing more than 16 percent of the total.

• As late as 1970, with both the draft and American involvement in Vietnam winding down, African Americans still accounted for 16 percent of the inductions.[5]

13.

Changing the World with a Song

Terry Callier

When Gamble and Huff split with Mercury in 1969 and no longer were my producers, I was devastated. After writing and producing hits like "Only the Strong Survive" and "Never Gonna Give You Up" and developing such a great rapport with those guys, it would be hard starting over alone or with someone else. But the reality was, I had three years remaining on my contract with Mercury, calling for three albums a year. I was in a terrible dilemma: Should I risk my professional reputation recording substandard material? Or should I use what I had learned over the years to lay the groundwork for developing songwriters who would supply me—and others—with quality songs for a lifetime? I chose the latter.

But where was I to find the writers? How would I finance such a venture? When would I start?

Terry Callier

All of these questions were answered when I went to Irving Steinberg, president of Mercury, and laid out my plan. Steinberg immediately got on the phone to Chappell Music, a large New York music publishing firm with ties to Mercury. The Jerry Butler Songwriters Workshop was soon born.

Chappell gave me a $150,000 advance to rent space, hire writers, and develop the program. One of the first people we hired was Terry Callier.

Terry is a throwback to the peace-and-love idealists of the sixties. He literally lives his songs. For instance, when he sings about how we all should love one another or about self-sacrifice, he can point to episodes in his own life as testimony.

Take, for example, the episode with his daughter Sundiata, then twelve years old, who announced in 1983 that she wanted to live in Chicago with Terry rather than in San Diego with her mother, from whom he was divorced. At the time, even though he had released five albums, he had no way of supporting her. "I could make rent but not much more," he said of his then shaky economic situation.

But instead of turning his back on Sundiata, whose name translates as "sun queen" in Africa's Mali language, Terry traded in his guitar for a computer, becoming a computer programmer for the National Opinion Research Center, an affiliate of the University of Chicago. Fifteen years later, he still has his day job and is still with Sundiata, who recently graduated from Northeastern Illinois University.[1]

"In the mid to late sixties everybody thought that if they could get the right chord pattern and the right set of words they could change the world with a song," said Terry, describing his take on the mood of the sixties. "Everybody believed that was possible. It was like searching for the Holy Grail. That's why a lot of songs from that era are structured the way they are, why they speak outright about love and peace and truth and freedom. That's what was in their hearts at that time."

What was in Terry's heart in the sixties and on through the nineties was his love for his daughter and a passion for music. Terry's musical tastes developed early, beginning with his mother's record collection, which included Nat Cole, Billie Holiday, and Louis Jordan. Then, as an eighth-grader at Scxton (we were in kindergarten together), he turned to doo-wop, forming several groups before going to high school and singing with still more doo-woppers. He got into folk music at the University of Illinois in Champaign, Illinois, because "that's what was happening at the time."

Also happening at the time was the John Coltrane Quartet, which Terry got to see perform for the first time in 1964 in Chicago. Terry was so captivated by the quartet's style that he changed his own.

"The quartet [consisting of Elvin Jones, McCoy Tyner, Jimmy Garrison, and Coltrane] was performing at the old Mckee's Disc Jockey Lounge at 63rd and Cottage Grove, right next to the El stop. I was a little excited, so I got there kind of early.

"When I got to the door of the club, I heard this hammering. It was about an hour to showtime, and the first thing that jumped in my mind was, What can these people be building in here? It's almost time for the show to start. When I walked in, it was Elvin Jones nailing his drum kit to the floor."

As the evening progressed, Terry began to understand exactly why Jones was doing all that hammering: intensity. Jones played with such driving force that his drums had to be anchored to the floor. And it wasn't just Jones. "They all played hard," he said. "I had never seen anything like that in my life."

After the show, he realized that he hadn't been nearly as committed or intense in what he was doing. "I had to integrate some of that in my presentation," he said of his decision to stop playing and singing altogether so that he could concentrate on revamping his style.

"It took about eight months to get it together, but I was nowhere near into what I was doing as they were. I didn't expect to become a jazz musician, and I certainly didn't expect to become a John Coltrane, but I knew that I had to have something of that intensity, something of that dignity. Just the way they carried themselves on stage, I had never seen before.

"When I went back into the clubs, I was still doing a lot of the folk repertoire, but I also had started doing my own things."

It was around that time that Larry Wade, his old chum from high school, showed up. "He came by my house one evening and told me about the Jerry Butler Songwriters Workshop, which was giving some writers an opportunity to receive an advance against royalties every week from Chappell Music. The only thing we had to do (we had to sign a contract, of course) was show up and write songs, or even not show up and write songs, because it wasn't a military type thing at all. Guys would come and stay all night, or you wouldn't see guys for a week or so.

"That wasn't what was important. What was important was that every two or three months there would be a demo session, and the writers would either perform their own tunes or have other artists perform them. Everybody looked forward to that and wanted to be ready for it.

"There were some very gifted people in the workshop. The most influential, in terms of musical success, were Marvin Yancey and Chuck Jackson. They had a group themselves that recorded a couple of hits, and they also produced Natalie Cole's first three albums, which all went gold."

The Callier-Wade duo also scored big, penning a Top 20 hit for the Dells called "The Love We Had Stays on My Mind." Recalling how the Dells wound up with "The Love We Had," Terry said with a laugh, "We didn't know it was specifically for them until after they heard it and said, 'Yeah, that's for us.' Actually, Charles Stepney, who was producing their album, asked us if we had anything that we thought the Dells might be interested in, and that was one of the things we showed them." The Dells eventually selected five Callier-Wade compositions for their *Freedom Means* album.

While he was working on the album, Stepney (who also arranged and produced some of Earth, Wind, and Fire's biggest hits) asked Terry if he had anything he wanted to record for himself. This led to Terry's recording *Occasional Rain,* the first of three albums for Cadet, a subsidiary of Chess Records. *What Color Is Love?* and *I Just Can't Help Myself* were the others.

Originally, *What Color Is Love?* was planned as a double album. But in 1974, just as Terry was putting the final touches on it, Chess was sold to pop-oriented GRT, and the album was shelved. "They weren't about to put out a double album," he said, "especially since the first album didn't do all that well." This was in reference to Terry's first go-around with Chess in 1963, when the label released his first single, "Look at Me Now." The record had "a lot of critical acclaim and a lot of nice write-ups, but it didn't sell many copies."

When the workshop disbanded in 1976, Terry had spent nearly six years there—"six years of some of the most instructive, beautiful, enlightening times of my life, as far as music is concerned," he said. "The workshop gave me a chance to really concentrate on writing and get inside the craft."

Terry performed in a few clubs after the breakup of the workshop until 1982, when he took his "last money" into a studio and recorded a two-sided single: "I Don't Want to See Myself (Without You) and "If I Can Make You Change Your Mind."

Nothing much happened with the single, and he soon resigned himself to a career in computer programming. Also by then, Sundiata had come to stay with him, and for the next few years he settled into the life of a loving parent. But in 1991, in an odd twist of fate, Terry got a call from Eddie Tiller in London, informing him that "I Don't Want to See Myself" had become a major acid jazz hit there. Tiller, who owns Acid Jazz Records and also works as a deejay, told Terry that he had been playing the twelve-inch in clubs and was getting a "heavy fan reaction." He felt that if he and Terry could come to some kind of an agreement to re-release the tune, it would do well.

"We didn't have any problem coming to an agreement, and he re-released it almost immediately, and it did do quite well," said Terry.

"He brought me over to England in '91 to do a small club called the Jazz 100 Club and one of the weekend musical festivals there. Then, in '92, I received a call from a man named Giles Peterson, who owns a label in London, and a man named Russ Duberry, from Brighton in the United Kingdom—both of them are deejays—and I was invited to perform at a festival called the Brighton Jazz Bop. Between 1992 and 1995, I was in England maybe eight or ten times. In Europe the people are more accepting of my music."

As a result of the shelved 1974 session, Cadet had "a lot of things left over that weren't touched at all," said Terry. Now, with the resurgence of his career, some of those cuts are being released by the MCA label. As of this writing, the CD package (anthologized in Britain under the title *The Best of Terry Callier on Cadet*) is "doing quite well in Europe" but not so well in the United States.

Terry signed with Verve Records in 1995 and recently recorded a new CD called *Timepiece*. Pharaoh Sanders plays saxophone on the title cut. "I never had a chance to play with Coltrane," said Terry, "but Pharaoh did. Since I was so influenced by Coltrane's work, when we went into the studio it was like we had been playing together for twenty years because of the way the song went down and what Pharaoh plays. That was because we were meeting on Coltrane's level."

He added that even though he was playing at Coltrane's level, at his intensity, he didn't have to nail his guitar down.

Samm Brown

Imitation, I am told, is the sincerest form of flattery. That being the case, I am sincerely flattered that Samm Brown modeled his Songwriters Workshop after the one I started in Chicago in the early seventies.

Brown's workshop, based in Los Angeles, has been going strong for more than thirteen years, with the only difference between his and mine being methodology. Brown takes more of an academic approach, whereas in my workshop we would hear lyrics and melodies in our heads and write them down, sometimes working alone and other times in collaboration with others. Brown, on the other hand, teaches the elements of songwriting. "I literally break a song down and articulate what works and why it works," he explained.

Brown, who began studying classical music at the age of six, took a circuitous route to songwriting, stopping first at the University of Maryland for his bachelor's and then at Columbia University for a master's in journalism, minoring in music. He eventually wound up in Chicago as an on-camera news reporter for WLS-TV, the local ABC affiliate.

"It was sort of a compromise with my father," he said of his decision to straddle careers. "My father was a career Army officer. When I let it be known that I was interested in going into show business, he said he wanted me to go to college and be a lawyer. He thought I would make a great lawyer. He used to say all the time, 'The black race doesn't need another hoofer, tap dancer, singer, musician, boxer, baseball, football, or basketball player. We need doctors, lawyers, and judges.'

"I didn't want to be an attorney. I was on the school newspaper in high school, and journalism always interested me. I liked words and telling stories, so I majored in journalism."

I met Brown shortly after he landed the job at WLS. An article in *Time* about my songwriters' workshop prompted the meeting. "Having been a fan," Brown recalls, "I cut the article out, put it in a file and later presented it at a staff meeting at WLS. 'I want to do a feature story on Jerry Butler,'" he told the group.

That was in 1971, and we were just getting started with the workshop. The studio hadn't been built yet; a piano was the only furniture we had.

One day, while working on the workshop story for WLS, Samm, as he puts it, began "noodling" on the piano.

"I didn't know you played piano," I said.

"Yeah, I really want to be in the record business and not in television."

"Well, if you ever want to get in the record business and be a songwriter, look me up."

He took me up on my offer sooner than I expected. A few months after our conversation, he was fired. "They said they were letting me go, but I call it being fired," he said, explaining that his contract wasn't renewed but that the position was held open. "It had to do with me being the most visible black face at ABC. Other blacks were behind the scene.

"At that time affirmative action was in full bloom. The unions were closed to blacks, so they had to let blacks in on various programs to learn the craft. Up until that time, it was a father-son kind of thing, or an uncle or other male in the family, because there were no females in those unions, either. The father would have a job, the uncle would have a job, and as the kids learned the craft and reached a certain age, they would be brought into the union. That's how that went. Black folks just weren't in that."

What precipitated his firing, he says, was that because of his high-profile job, blacks at the station would always come to him with their problems. He eventually agreed to "head up this somewhat loose-fitting, ad hoc committee of black folk at the station and present their grievances.

"In our only meeting, John Severino, who was the station manager at the time, went around the room—there must have been about a dozen or so black guys there—and asked, 'What is the grievance?'

"I was stunned. Everyone said, 'Oh, there's no problem. Everything's fine.' I was left, as the saying goes, 'twisting slowly in the wind.' The guy who didn't have a problem, but was trying to do something to help everybody else, was the one who got fired. I think I was called in that meeting a 'demagogue' and a 'troublemaker.'

"As we left the meeting, I said to one of the guys, 'You know, you're the one who came to me bitching about how the white guys were treating you, and you didn't say a thing [in the meeting] about any of that.' He said, 'Samm, I've got a wife and six kids, and I really need this job. I didn't think you were really going to do anything about [the grievances].'

"So they fired me. I was given an opportunity to go to ABC in New York for a higher salary, but before I made that decision, I thought I would look Jerry Butler up. So I did."

When he showed up at my office, I said, "Brown, I can't pay you what they paid you over at ABC."

"Well, what can you pay me?"

"I can do about a hundred dollars a week." I said it with a straight face, but I knew Brown was doing all he could to keep from laughing. At that time, Samm was making easily forty or fifty thousand dollars a year. He was young and single, and doing quite well. But he wanted to be in the music business.

He took the job, which wasn't a job, really; it was more like an advance against royalties. Yet, he says, "it was a move that, even to this day, I look back on and have no regrets in making. It was the right move."

During his stint at the workshop, Samm met other young musicians and aspiring songwriters, among them Chuck Jackson, the younger brother of the Reverend Jesse Jackson, and Marvin Yancey. While at the workshop, Chuck and Marvin wrote and produced Natalie Cole's first big hit, "This Will Be," a song originally meant for Aretha Franklin. My brother Billy was also in the workshop. So was Terry Callier, who wrote "The Love We Have Stays on My Mind" for the Dells; and Lenron Hanks, whose "Back in Love Again" literally made Jeffrey Osborne and LTD. And then there was Zane Grey, who collaborated on my hit "Ain't Understanding Mellow." Looking back on it now, Brown calls those songs the "super-standard R&B songs of the era."

Because he could write music and arrange, Brown was asked to transcribe the songs that Marvin and Chuck wrote. "They'd write it, and I would go over to their house and write it out," he says, describing how he produced what we in the business call lead sheets—a sheet of music that shows, among other things, what key the song is in, the chords, and the notes. The lyrics are written beneath the notes. The sheet is then given to a copyist so that it can be copyrighted.

Nothing lasts forever. Brown left the workshop after two years—I'm surprised he lasted that long—and moved to Los Angeles, where he later produced and co-wrote "One Day in Your Life," Michael Jackson's first hit in the United Kingdom. "One Day in Your Life" gave Samm the distinction of being the only record producer other than Quincy Jones and Freddie Perrin to have a number 1 international hit with Michael during the seventies and eighties.

Besides Michael, Samm's songs have been recorded worldwide by such diverse artists as Johnny Mathis, Gloria Gaynor, the Supremes, the Miracles, the Jacksons, Al Wilson, Maxine Nightingale, Andre Kostelanetz, Hitomi (Penny) Tohyama, Majesty, and Demis Roussous. He also produced my album *The Spice of Life*.

Samm was the Jacksons' arranger and musical director for their Emmy-

In 1977, powerful publisher Chappell Music sent its big guns to the Songwriters Workshop to announce the release of the *Suite for the Single Girl* album for Motown. *From left.* Vice President Buddy Robbins; President Norm Wisner; Vice President Richard Robinson. My brother, Billy Butler, and I round out the picture. Photo by Lee Snider, courtesy of Annette Butler.

nominated CBS musical variety show, and musical director/arranger/conductor for several major stars on their domestic and/or world tours, including the Jacksons, Donna Summer, Lola Falana, Al Wilson, Peaches and Herb, and Maxine Nightingale.

A recipient of numerous RIAA-certified gold and platinum awards for songwriting, arranging, and producing, Samm has also received several ASCAP awards, including awards from the UK, Brazil, and Japan. He is also a former staff writer and producer for Motown Records, and a staff writer at Almo-Irving and Jobete music publishing companies. A past chairman of the NARAS Institute, Samm has served on the NARAS Board of Governors (Chicago Chapter), was a member of the 1983 Producers' Grammy Screening Committee, and is a frequently requested guest speaker on songwriting at the Los Angeles Songwriters Showcase. Samm also teaches a songwriting workshop twice a month at the National Academy of Songwriters.

For the past three years he has hosted his own show on public radio called "Samm Brown's For the Record," featuring interviews with record industry people who work behind the scenes: lawyers, promotion and A&R people, and publishers, among others. Guests have included Eartha Kitt, Donald Passman, and, he says proudly, the last interview with Johnny "Guitar" Watson before he died. I also was a guest on Samm's show.

Another show that Samm hosts and produces, "Beneath the Surface," which features news and political-social commentary, "satisfies the journalist part of me," he says.

And if that is not enough, he manages to squeeze in managing a singing group, U4Ea! "That's why I'm single, unmarried, and don't have any kids," he says, laughing. "I don't have time to get a toehold anywhere."

Patti LaBelle

A friend will joyfully sing with you when you are on the mountain top, and silently walk beside you through the valley.

—ANONYMOUS

Even though we haven't seen each other in years, I still count Patti LaBelle among my friends. People like Patti don't change like the weather: fair one day, cloudy the next. They are like the sun: warm, nurturing, constant, enduring. You don't have to have a hit recording or TV show to remain friends with Patti LaBelle. You either are or aren't her friend. Ask anyone who really knows her; they'll tell you.

I never knew, until I read her bestselling memoir *Don't Block the Blessings,* that Patti was going through so much pain over the years. I guess no one knew, except those who were very close to her. Over a ten-year period, Patti lost three sisters and her best friend. But like so many of the people I write about in this book, she worked her way through it—all the while remaining a down-to-earth "woman of substance," as *Entertainment Weekly* once described her.

Like so many of the great artists, musicians, songwriters, and managers who intersected my career, Patti came out of Philadelphia. I don't know, maybe it's something in the water there that produces such talent. Think about it: Bill Cosby, Patti, Dee Dee Sharpe, Kenny Gamble, Leon Huff, and Grover Washington, to name just a few—all from Philadelphia.

What stands out in my mind about Patti—and, for that matter, Nona Hendryx—is an incident that occurred in the mid-seventies. We were playing

Patti LaBelle

Basin Street West in San Francisco, and a columnist out there wrote something to the effect of, Why is someone as great as Patti LaBelle singing backup for Jerry Butler?

I have a problem with journalists who don't do their jobs. True, it was a legitimate question: Why *was* Patti singing backup? And it is also true that he had a right and an obligation, as part of his job, to ask the question. My point is, he asked the wrong people—the public—and by doing so made it more a rhetorical question than a question in search of an honest answer. He should have asked Patti or me *first*.

If he had asked me, I would have told him that it wasn't about greatness —it was about friends helping each other out in a time of need; it was about two gracious, fantastic women who needed work, and a very grateful performer who needed their help. It was about loyalty and caring; about comradeship and understanding the nature of the business we were in. It was about respect.

It's been said that "greatness is not found in possessions, power, position or prestige but, rather, in goodness, humility, service and character." Patti LaBelle and Nona Hendryx have demonstrated over the years that they have an abundance of humility and goodness in them. To me, that adds up to character.

When I approached Patti, Nona, and Sarah Dash about working with me in San Francisco, they weren't gigging and I was. I said, "Look, you all can help me and I can help you. I can help you by giving you some bread to put in your pockets, and you can help me get through this week at Basin Street West, because I don't have any backup singers." Patti and Nona said, "Yes, we'll do it." Sarah thought it was beneath them, and she didn't want to come. But we had a great time.

"It was great," said Nona, not of that incident specifically but of the camaraderie that existed among entertainers of that era. "We were like family. We rooted for each other. We stood in the wings and watched each other and applauded. We missed each other when we were apart. When we did perform together again, we were genuinely happy to see each other. I miss that, the camaraderie. You don't really have that anymore."

She also misses the good-natured fun we had. "We used to play tricks on one another," she said, laughing. "Like the time we were performing with the Impressions at the Uptown Theater in Philadelphia. We stuffed their shirts with paper and filled their shoes with water.

"But they paid us back. At the end of the engagement, Jerry, Curtis, and Sam came to our dressing room and sang 'Goodnight Sweetheart' in wonderful harmony. We were touched. When they finished and as we hugged them goodbye, they stuck us with pins!"

Smokey and Claudette Robinson, of the Miracles, remember other ways we supported each other. "Jerry and Annette saved us from starvation," said Claudette, recalling the Miracles' early days on the road. "We always ate well when we were on tour with them."

"People used to try to stay where Jerry was staying because Jerry could cook like somebody's mama," added Smokey. "We all tried to stay where he was because he was going to cook dinner one of those nights. We were going to eat."

Annette and I learned early on how to economize. Not that we were cheap or anything like that. I was simply using the skills I learned at Washburne Trade School in Chicago, where I studied to be a chef. I rationalized that when we are at home, I go to the supermarket to shop for fresh ingredients, so why not do it on the road? Why not help my friends?

Artists help one another in other ways as well. "Curtis and Jerry helped me write my first song," said Nona. "They helped put the chorus to it. I am really grateful to them." Nona has since gone on to write several hits for LaBelle and others.

Smokey Robinson. Photo by Charles McMillan.

And this from Smokey:

"When we first started out, we didn't know from a hole in the ground. I remember we were at the Uptown Theater in Philadelphia. We used to run out onstage, sing our song, "Bad Girl," then run offstage. We'd run out there, sing our song, run back. One day Jerry came to our dressing room and said, 'Look, I want to tell you guys something. You've got to be cool.' We listened to him because he was the Iceman and he had been performing for a couple of years before us."

I remember telling them, "When you enter a stage, you should *walk* on, not run." I merely passed on some of the things people like Phil Moore had taught me. Smokey says I was "instrumental in giving the group some of the best tips we ever got to be performers," adding, "I love Jerry Butler. Jerry Butler is my brother."

Several top-name performers have sung backup for me. Among them are Patti Austin, Nicky Ashford and Valerie Simpson, Melba Moore, and Cissy Houston. And in each case, it had nothing to do with who was perceived as "great" at that moment in time. They simply were being paid to do a job.

It was in that spirit, then, that Patti and Nona agreed to work with me. And

Were we ever that young? *From left:* Claudette and Smokey Robinson; Annette and Jerry Butler; and the late LaVern Baker.

it was in that spirit that I worked with Patti when my career was waning and she had become this gigantic megastar following the breakup of LaBelle.

Patti wrote in *Don't Block the Blessings:* "One of my most memorable engagements was the week I spent with Jerry Butler at Broadway's Winter Garden Theater in 1980. I was happy to be reunited with 'The Iceman,' who I hadn't shared the stage with since the Bluebelles used to open his show and then sing backup for him."[2]

It was a memorable week for me, too, because I got to work with one of my favorite performers. Patti *is* an amazing performer.

Robert "Boogie" Bowles

Starting with Curtis Mayfield, I have been lucky enough to surround myself with some dynamic, creative musicians, many of whom have since gone on and done well for themselves in the music business. Besides Curtis, those who most readily come to mind are

From left: Freddie Perrin (piano); Pancho Morales (percussion); Hassan Miah (not visible); Robert Bowles (guitar); and Dave Green (bass).

• Phillip Upchurch, a guitarist just out of Chicago's Marshall High School, who played for me for about a year before going with Dee Clark. Phil, who had an instrumental hit, "Can't Sit Down," for Vee Jay, was recently honored by the Rhythm and Blues Foundation.

• Freddie Perrin, a pianist and my former bandleader from 1970 to 1973, who left to write and produce the Jackson's Five's first hits, "ABC" and "Just One More Chance."

• Idris Muhammad, one of the best jazz drummers on the scene today, who played for me between 1960 and 1963.

• Billy Butler, songwriter, guitarist, brother.

I don't take credit for "discovering" any of the people I've mentioned above, but I do take credit for discovering a young man I met in Boston in 1968 named Robert Bowles. Boogie, as he is known, came to work for me when my guitar player couldn't make a gig. I asked my drummer, Hassan Miah, to find somebody *quick.*

"I was the guy," said Boogie, recalling the day. "We kind of ran over some music and I did the gig.

"After the show I went to get paid, thinking I was going to get about twelve dollars, which was about what people were getting around that time, but they gave me fifty dollars. I was like, wow, fifty dollars to do a one-nighter! Things have changed."

Indeed, things have changed considerably since then, for Boogie and for me. For one thing, musicians now get paid about $400 a night. As for Boogie, now fifty, he became my bandleader, taking over from Freddie Perrin after Freddie left to produce for Motown.

Boogie stayed with me for about seven years before following Freddie to the West Coast in 1975 and playing on some major recordings. Among them were the seventies disco standard "I Will Survive" with Gloria Gaynor and "Reunited" with Peaches and Herb, "Shake Your Groove Thing," and "Hello Stranger." Boogie also produced Tavares's hit "Check It Out." He has been playing guitar for Smokey Robinson for the past eleven years.

A native of West Virginia, Boogie was enrolled at the famous Berklee School of Music in Boston when I met him. At night he moonlighted, backing up local groups like Chubby and the Turnpikes. He also played behind Martha and the Vandellas whenever they came to town.

But I was the only one who asked him to go on the road. Thus he gives me the credit for rescuing him from more gigs with Chubby and the Turnpikes. I put him "on a higher level," he says.

But the thing that kept him going all these years was his "feel and creativity, the ability to create licks and grooves. Being a guitar player, those are very important elements."

Before hooking up with me, he was more of a jazz musician. "Jazz was swinging all the time, but it wasn't enough," he says. "I had to have something with a little more funk." He found it playing guitar on the session in which I recorded "Never Gonna Give You Up" with Kenny Gamble and Leon Huff.

"The groove was chink, chink, chink. Chink, chink, chink . . . ," said Boogie, humming what sounded like the intro to "Jingle Bells." " . . . Never gonna give you up," he continued, singing the first line of the song. "I came up with the groove for that."

"It's interesting because Freddie Perrin, in one of his sessions years later, said, 'Man, you know that groove you played on "Never Gonna Give You Up"? Play that, that Jingle Bell groove.'

"I remember [at the original session] when I started playing that, Leon Huff came over and said, 'Don't play that. Don't play that.' But then Kenny Gamble said, 'What are you playing?' I played: Chink, chink, chink . . . I said, 'This is the kind of feel I got.' He said, 'Play that!' That's the way they did it. You start playing, and the producers, they come by and try to assemble it. You know, the groove, the track, whatever.

"Producers generally have their own team of people they feel comfortable with, and they don't like to work with other people. I mean, if they're having a success, they want the same team of musicians, especially in the rhythm section, because in those days, Gamble and Huff, Freddie Perrin, and those people, they would just put out a chord chart and you would create. You would create a groove, a rhythm, a lick. These things were very important in making a hit record.

"Gamble and Huff had their own team. But Jerry said, 'Hey, man, I'd like to bring my cats in.' So he brought in Freddie Perrin, who played vibes, and me on guitar. The rest of the musicians on that session were from Philadelphia, the regular guys that Kenny Gamble and Leon Huff used.

"When I went out to L.A. and started doing sessions, the first thing they said was, 'How does it feel, man?' And I would say, 'It feels good. Now let's fix a few notes.' But if it doesn't feel good, it won't work. How does it make you feel? That's the bottom line.

"That's the stuff you can't teach. That's the stuff like when Michael Jordan fades, goes left, pulls back, and hits, they don't teach that shit. That's the real shit. That's what music is all about. You've got to ask yourself all the time, 'How does it feel?' If it feels good, you can get the other stuff going."

Boogie credits Freddie Perrin with getting him involved with producing records and moving to the West Coast. "Freddie always wanted to be a producer," he said. "To show you how naive I was, I didn't even know what a producer does. I said, 'Freddie, what do you do?'

"I produced the group Tavares and got them a deal with Capitol Records, a thing called 'Check It Out.' The way I found out what a producer does, I called up a guy in Philadelphia and said, 'How do you become a producer?' and he told me, 'Go make a record.' Oh, is that all there is to it?"

Boogie, who is white, said he never really had a problem with being the only white musician, or white person, working on a show of black rhythm and blues artists. "I never really had a problem with that," he said.

"It's because of my upbringing. I'm originally from West Virginia. I was born and lived on a river bank. I lived around black people and white people. In the South, certain parts of the South, black people and white people all lived together. And at that time that's the way it was. The only thing I knew was rich and poor. My mother and father never taught me black and white. There was a [black] family called the Robinsons who lived a couple of houses down from where I lived, and they had the best house in the neighborhood. The man of the house was a bricklayer.

"I was always around black people. I started feeling the racial tensions as I got older and moved into Boston and Chicago, especially when I moved to Chicago."

Boogie remembers one incident in particular, back in the seventies when we were working at the Apollo Theater. "We were out in the theater getting some popcorn, and I was there getting something, and this one cat, this brother behind me, said, 'Yeah, man, I wanna put in my order just as soon as whitey here gets his shit together.' I said, 'Hey, man, I'll just move aside. Go on.'

"I had something happen to me which hurt me, back when O. J. was having his problems. Some motherfucker I was working with called me Mark Fuhrman. That's some cold shit, man. I knew this motherfucker a long time, too, man.

"But, you know what? Let me tell you something. It's about security, how a person feels, if they feel insecure or whatever. If you find somebody and they're secure in who they are, they're going to be okay. People are people. I'm married to a Japanese girl now. Before, this girl I was damn near married to for thirteen years was black. And, of course, I was married to a white girl.

"People who have problems, in terms of racism and all, they are just insecure within themselves. If they've got something bad to say to you, man, it probably ain't you; it's them. They've got the problem.

"Jerry used to say, 'The reason I got the white boy over here is because he's certified, qualified, and bona fide.' That was his three things. I know Jerry was looking at me and he was saying, 'This is my employee. But Boogie is doing a job for me. He's doing the job; he's reliable; he's doing the job I want him to do. I don't care if the man's white. Boogie is doing for me what I need now.' I like that about Jerry. It shows integrity."

This reminds me of an incident in 1970, following an invitation from Amiri Baraka for us to perform at the Congress of African People (CAP) convention in Atlanta. When we arrived, I saw Ron Karenga, Stokely Carmichael, and a whole bunch of folks from the Black Power movement milling around. Right away I felt that we were in for a tough time.

On the day we were to perform, the lineup called for the late civil rights leader Whitney Young to speak first; then we were to perform, and Minister Louis Farrakhan was to follow us. All day I was concerned about the attitude of the crowd, so I finally pulled Baraka aside and said, "Man, I don't think we should go on." He said, "Why not?" I said, "I've got these two white fellows in the band [Boogie Bowles and bassist David Green]." He said, "Are they with you?" I said, "Yeah." He said, "Well, that's cool." I said, "I don't think so, because the brothers and sisters out here are on a serious, militant kind of trip." Calming me, Baraka said, "Jerry, it'll be all right." I said, "Okay, I'll leave it to you."

The program started out as planned, but when Young, a fair-skinned integrationist, started to speak, someone in the audience yelled out, "*Whitey Young!*" That got them started. The booing, heckling, and cussing got so bad that Young gave up and walked off the stage.

We were up next. Boogie and David had to hook up their amplifiers, and just as I had suspected, when they walked onstage, all hell broke loose. Shouts of "Get them whiteys off the stage!" rippled through the audience. Boogie looked around and saw me and said, "Hey, Ice, what should we do?" I said, "Get your ass off the stage before we all get killed!" At that, Boogie and David literally ran off the stage.

The program went on as expected as things settled down, with Farrakhan due up next. As we were coming offstage, going up the stairs leading to the dressing rooms, we saw Farrakhan standing at the top of the stairs with a phalanx of Fruit of Islam (FOI) guards in front of him. They immediately started rushing down the stairs like storm troopers, pushing people out of their way. I was really peeved at that. I understood that they were trying to protect Farrakhan, but I felt it was a little excessive. No one backstage was going to do anything to Farrakhan.

Years later, in 1986, when I was elected to office, Farrakhan's secretary called and invited me "to join the Minister" for lunch at his home. I accepted the invitation because, at the time, I was in the process of going for my thirty-second degree with the Masonic Order. An old man by the name of Levi Morris, who was one of my instructors, had said to me, "Brother Butler, any differences that you have with anybody, you ought to try and resolve them now so that you can be free to go on with your life." For a long time I had held that CAP incident in Atlanta against Farrakhan, not so much him personally, but since he was the head of the organization, I felt that he should take full responsibility for it. Having lunch with him would give me the opportunity to air my grievance.

I drove to this home expecting to see a bunch of other people there. But to my surprise, the luncheon was arranged for just Minister Farrakhan and me. While we were talking, I finally said to him, "Look, I didn't want to say this to you because I don't want it to come between us." He said, "Brother, what is it?" I began relating the CAP incident, and at the first mention of the Congress of African People, he said, "Yeah, I remember that." I told him that I felt personally offended by his FOI for the way they acted, because neither I nor any member of my band held any animosity toward him or anyone else in the Nation of Islam. Farrakhan, with deep sincerity, said, "Brother, I apologize for that." We embraced and went on with our lunch. It felt good. I felt good about getting it off my chest; I felt even better when he acknowledged it.

The CAP incident bothered me for another reason. I didn't want the ugliness, the utter stupidity, of racism to be used to deny white performers an opportunity to perform freely as it had been used against blacks, who, as I have duly noted throughout this book, were forced to comply with and suffer through America's outlandish de facto apartheid system for so long. To me, racism perpetrated by black people is just as bad as—or worse than—white racism. I want no part of it. I felt the same way about Boogie and David as Nat Cole felt about Jack Costanzo, the white bongo player who joined his trio in the late fifties. When asked why he had hired the bongo player, Nat replied, "I hired the man I thought would do the best job." Costanzo also was hassled by white and black racists for playing with black musicians.

Boogie, meanwhile, said he has been "blessed with being on teams with some great people. That's the whole thing. I had a certain talent, and all the people I've ever worked with had a certain talent, in that we did something significant. I like to be involved in significant things.

"Probably the best song I did was 'Reunited.' I played all the guitar work on that. I hear those licks all the time. They keep repackaging this stuff. These tunes and these licks will be heard for years and years. That's because they are good songs.

"As I get older and they keep playing these songs, they bring me back. I can remember sitting there in the studio playing them. I hear those licks and I say to myself, I created those licks. I've been very lucky."

Bobby Scott

I have met some colorful characters in my day, especially musicians, but none more colorful—or memorable—than Bobby Scott.

It's odd how we met. I was performing in Norfolk, Virginia, when, about three in the morning, I was awakened by a phone call to my hotel room.

"Hey, Jerry," said this soft, Wolfman Jack–type voice, speaking almost in a whisper, on the other end. "This is Bobby."

"Bobby who?"

"Bobby Scott. I'm doing a movie called *Joe*, man. It's one of these crazy things, you know. It's like this guy, he's a real straightlaced whitey. Got this daughter; she's a teenager—you know, daddy's little girl. She's chasing around with this hippie motherfucker, smokin' dope and carryin' on, and the old man kills him, or plots to have him killed, and I'm writing this song, man, and I need somebody who can tell a story."

"Is that why you called?"

"Yeah, man," he said, "because you can tell a *sto-ry*."

At first I thought I was dreaming, because it seemed so unreal: a stranger calling me at three in the morning, offering me a chance to sing in a movie. Either I was dreaming or someone was playing an awfully bad joke on me.

"When are you going to do it?" I asked.

"Tomorrow."

"What!"

"Tomorrow."

"Man, I can't learn a song overnight!"

"Hey, man," he said, "it ain't much music. It's a *sto-ry*. C'mon. I'll send you a ticket; get on the plane; you come in here; I'll be in the studio; this is the address of the studio; take a cab on over there; hour—hour and a half, you're out of here. You're done.

"Let me sing it for you." He began singing and accompanying himself on the piano:

> Where are you goin'?
> Tell me what you want to be.
> You're coming of age,
> But you're lost on a page
> No one can see . . .

It didn't take much convincing after that—in fact, none at all.

"It's great," I said.

"You like it?"

"Yeah, man, it's a monster."

"Let me play a little bit more for ya . . . "

"No, that's okay," I said.

"C'mon, man," he said, trying to squeeze in a few more bars. "Talk to me! Tell me how good it is!"

"Naw, man," I said. "I've gotta get the hell outta here."

When I hung up the phone, I still wasn't sure about this character, so I called Phil Moore later that morning. "Bobby's cool," said Phil, adding that Bobby had written a hit or two. I was finally convinced, and I got on the plane to New York.

When I arrived, I went directly to the studio. Inside, the first person I saw was this tall white guy, his face all red, sitting at the piano with a bottle of J&B.

"Hey, my man!" he said, getting up to greet me. "Come on in here." He turned to the orchestra: "All right, guys, the singer's here. Let's try it." He started singing, and this time the orchestra fell in behind him. The strings were so beautiful, you wanted to cry.

When he finished, I said, "Bobby, why don't you sing it yourself?"

"Naw, naw, naw, man," he said, waving off the suggestion. "I don't wanna sing. I want *you* to sing it. C'mon."

I did maybe three or four takes on it, and he said, almost in a whisper, "That's great, great. You didn't get a hundred percent of the melody, but you got enough. Ninety percent. I'll take that. Great, man, great."

He took another swig of scotch. "Shit!" he said, and yelled out to the engineer, "Hey, man, play that shit again. Yes! . . . " His words trailed off as he bobbed his head approvingly. "Tell a *sto-ry,* Jerry!" he shouted, swaying from side to side, his head thrown back, eyes closed. "Make it real!" He was fun to watch.

After the session, I had some time to kill before going back to Norfolk to finish the gig. So Bobby and I hung out for a while in Manhattan, going to lunch and whatnot. I got to know a little bit more about this stranger, including that he was part Irish and part Native American and occasionally earned his living as a mercenary. "I do things for people," is all he would say about that. I didn't pry.

The time we spent in Manhattan turned out to be one of the most memorable days of my life. I didn't want to go back to Norfolk. I wanted to continue hanging out with this interesting, wildly entertaining, crazy human being.

I saw Bobby only one other time after that, just for a few minutes. To this day, I don't know if he's dead or alive.

Shortly after the movie came out, someone told me, "I just came back from Australia, and you know what's big over there? Your theme song from *Joe.* Some disc jockey over there plays it religiously every night. He says you tell such a beautiful story."

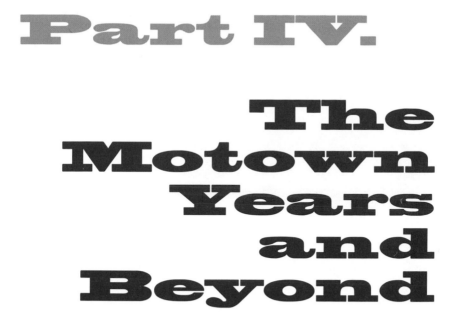

Part IV.

The Motown Years and Beyond

14.

You've Got What It Takes

Berry Gordy and Ewart Abner: Two Men of Vision

When I signed with Motown in 1975, I had the distinction of recording for two of the world's largest and most successful black-owned record companies: Vee Jay and Motown. When I left in 1978 to sign with Philadelphia International, I had the distinction of recording for the three most successful black-owned record companies. Not many people can say that.

Motown, by far the most well-known of the three, boasted at one time a roster that included Smokey Robinson and the Miracles, the Temptations, the Supremes, the Jackson Five, the Marvelettes, Marvin Gaye, Gladys Knight and the Pips, Martha and the Vandellas, the Four Tops, Stevie Wonder, and Mary Wells.

Motown's founder, Berry Gordy, started his career in the music industry as a producer-songwriter. In 1959 he had his first success with "Reet Petite," which was recorded by Detroit-born Jackie Wilson, who had replaced Clyde McPhatter as lead singer of the Dominoes. The next year he wrote "Lonely Teardrops" for Wilson and started the Jobete Publishing Company. At the same time, Gordy began to produce records for the Miracles, Eddie Holland, and Brian Holland.

At the urging of Mable John (Little Willie John's sister) and Smokey Robinson, Gordy borrowed $800 from his family, rented an eight-room house at 2648 West Grand Boulevard in Detroit, and started Motown Records.

In 1959, its first year of operation, Tamla Records, a Motown subsidiary, scored a minor hit with its first release, Marv Johnson's "Come to Me." Later that year Gordy co-wrote and produced "Money," which was recorded by Barrett Strong and reached the number 2 spot on *Billboard*'s R&B Chart. In November 1959, Gordy recorded "Bad Girl" by a young William "Smokey" Robinson and the Miracles, which reached number 93 on the pop charts with the help of national distribution by Chess Records.

It was Smokey who convinced Gordy that Motown should distribute its own records. In 1960, Gordy co-wrote and distributed "Shop Around" by Smokey and the Miracles, which was a number 1 hit and established Motown as an important independent company.

Over the next four years, Gordy, capitalizing on the girl-group craze, produced hit after hit from the likes of the Marvelettes, Martha and the Vandellas, and the supreme girl group, the Supremes.

By the mid-1960s, Gordy had assembled a Motown team that could take poor black youths from Detroit and teach them to talk, walk, and dress like successful debutantes and debonair gentlemen.

Gordy combined the polished images of the Motown acts with a gospel-based music that could appeal to mainstream America. In place of the blues and R&B, he favored a distinct music grounded by an insistent pounding rhythm section, punctuated by horns and tambourines, and featuring shrill, echo-laden vocals that bounced back and forth in the call and response of gospel. Aiming for the mass market, Gordy called the music "The Sound of Young America." He affixed a sign over the studio that read "Hitsville U.S.A."

The songwriting team of Brian Holland, Lamont Dozier, and Eddie Holland joined forces in 1962 and perfected the formula of success that they had discovered with their composition "Where Did Our Love Go."

The Motown sound can be directly attributed to the in-house rhythm section known as the Funk Brothers, headed by Earl Van Dyke, a former jazz pianist who toured with Lloyd Price. Drummer Benny Benjamin and bassist James

Jamerson, who had backed Jackie Wilson and the Miracles, were the nucleus. Together with a few other musicians, the Funk Brothers provided the trademark percussive beat of the Motown sound.

During the mid-1960s, Gordy established a music empire that included eight record labels, a management service, and a publishing company, and grossed millions of dollars a year. From 1964 to 1967, Motown had fourteen number 1 pop singles, twenty number 1 singles on the R&B charts, forty-six more Top 15 pop singles, and seventy-five other Top 15 R&B singles. In 1966 alone, 75 percent of Motown's releases made the charts.

In 1967 the Motown empire began to decline. By the time I arrived, Motown had uprooted its operation and moved to Hollywood. Florence Ballard of the Supremes had gone. So had David Ruffin of the Temptations, and Gladys Knight and the Pips, among others. Tammi Terrell had passed, and in 1968 the highly successful songwriting-production team of Holland-Dozier-Holland quit and filed suit against Motown.

Even though Motown was regularly turning out hits, I realized when I signed with them that this wasn't the same company that had produced "Shop Around," "Ain't Too Proud to Beg," "My Girl," "I'll Be There," "Baby Love," and "Stop in the Name of Love." The same name and some of the same people, but not the same spirit.

The Motown that I signed with seemed preoccupied with movie-making. In 1972, it had scored a huge success with *Lady Sings the Blues,* starring Diana Ross in her first film role. Three years later Motown released *Mahogany,* another film starring Diana, and, following that, *The Wiz,* starring Diana and Michael Jackson.

It was the best of times and the worst of times for me. The best of it was reuniting with Ewart Abner. The worst was not being able to come up with the mega-hits needed to further enhance Abner's reputation as an astute businessman and record industry genius.

Ab, as he was called by many in the industry, joined Motown in 1967, brought in by Berry Gordy himself. He became Motown president in 1973, serving for two years before leaving to manage Stevie Wonder. Just before he left, he called me. "Hey, baby," he said. "I know your contract is almost up at Mercury. What do you think about coming to Motown?"

"I'd be delighted," I said. We came to terms right over the phone, and when my contract was up at Mercury a month or so later, I joined a roster that included Lionel Ritchie, Stevie Wonder, Smokey Robinson and the Miracles, the Jackson Five (sans Michael), and Diana Ross, whose recording of the theme from *Mahogany* ("Do You Know Where You're Going To") went gold later in the year. I was in great company and I knew it. Not that Vee Jay and Mercury didn't have some dynamite acts, because they did; it's just that this was *Motown,* man! You can't get much better than that.

Or can you? Immediately after I signed, I felt that I had made a mistake. From the beginning, I felt like I was always on the outside looking in—you know, the feeling you get when, say, you're the new guy on the team and nobody passes you the ball. I was Ab's boy, not Berry's or Smokey's. Ab wanted me there, not them.

As I have recounted throughout this book, Ab had a great influence on my career. I admired him profoundly. So it was with deep, deep sorrow that I learned of his death December 27, 1997, of complications from pneumonia. He was seventy-four.

The memorial service, held January 8, 1998, at the Forest Lawn Glendale Mortuary in Los Angeles, was evidence of his popularity and the respect he commanded in the industry. The music industry elite overflowed the chapel, where they heard tributes from Stevie Wonder, Berry Gordy, and others.

I first heard about the memorial services from Stevie, who called me in Chicago and offered his private plane to fly me to Los Angeles. What is that old saying, when it rains, it pours? A few days before Stevie's call, my mother had passed. As much as I wanted to attend the services and pay my respects to Ab, the man who had contributed so much to my growth as an artist, I had to decline Stevie's generous offer. Two days after the memorial service, we buried Mama. Two people whom I dearly loved and respected died within a two-week span.

Carl Davis, who received his first million seller at Vee Jay for producing "The Duke of Earl" with Gene Chandler, said of his lifelong friend, "Abner was one of the few men I know who had the charisma to make you feel better just being around him. He was able to relate to people of all walks of life, from a homeless person to the president of a company. He was a man for all seasons; he will be missed."

Shortly before he died, Ab was interviewed for the PBS program *Record Row.*[1] The program chronicled the rise and fall of several recording companies located along a three-block stretch of Chicago's south Michigan Avenue known as Record Row. Vee Jay, Chess Records, and Brunswick Records were among those featured in the program.

"It was amazing that this was black music and there weren't any black entrepreneurs in it," Abner said of his reason for taking the Vee Jay job. "Calvin knew talent, and Vivian understood what was happening and could play it. But they didn't have knowledge of the industry or the background to take it beyond where they were. I had some dreams and a vision about it."

He said he watched Chess Records make money off of blues singers Muddy Waters, Howlin' Wolf, and Willie Dixon. When he took a look at Vee Jay's roster, he said, "Hey, man, there's talent here. We can do that."

He was promoted to general manager and, two years later, president. In a few short years his dreams and vision began to take shape. Building on the company's blues base, he signed several new blues acts, including John Lee Hooker and Jimmy Reed. Turning his attention to his first love, jazz, he signed jazz trumpeter Lee Morgan and saxophonist Wayne Shorter to the label and steered Eddie Harris's *Exodus to Jazz* to become the first jazz album to be certified in the Gold Jazz category. On the rhythm and blues and gospel side, he signed acts like the Impressions, the Staple Singers, the Dells, the Pilgrim Travelers, and Lou Rawls. Before it was over, Ab had transformed Vee Jay from a fledgling upstart into the nation's largest black-owned record company and one of the most respected in the industry.

Then suddenly, everything began to unravel. Relationships between the Brackens and Ab, who owned a third of the company, had become strained, exacerbated by the Brackens' desire to slow things down. "If you retrench now," Abner told the Brackens, "we'll be little again. I don't want to be little again." But the Brackens persisted. Finally Ab said, "If I can't run it, I can't be here." And he soon departed. "[It was] one of the darkest, unhappiest days of my life," he said on the *Record Row* program.

Ab was serving as executive assistant to Gordy and executive vice president of Jobete Music and Stone Diamond Music at the time of his death.

There Are Songwriters and Then There Are Songwriters

A lot of the stuff I recorded for Motown got swept aside because I came in when Abner was going out. I really didn't fit the Motown formula. I think part of the reason for my feeling like an outsider was that I didn't live in Hollywood, where I could just hang around every day and pester the shit out of people. I went out there, did what I had to do, and came back to Chicago. In retrospect, you can find all kinds of reasons why something didn't work. But if there was one thing that had to do with my rather nondescript career at Motown, it was the fact that I lived in Chicago and Motown was in Hollywood.

One of the first producers Motown assigned to me was Marv Davis, who had a ballad, "This Is Your Life," that he wanted me to do. When I heard the demo, I recognized the lead singer (who I later learned was Lionel Ritchie) as one of the kids I had met a few years earlier when I performed at the Tuskegee Institute in Alabama. I remembered it well because a group of Tuskegee students calling themselves the Commodores did the sound for the show and screwed it all up. I simply chalked it up to their being college kids who were doing the best that they could. We got through the show without any problems, so there was no harm done.

By the time I got to Motown, however, the Commodores—those same kids who had screwed up my sound—were already there. They had just recorded "Love Is Slippery When It Is Wet," which was real funk. They were chasing the funk thing, real commercial but dumb kind of stuff.

When I heard "This is Your Life," I said, "That's a smash." Suzanne DePasse, then head of A&R, said to me, "Well, we're not going to put it out on them because we're taking them in a different direction." I said, "Cool," and Marv Davis and I went into the studio and recorded it. It was good, but it was not as good as Lionel Ritchie's version.

When the Commodores' manager, Benny Ashburn, heard our version of it, he literally pitched a bitch and read the riot act to Suzanne, who had a change of mind and decided not to release *my* version of the song as a single, opting instead to put it on my first album.

I was with Benny Ashburn on that one because it was a smash song, and later proved it. When I heard Lionel Ritchie sing it, I remember telling Mark, "We can cut it, Mark, but we ain't going to do it like this." He said, "But Jerry, your voice is so much better."

"It ain't about voice," I said. "This is about attitude, about feeling. This is *this* boy's song." Just like "I've Been Loving You Too Long" is Otis Redding's song, "This Is Your Life" was Lionel Ritchie's song. Anybody could do it, because it was a good song. But nobody could do it like he did it.

And that was the piece that kept getting missed. They always assumed that you could take any great song and do it. Sure you can. But can you do it with the same conviction, the same feeling, the same reality that the writer brings to it, the person who stitched it all together and knows how all the seams are supposed to fit? The whole attitude in just *how* to sing it gets wrapped up in that.

You take a song like "Make It Easy on Yourself," for instance. I sang it; it was a good song; it sold some copies. The Walker Brothers came along and sang it; it sold some copies. Dionne Warwick sang it and sold some copies. I learned it from Dionne. So Dionne was actually copying me copying her. The bottom line is, yeah, Dionne, the Walker Brothers, and Jerry Butler all interpreted a good Hal David and Burt Bacharach tune. But Lionel Ritchie was different: He was interpreting his own stuff, which took it to another level. Not only was he the singer, he was the writer. He knew where all of the nuances were. It was his inspiration.

It's like what Bobby Blue Bland once said about me: "If Jerry Butler never sings anything else in life, he sang the shit out of 'For Your Precious Love.' Ain't no need for anybody to be fucking with that but him." I think that is the greatest compliment that has ever been paid to me.

I feel the same way about B.B. King doing "Lucille," Smokey Robinson doing "Ooh, Baby, Baby," Curtis and the Impression singing "Say It's Alright." I don't care how well you sing those songs, you'll never be able to approach the original artists.

That brings me to my whole philosophy about songwriting. A good song conveys universal, human emotions. That's why, when radio and TV programmers try to separate songs into categories of R&B and rock and roll, they do it for discriminatory reasons, not because white people's tastes are different from black people's. Sure, white people will have a hard time relating to songs that come out of the Southern Baptist, down-home blues tradition, because they weren't raised with that. But it does not mean that whites can't relate to "Ooh, Baby, Baby" or, vice versa, that blacks can't understand "Make It Easy on Yourself."

It has to do with culture. When you think in terms of writers from the South, for instance, the guys who wrote "Midnight Train to Georgia" by Gladys Knight and "Buy My Suitcase," the thing that Brook Benton did, there's a commonality there between the stories. Whether you were white or black, if you were from the South, you knew what those stories were about: this guy leaving Georgia to go to New York to become famous:

> He's leaving on that midnight train to Georgia . . .

He got kicked around and now he's going back. Going back home, as a lot of people do when they go chasing their dreams and things don't work out. They wind up packing their stuff and going back home,

> To a simpler place in time . . .

That's a northern story and a southern story. It's a white story and a black story. It's a story. That's where the universality of music comes in.

For a long time, listening to Aretha Franklin recording in Muscle Shoals, nobody knew those were white guys playing behind her. They just knew it sounded good. They didn't care if they were white or black. That was sanctified and holy. It didn't have anything to do with color. It just had to do with the groove.

It's like basketball players. You always want to say this basketball player is better because he's black. Basketball players are good because they can put the ball in the basket. Larry Bird in his prime made a whole lot of black basketball players look inept. I thought of Jerry Leiber and Mike Stoller as the Larry

Birds of music: not a whole lot of natural talent, but guys who worked hard at being two of the best professional writers ever.

They were big with the Drifters: "Under the Boardwalk," "A Rose in Spanish Harlem." They also were famous for writing novelty songs like "Yakety Yak" by the Coasters. They wrote novelty, they wrote beautiful, they wrote, they wrote. Some people have that ability to go from comedy to love songs. Leiber and Stoller were like that. They were the consummate professional writers, always working at their craft.

One of my favorites was a song they wrote called "Where's the Girl?" about a dresser drawer filled with old hairpins, lipstick, a bottle of perfume, and lord knows what. But where's the girl? In the story, all the stuff she used was there, but where's the girl? This guy wakes up in the morning and starts: "Where's the girl?" Then he begins reminiscing about all of the things that they used to do, all the things she used to have.

Never sold anything, never sold a lot of albums, but it was a real pretty song.

Another favorite was "I Don't Want to Hear It Anymore," written by Randy Newman. Calvin freaked out over this song. "Oh, Jerry, you gotta recut this!" he said.

> She don't really love him,
> But that's what I heard them say.
> She sure wasn't thinking of him,
> Not today.
>
> I saw her yesterday,
> With that guy from room 149,
> Standing there together.
> They looked so fine.

He was listening to the gossip, and then he says:

> I don't want to hear it anymore.
> Oh, I don't want to hear it anymore,
> Because the gossip never ends
> And the heartache soon begins
> They talk too loud.
> And the walls are much too thin.

Was it black? Was it white? It could have been anybody's song. That's the beauty of the music, because it tells these stories. When you get to the meaning of the stories, they don't have Jewish or Polish or Irish or Italian or African on them. They have human on them, the pain that humans suffer. Maybe the setting is Ireland or Africa or Poland, but the bottom line is, these human emotions called jealousy, hatred, love, pain, and sorrow are just that: human emotions. They happen to everybody. That's what makes music universal. Music expresses the emotions. The surroundings and the setting become less important.

That's also true of Freddie Perrin and his wife Chris, who were writers on a lot of the Jackson Five songs. When you see the credits on the records, you will see "F. Perrin" or "C. Perrin." Sometimes she would use her maiden name.

Chris Perrin wrote a lot of the lyrics to those songs. Freddie was a good lyric writer, but he was more of a musician and gave more musical structure to the songs. She kind of added in the lyrics.

Chris reminded me a lot of Linda Creed, who wrote with Thom Bell and the Stylistics. She wrote "You Are Everything and Everything Is You." She also was one of the people who was involved with Mighty Three Music during its early stages. I wrote a tune with her called "Walking Around on Teardrops." It was Linda Creed, Thom Bell, and me.

Both Chris and Linda are Caucasian. And the songs they wrote had nothing to do with some abstract notion called "crossover" or "rhythm and blues" or "pop," or the latest buzzword, "market segmentation." They, like every songwriter I know of, simply write for and about people.

Bill Cosby

The tears of a clown . . .

—EXCERPT FROM SMOKEY ROBINSON'S HIT "TEARS OF A CLOWN"

There is a scene in Ruggerio Leoncavallo's famous opera *I Pagliacci* (Clowns) where Canio, the main character, tells of his suffering at having to perform despite his grief. I thought of that scene when I heard the news of the tragic death of Bill Cosby's son, Ennis, in January 1997. Cosby's new show was in production at the time, and like Canio, he had to continue trying to make people laugh despite his grief. Where Canio's grief was make-believe, Cosby's was real.

I mention this here because I think Bill Cosby typifies all that is remarkable and admirable about "survivalists," the term I use for people who face the worst that life throws at them and yet manage to overcome adversity with grace and forbearance. Some call it courage under fire; I call it character, and Bill Cosby has it in abundance.

I first met Cosby in the summer of 1963, about two years before he co-starred with Robert Culp in the television adventure series *I Spy*. He was already a popular nightclub draw with his stand-up comedy routines. Cosby's stature at that time was a breakthrough for blacks. The *I Spy* series earned him three of his five Emmys.

My manager in 1963 was Irv Nahan, a former truck driver who struck it big managing and booking acts such as the Harlem Globetrotters, the Drifters, and the Coasters, to name just a few. Irv lived in Philadelphia, Cosby's hometown. Cosby's cousin and manager, Del Shields, brought Bill by Irv's office one day while I was there. Shields, a popular jazz disc jockey on radio station WDAS in Philly, was looking to book Bill on the "chitlin circuit." Irv knew a lot about Cosby and liked his act. But he felt that Bill's comedy style was "too clean" for such notoriously tough audiences as the Apollo's and other theaters on the circuit. I saw firsthand how brutal such an audience could be when I appeared with the late Godfrey Cambridge (1933–1976) at the Apollo for a week-long engagement in 1962. Godfrey, a highly respected stage actor who starred in plays like *Purlie Victorious* (1961), thought he'd try out his urbane stand-up comedy routine before a black audience.

It was a disaster. Godfrey was barely into his act when the catcalls started coming from the audience: "Get off the stage, niggah!" "Git yo' fat ass outta here!" The boos and heckling were thunderous. Godfrey was stunned. Tears rolled down his cheeks as he ran off the stage. He left the show in midweek, never again to appear on the chitlin circuit.

That's what Cosby was up against, and Irv knew it. He gracefully declined to book Del Shields' cousin, and in doing so, I think, preserved the career of one of the nation's top comedic geniuses.

In the ensuing years, however, I worked several shows with Bill, including the Music Carnival Theatre in Cleveland, where I was his opening act.

But my most memorable time with Bill came in 1975, shortly after I signed with Motown. Bill heard that I was in town recording an album for Motown, and he invited me to his Hollywood home to listen to some songs he had co-written with one of his friends. He thought the songs would be great for the album.

After dinner, Bill, his co-writer, Annette, and I retired to the Cosbys' spacious living room while his lovely wife Camille attended to Ennis, then about five years old, and her other children, in another part of the house. Bill passed out his favorite cigars to the men, and we all lay back, blew smoke rings, digested the meal, and listened to the music.

When the songs finished playing, Bill turned to me with this proud look on his face and said, "What do you think?"

"I don't like 'em," I said without hesitation. At first he thought I was kidding. He asked again, this time with his famous broad-faced grin. "Really, what do you think?"

"They stink," I said. The songs were blues songs, not my bag at all. But I saw where I could have some fun at Bill's expense, so I pretended that I absolutely couldn't stand them. I had planned to eventually come clean and let him know that I really wasn't that down on the songs. But things started moving too fast, beginning with Bill proselytizing in earnest.

"You liked the background singers, right?" he said.

"Nope."

"What about that first tune—you know, the part where they go . . ." and he began singing the tune.

"It stank, too," I said. Cosby was speechless. Annette began tugging at my sleeve, concerned that I was being too direct. "I'm sure Bill wants me to be honest," I told her.

"I do," he said. "But tell me this, Jerry," he began in classic Cosby style. "You mean to tell me that you have come to my home, ate up all my food, smoked my cigar, and think you're going to get out of here without recording my tunes?"

It was my turn to be speechless.

"Give me my food back," he said. "And give me back my expensive cigar!" He stood there fuming in mock anger. I started laughing.

"This isn't funny," he said. "Get out of my house!" he bellowed, while standing with his arms folded across his chest, pouting. I couldn't stop laughing.

I didn't hear from Bill until two years later. I had asked him to make a guest appearance on a talk show pilot I was hosting for PBS. On the day we taped the show, Anna Morris, my producer, tried frantically to reach Bill in Los Angeles to remind him of the taping. She finally caught up with him on the tennis court. He had indeed forgotten about it. That evening, however, still dressed in tennis attire, Bill Cosby flew into Chicago, raced over to the TV studio, apologized for being late, and gave one of the best interviews ever.[2]

I have immense respect and admiration for the man. There is no finer human being on this planet. I cannot begin to understand the pain he and Camille suffered over the loss of Ennis. But I do know that somewhere in Heaven an angel waits to greet a very special person.

Richard Pryor

Moms Mabley used to say all the time, "You can tell the great comedians because great comedians always make fun of themselves."

The genius of Richard Pryor, I believe, is that he could take his own life experience and make a joke out of it. Who else would think of shooting up his car, then walk onstage and make a monologue out of it? Who else would talk about setting himself on fire while fooling around with drugs? All through his life, when he was making stories, he was making stories about his own life experiences. That's what made it so funny.

My first work with Richard Pryor was at the Apollo. He was just a skinny little kid then. I didn't know anything about him. When I first saw his show, I said, "This cat is really crazy." He was making faces and all kinds of funny sounds, and running back and forth across the stage—something which didn't go over so well with those legendary Apollo Theater audiences I mentioned earlier.

Richard's humor would sometimes go over the edge. That is, it would go from humor to tragedy. For instance, when he talks about the wino and the junkie: "Look at that boy," said the wino. "Started messin' with that dope. I remember the time when he could keep numbers in his head. Didn't need no paper or pencil. Now the nigger can't remember his name."

"Pryor was one of the first black comedians to use the 'N' word in his routine," Fred Jurek wrote in a 1996 article for *Comedy* magazine. "He used it often and with effect. . . . He kept hitting the nerve of racism in America."

Reviewing Richard's autobiography, Jurek replayed one of his comedy routines:

> Cops put a hurtin' on your ass, man. White folks don't believe that shit. "Oh, come on, those beatings," white folks say. "Those people are resisting arrest. That's because the police live in your neighborhood. White folks get a ticket, they tell the officer "Glad to be of help." Nigger got to be sayin', "I—am—reaching for—my wallet—for—my license. I don't want to be no Mother F*#@in' accident."

In a May 1995 interview with *People Online,* Richard, who grew up in Peoria, Illinois, painfully revealed that when he was six years old he was molested by a teenage pedophile named Bubba. "For a long time," Richard said in the interview, "I tried not to think of it." It was one of many episodes in his troubled life that eventually led him to drugs.

He eventually joined the army and was sent to Germany. After his military stint, things started moving fast for Richard: *The Ed Sullivan Show,* jobs with Redd Foxx, nightclubs, *Saturday Night Live,* hit recordings, and movies.

In 1975, we—Mama, Annette, the boys, and I—were staying at the Sunset Marquis in Hollywood while I was recording for Motown, and Richard showed up one day with his girlfriend. "Sit down, bitch," he said—that's the way he talked to her—and before I could say anything, Mama said, "Now, you cut that out." "Yes, ma'am, Mrs. Butler," he said.

I'm no psychologist, and I certainly don't try to be, but I think Richard's disrespect for some women, as demonstrated in a lot of his material, stems from his growing up around pimps and whores in Peoria. Showing contempt for one's girlfriend by calling her a bitch—especially among strangers—is par for the course for pimps, who I think are the most scurrilous scum on the face of the earth, right up there with child molesters and men who abuse women. But don't get me wrong. I'm not judging Richard or in any way insinuating that he has a pimp's mentality. I'm just making an observation. I deeply admire and respect Richard for having the courage to at least try to fight his addictions, and for his ability to laugh at himself while allowing others to laugh with him.

It also was typical of Richard that whenever I performed in Los Angeles, especially at the Troubadour, he would drop in with a huge entourage and sit in the front row. I guess he liked my show.

But my most indelible memory of Richard was the time we worked together back in the mid-seventies at Detroit's Clint Fisher Theater. I opened the show for Richard, who at the time was hot, hot, hot, having just released *Bicentennial Nigger*, in which he explored two centuries of white oppression.

The way he set it up with the flag, everybody was laughing when he first started, but by the time he got to the end of it, everybody was almost in tears. I said to myself, This man is beyond being a comedian. I mean, here is real genius and artistry.

We were there for a weekend, and it was wall-to-wall for all the shows. On the first night Mac (Charles McMillan, my manager) came down to the dressing room and said, "Richard asked if you would come down to the dressing room. He wants to say hello to you."

So I went down to the dressing room and sat down. Richard was just sitting there and I was just sitting there, both of us staring down at the floor and then up at the ceiling, silent. This went on for about ten minutes, until finally he said, "Now that you're down here, I don't know what the fuck to say." We started laughing. When we stopped, I got up and left.

Richard had this double platinum album for Warner Brothers Records, and they wanted to present it to him onstage that night. They called him onstage and brought out these beautifully framed gold albums. The presenter from Warner Brothers said, "On behalf of Warner Brothers Records, we present these two albums to Richard Pryor for . . . blah, blah, blah." When he finished, the audience stood up and applauded wildly. When the applause subsided, Richard said, "Can I pawn these motherfuckers?" We were off to the races again.

Later that night, Mac came back to the room and said, "Jerry, guess what?"

I said, "What?"

"They gave us twenty-five hundred dollars too much."

I said, "Give it back."

"Why?"

I said, "Because they may be testing you. They may have done it on purpose. And even if they didn't do it on purpose, when they settle up tonight, they're going to know that somebody got too much money. If I'm going to get busted for taking some money, I don't want it to be for a lousy twenty-five hundred dollars. We don't want that kind of a reputation."

So he took the money back. When we finished the engagement, they gave us a bonus—you guessed it—twenty-five hundred dollars.

Recently, when I read Patti LaBelle's book *Don't Block the Blessings,* I learned that Richard gave Patti a Rolls Royce after one of their shows. I have but one thing to say to that: Richard, you dirty so and so, you owe me one.

Jackie "Moms" Mabley

Moms Mabley will always be remembered as one of my favorite people. When I first saw Moms, I thought she was a man in drag. She didn't have any teeth, wore an old dress, and talked in that patented gravelly voice of hers.

The first time I worked with her was at the Howard Theater in 1959. She was standing out back with this outfit on, and everybody was talking to her. "Who's that guy dressed up like a woman?" I asked. Somebody said, "Oh, that's the comedian."

I found out later, when she showed me some pictures, that she had once been part of a chorus line. When she put her teeth in, put on some makeup, and dressed up, Moms Mabley was a stately, handsome woman, even in her old age. In her comedy routines, however, she would always talk about these self-deprecating situations, poking fun at herself. She was a very funny person.

Born Loretta May Aiken on March 19, 1897, in Brevard, North Carolina, Moms is the all-time favorite female comedian on the *Billboard* charts, placing thirteen albums in the Top 200 during the sixties. Her albums *At the "UN"* (1961) and *Young Men Si, Old Men No* (1963) hit number 16 and 19, respectively.

Moms, with her mealy-mouthed, rubber-jawed delivery, was a lot like Richard Pryor as she went about creating self-deprecating, real-life female characters. For example, Moms would come onstage, cross her legs, and say, "Yeah, child, you gotta cross 'em real fast, because they'll look. Don't care how old you are." Most of her material poked fun at growing old. She was a regular on TV talk shows.

The thing I remember most about Moms is how she would always cheat at

Moms Mabley (*left*) and Jerry's mother-in-law, Ozell Smith

cards. She loved to play cutthroat pinochle and would cheat throughout the game. But if you caught her at it, she would get mad, throw her cards in the air or down on the table, and stalk out of the room.

Moms, Georgie Woods, and I, or Brook Benton, Moms, and I would always be back in the dressing room during the shows playing pinochle. Sometimes Dionne Warwick would join us.

Moms used to call Brook Benton and me her "adopted sons." She would always try to do things for us, including writing a song for me called "Butterfly," which I later recorded.

> Butterfly, please be careful of your wings.
> Be careful of all the hurt tomorrow brings . . .
> When you're tired of dancing and being caressed,
> Butterfly, I'll build a nest for you . . .

Moms passed May 23, 1975. She was seventy-eight.

Dinah Washington

Dinah was another one of my favorites, even though she tried very hard throughout her career to make me and others dislike her. Permit me to be a psychiatrist for a moment. I think Dinah's rudeness and frankness were part of the defense mechanism she developed over the years.

Born Ruth Lee Jones in Tuscaloosa, Alabama, in 1924, Dinah moved with her family to Chicago in 1931. As a youngster, Ruth was nicknamed "alligator" because of her rough skin texture. She also was teased about being overweight. That's why I think that being abrupt and frank with people was sort of like payback for some of the abuse she took as a child.

I remember one incident in particular. Dinah invited Annette and me to a party at her duplex apartment in New York. Among the invitees was Little Esther Phillips, who had just scored a big hit with "Release Me" on King Records. Esther had a serious overbite and was quite sensitive about it. Just before the party, however, she had corrective surgery on her teeth and gums.

Dinah was standing at the top of her spiral staircase when Esther came in. "Well," Dinah grunted, "it looks like 'Release Me' has done wonders for somebody's mouth!" Esther shouted, "Bitch!" and ran up the stairs after Dinah. It took half of the party-goers to pull them apart.

At the age of sixteen, Dinah joined gospel legend Sallie Martin's all-female group as the pianist and vocalist and toured nationally with them. She left Martin in the early 1940s and began singing blues and jazz at clubs on Chicago's South Side. It was during this period that she began copying the style and repertoire of Billie Holiday, who often appeared in Chicago.

In 1943, Joe Glaser heard her sing and signed her as the female vocalist with Lionel Hampton's band, which he managed. To launch her new career, Hampton suggested that she change her name to Dinah Washington. In December 1943, she appeared at the Apollo Theater, where music critic and songwriter Leonard Feather saw her and arranged for her first recording session with Keynote Records. She went on to become known as the "Queen of the Blues" during a fifteen-year career with Mercury Records.

There's a story that people like to tell about Dinah and Brook Benton, who had several hits together on Mercury Records: "Rockin' Good Way (to Mess Around and Fall in Love") and "Baby (You've Got What It Takes)." As the story goes, during the recording of "Baby (You've Got What It Takes)," Brook kept coming in at the wrong place, and Dinah, a notorious one-take artist, got tired of it. Also, in those days, when someone goofed, everybody had to do it over again. Dinah said she would sing it one last time, goof or no goof. What follows is an excerpt from the final, "best" take:

DINAH: Ooh, it takes a lot of lovin' to make my life complete.

BROOK: Mmm, and it takes a lot of woman to knock me off my feet. And baby, you've got what it takes.

DINAH: I said,

BOTH: Mm, mm, mm, uh-huh, mm, mm, mm.

DINAH: Ah, ah, hah.

BOTH: Mm, mm.

BROOK: You know you've got just what it takes!

BROOK: Because it takes more than an effort to stay away from you. It'd take more than a lifetime to prove that I'll be true.

DINAH: But it takes somebody special to make me say, "I do."

BROOK (*spoken*): "Oh, yeah."

DINAH: And baby, you've got what it takes.

DINAH: Ah, ah, hah.

BOTH: Mm, mm, uh-huh, mm, mm, mm.

BOTH: Mmm.

BROOK: You know you've got just what it takes.

DINAH: Because it takes oh, yeah.

DINAH (*spoken*): "You're back in my spot again, honey."*

BROOK (*spoken*): "I like your spot."*

DINAH: To stay away from you.

BROOK (*spoken*): "I can't stay away from you."

DINAH: It takes more than a lifetime, daddy, to prove that I'll be true.

DINAH (*spoken*): "NOW it's you."*

BROOK: But, it takes somebody special

DINAH (*spoken*): Like me, baby, to make me say, "I do."

BOTH: And baby you've got what it takes.

The record, released by Mercury in 1959, peaked at number 5 on the *Billboard* rhythm and blues chart.

Once I went to the Apollo to see Dinah's show. She came onstage in a sultan's chair, carried by some muscle-bound guys all decked out in G-strings. They set the chair down in the middle of the stage, the curtains opened up, and she stood there in this flowing blue gown, with a crown and all this glitter and stuff on her. She looked like a queen. The audience was in an uproar. I mean, this was pure show business.

She had her sons performing with her. They did a little tap dance routine with a cane and a hat. Midway through the show, Dinah had to go and change clothes, so she told the audience, "While I go and change clothes, my sons are going to entertain you." She turned and gestured for her sons: "Come on, darlings!"

As soon as her sons started out onstage, a lady in the front row got up and started to leave. Dinah stopped the music. "Bitch, don't you walk out on my children!" The lady turned around, pleading, "Dinah, I gotta pee." Dinah said, "Well, hurry back." The audience was rolling on the floor, and Dinah was laughing, too. It was classic Dinah Washington.

I recall the first time I met her. This was about a year or two before she died.[3] It was in Chicago. Roy Hamilton took me up on South Parkway (now Martin Luther King Drive) to Robert's Show Lounge. We went back to her dressing room, and she had a pot of chitlins on. I didn't realize at the time that Brook Benton had been a truck driver, and that he and Dinah weren't getting along too well. Roy said, "Dinah, I want you to meet Jerry Butler." She turned around from her pot of chitlins and said, "And what kind of truck do you drive?" I didn't know what to say because I didn't know what the joke was all about.

I never worked with Dinah, but the Dells worked with her all the time. They sang backup for her. Matter of fact, there's a story that's been around for a while about the time she bought uniforms for the Dells for an upcoming show

* Indicates ad lib between Dinah and Brook.

in Canada. So they went up to Canada, and one day they were lying around the pool with some of the local girls, having big fun. But when they came back to their room, Dinah had put all of their uniforms in the bathtub and set them on fire.

That's the other thing about Dinah. She was a very jealous woman. She had six husbands, including movie actor Raphael Campos and Detroit Lions football player Dick "Night Train" Lane.

You hear all these stories about her, about her temper and abrasiveness, but the fact remains, she was one heck of a talent.

It Takes Two

One of my most memorable experiences at Motown was recording alongside Thelma Houston, one of the most talented vocalists of this or any generation. Our *Thelma and Jerry* album marked the next to last time I teamed with a female vocalist to record a single or an album.

My first teaming with a female vocalist was on "Let It Be Me" with Betty Everett, who is best remembered for her huge hit in the sixties, "The Shoop Shoop Song [It's in His Kiss]." Following its release on Vee Jay in 1964, "Let It Be Me" reached the Top 10 on the rhythm and blues charts. It was part of an album that Betty and I recorded entitled *Delicious Together.*

The events leading up to our teaming began early in 1964, when Annette and I were in the Bahamas and took in a nightclub. A local band played the tune, which had been a hit by the Everly Brothers. Annette and I couldn't get the tune out of our heads, and we sang it in harmony all the way back to our hotel.

When we got back to the States the following week, I told Calvin about the experience and suggested that I sing a duet with someone.

"I've got just the person for you," said Calvin. "Her name is Betty Everett."

Betty and I took an entirely different approach to the song than the Everly Brothers. For one thing, the Everly Brothers were two men singing

God bless the day I found you.
I want to stay around you . . .

We took it and slowed it down, funked it up some, and gave it a little more oomph. The result was a more romantic song, an expression of love from a man to a woman, and vice versa. I believe we put it in its proper perspective.

Betty and I did several other duets at Vee Jay, including "Smile," "Ain't That Loving You Baby," and "Love Is Strange," the Mickey and Sylvia hit.

After Vee Jay folded in 1967, Betty went to ABC without success before

recording "There'll Come a Time," her last Top 40 hit, for British-based Uni in 1969. This song was her first entry in the soul charts, where it went to number 2. Betty had five more entries in the soul charts on Uni and Fantasy by 1971.

Gladys Knight and
Jerry

Betty also had a hit with "You're No Good," which was covered by Linda
Lewis in 1975 and went Top 10 in the UK, and number 1 in the United States
in a version released by Linda Ronstadt.

Following Betty, I next teamed up with Brenda Lee Eager on "Ain't
Understanding Mellow" for Mercury Records. Written by Homer Talbert and
Herscholt Polk while they were members of the Songwriters Workshop, this
song went gold in 1971. We also recorded Bacharach and David's "Close to
You" together, as well as another workshop song, "The Love We Have Stays on
My Mind," among other songs.

Brenda and I were featured on the cover of the January 15, 1973, issue of
Jet magazine, whose cover story was titled "What's Ahead for Soul Music in
1973."

My most memorable experiences with Brenda, however, were her electri-
fying performances onstage during the year or two we toured together. She was
a lot like Patti LaBelle and Gladys Knight, both of whom I toured and sang

M.C. Gary Owens with presenters Jerry Butler and Thelma Houston during the
festivities for the 15th Annual Grammy Awards, held March 3, 1973, at the
Hollywood Palladium in Los Angeles.

duets with, in her attitude toward performing: All three gave everything they
had for every song. Gladys, however, was a lot like Betty Everett, in that she
seemed to do everything so effortlessly. A lot of that had to do with experience,
which she picked up singing with her brother Merald "Bubba" Knight and
cousins Edward Patten and William Guest over four decades as Gladys Knight
and the Pips.

I also toured with the multi-talented Dee Dee Sharpe (she of "Mashed
Potatoes" fame) for three years, and co-produced an album for her on Philadel-
phia International. She was then known as Dee Dee Sharpe Gamble, wife of
Kenny Gamble, Philly International's co-founder and owner.

Other dynamite female vocalists I sang duets with were Tammi Terrell,
known as Tammi Montgomery when she toured with me, and Patti Austin, one
of the most professional vocalists I've ever known.

Which brings me to Thelma Houston, who is best known for her gigantic disco hit "Don't Leave Me This Way," the superb Harold Melvin and the Blue Notes track. Thelma's rendition of the song, one of the best songs from the disco era, won a Grammy in 1977. Thelma also participated on the soundtrack of the movie *Thank God It's Friday,* with the song "Love Masterpiece."

We recorded two albums together for Motown: *Thelma and Jerry* and *Two to One.* Both were delightful experiences for me because, here again, I was working with a consummate professional. When I think of Motown, somewhere in the back of my mind the name Thelma Houston always pops up.

My last duet with a female singer was on Philadelphia International. Debbie Henry and I recorded "Don't Be Like an Island" in 1980. She was the last in a long line of elegant, talented women that I recorded with, and I thank them one and all.

Part V.

The Political Years

15.

Summing Up

Stopping to Smell the Roses

As the decade of the eighties got under way, I found myself paying more and more attention to my surroundings and to the future. I later came to understand that this is common among men in their early forties, sort of like a rite of passage, or the early stages of male menopause. It's when you reach a point in your life where you realize that you have done a lot of things, met a lot of people, made a lot of money, but you haven't stopped to smell the roses. That is, you haven't stopped to ponder the simpler things in life, the common, everyday occurrences, such as watching the sun rise at dawn, listening to the sound of wind whistling through trees, observing an unusually starry night, enjoying the sound of children's laughter. For me, it was like an epiphany of sorts, a revelation, in which my yesterdays came into clear focus as I reassessed who I had been and where I wanted to go.

I soon came to the conclusion that I no longer wanted to be just an entertainer. Phil Moore was right: At twenty-three, I hadn't done anything to brag about. I hadn't lived as yet. Therefore, I hadn't earned the right to sing a song like "I Did It My Way." But at forty-three, I had indeed earned the right to sing such a song, just as Sinatra had when he was that age. What's more, I was *obligated,* by virtue of my age and experience, to pass on what I had learned, if not to my sons, then to the next generation of would-be singers, entertainers, business people, and parents.

Yet I didn't have a legacy—something that was truly mine—to pass on. I knew how to make records; I had done it a zillion times. I also knew how to find talented artists, write songs and get them copyrighted, assemble musicians, record songs, and, lastly, produce the record for distribution to the public.

What I didn't know was the management side of the recording business: motivating and leading people to a successful end, not only creating the product but marketing it as well. I felt it was important to know that aspect of it *first* before even thinking of trying to leave some kind of legacy.

Thus, my brother Billy and I and some of the guys from the Songwriters Workshop decided to use what we had learned from others to create Fountain Records. I had some experience running a record company from as far back as 1970, when I, along with my then manager and lawyer Bill Matheson and a group of Memphis doctors, formed an independent label called the Memphis Corporation. We converted an old filling station into a sound studio and produced some very good tracks on me as well as the Ohio Players. Unfortunately we couldn't sustain the operation, and it closed after two years.

My experience, however, went for naught. We had modest success with a single I recorded on Fountain in 1982 called "No Love without Changes" and, in the same year, an album, *Ice 'N Hot.* But that was about it. I am not a quitter, but I soon recognized that it was futile. The record industry had changed. As I noted earlier, if the Vee Jays and the Motowns could be squeezed by the majors, what possible chance did a Fountain Records stand? So after about two years of operation, we closed shop. We couldn't compete.

Meanwhile, I had gotten involved in a beer distributorship on the South Side of Chicago, the Iceman Beverage Company, that was doing extremely well. We were a multi-brand house, with brands like Pabst and Carling Black Label. We also distributed a beer from Holland called Skol and the top Japanese beer, Kirin, as well as some minor labels.

The beer business is a lot like the record business, in that there are a few major companies that control the market, and a lot of smaller companies that fight over what's left.

By 1983 I was spending so much time attending to the affairs of the beer business that I literally let the entertainment side go. Consequently, my bookings began to dip. Had it not been for the diligence of my longtime manager, Charles "Mack" McMillan, my singing career probably would have been over years ago. He kept me working and my name before the public. I owe a lot to that man, who, like Bill Matheson before him, has only a gentlemen's agreement with me.

As great as the Iceman Beverage Company was doing—perhaps we were doing too well—the company folded after a few years.

By then, I was already becoming deeply involved in my surrounding community: I served a few years on our local Parents and Teachers Association. I was a member of Operation PUSH, served on numerous boards, and participated in several fundraisers for political candidates. In short, I was becoming more politically active. I began to think that if I was going to leave a legacy of any kind, it more than likely would be something with a political tinge to it. Although by 1985 I was leaning in that direction, I was surprised by how fast I actually did take the plunge.

"Somebody Ought to Do Something"

At least once a year a news reporter or someone will ask me, "What got you interested in politics?" I generally respond, "I've always been interested in politics," which is true. Since I can remember, I have had an opinion about everything from the price of butter to the price of freedom. Everything is political to me. But when people inquire about my interest in politics, I guess what they really want to know is, "How did you get involved in government?" That's different.

I have a short answer and a long one. The short answer is that I thought I could make a difference. The long answer, which encompasses the short, is that I was challenged by a former business partner to try to make a difference. I remember it well.

It was a hot day in August 1985, and Ron Bogan, my partner in the ill-fated Iceman Beverage Company, was driving me home. All the way there I was going on and on about the late Larry Bullock, a state senator who reportedly had become involved with a notorious street gang. Also, I was peeved that Bullock, who is black, had sided with Ed Vrydolyak, a white politician opposed to Harold Washington, Chicago's first African-American mayor. "Somebody ought to run against this guy and get him out of office," I said. Ron laughed. "Yeah, it's always somebody else. Why don't you run?" His response had momentarily caught me off-guard. I reflected for a moment and then said, "I'm going to do it."

When I got home, I called Bobby Rush, who was the alderman in my district.* "Bobby, I want to run for state representative," I said. "What do you think?" He thought about it for a minute and said, "Let me call you back."

About fifteen minutes later he called back, saying, "Jerry, a lady by the name of Lou Jones ran for that seat a couple of times before, and she came real close to beating Bullock last time. The mayor has already endorsed her to run against him this time. If you got in the race, you probably would win because of your name recognition. But it would put a loser in Harold's column. And if Harold decides to endorse you or support you, rather than support Lou Jones, then he is going to look like a turncoat."

"I don't want to do that," I said. "I just want to get somebody in there who is more trustworthy." I was fired up by then and, remembering my conversation with Ron, said, "Where else can I be of use?"

Bobby was quick to answer. "Well, you know, the Supreme Court has ruled that seven wards on the South and West Side of Chicago must be remapped because there have been discriminatory factors in those wards, and the people who represent folks that live in those wards are not representative of the people." He added that Vrydolyak, then chairman of the Cook County Democratic Party, would have a lot to say about who was slated to run for seats on the Cook County Board of Commissioners, the government body that, among other things, is under state mandate to oversee the county's hospitals, jails, sheriff's department, courts, and property tax collection. With more than 5 million constituents, Cook County is the second-largest county in the United States, after Los Angeles County.

Fearing that Vrydolyak would fill those seats with his friends and cronies, Bobby said, "It sure would be nice if we had somebody with your name recognition heading up a slate of independent candidates to run against the regular Democratic slate."

I accepted the challenge and entered the race for one of seventeen seats on the Cook County Board of Commissioners.

Free Publicity

Shortly after I announced my candidacy, I had to go to Washington for an engagement. Before I left, I asked blues disc jockey Pervis Spann to produce a fundraiser for me at the Arie Crown Theater in McCormick Place. He agreed to do it.

Prior to that, Bobby Rush had taken me in to see Mayor Harold Washing-

* Bobby is currently serving his third term as an Illinois congressman.

Flanked by then alderman Bobby Rush (*left*), Mayor Harold Washington, and TV personality Sid Ordower, I announced my candidacy for Cook County commissioner in 1985.

ton about supporting my candidacy for the Cook County Board of Commissioners. Harold had basically said, "Jerry, I want to support you, but it's a little early yet. I don't want to come out and support you and find out you can't pull it off. I want to wait and see."

"I think that's a wise decision, Mr. Mayor," I said. "But you just watch my smoke. I'm going to get out there and campaign hard, because I believe I can win this thing."

However, when I came back from Washington, another alderman, Dorothy Tillman, had planned a big rally for Harold at the same time as my scheduled rally, and to my dismay, I learned that there had been no radio announcements or anything else done for my rally. Nothing had happened since I left town, and I had been gone about ten days.

I called Pervis and asked what happened. He said, "Well, Jerry, you didn't leave no money, so I didn't do nothing. I couldn't take *my* money and put it out there." I said, "Man, you know I would've made your money good." "This is politics," he said. "People don't do it that way. We like to get paid up front so we know we're going to get our money. Some of these politicians won't pay you." I finally said, "Okay, forget it."

So then we had a big meeting—Bobby Rush, my wife, and some of my supporters got together to try and salvage things. "What are we going to do?" someone asked. "The worst thing we can do," I said, "is wind up over at the Arie Crown Theater with empty seats, so *give* the tickets away." We had sold, I think, maybe 500 tickets at about $100 apiece, mostly to corporations and big-spender types.

The plan was to sell a thousand seats at $100 apiece, and the rest—Arie Crown holds about 4,500—at $10 to $25 so that the not-so-well-off people could participate.

The day before the show we learned that the mayor was going to come by and acknowledge his support for my candidacy. We had a little press reception before the show, and, naturally, wherever the mayor went, the TV cameras followed him. When he came to the press reception, which was held in a little room in the basement of Arie Crown, all the press came with him.

It was beautiful because all of the people who had paid $100 were in the room having food and other little comforts as part of the deal for donating the extra money. Apparently a reporter asked one of the donors how much he had paid to come to the event. The man said $100. So the reporter figured that at $100 for 2,500 people, which he estimated the crowd to be, I had made $250,000.

The following Sunday the front page of a major newspaper ran a head-line that read, "Jerry Butler fundraiser at McCormick Place raises $250,000." That put me in the category of the Vrydolyaks and Hynes and all the big guys in town. The bottom line was, we made a little money but nowhere near the $250,000 that was reported. But the perception was there, and because it was in the papers and all over the front page, it was the biggest news in the county.[*] And it happened just one week before the election.

We were extremely fortunate. During that same campaign, we did a fund-raiser for my Masonic lodge. NBC News was doing a special about the rhythm and blues singer running for the Cook County Board and sent a news crew out to tape part of my performance. Our little Masonic event turned into a great big

---

[*] The reception also made news in France. My niece, Lisa, had an eleven-year-old ex-change student from Rheims, France, visiting with her during that time. She brought him to the reception and introduced him to the mayor. When the boy returned home, he wrote to Lisa, saying that a picture of him shaking hands with the mayor had been published in one of the local newspapers.

After years of study, in between working at my day job as a Cook County commissioner and as a weekend entertainer, I finally reached my goal: a master's degree in political science from Governors State University, presented by university president Paula Wolf on June 5, 1993.

hoopdeedoo because NBC was there filming. That also ran about a week before the campaign.

Another stroke of luck: My wife and I were down in Atlanta, on our way to Disney World, when I got a call from Anna Morris in Chicago wanting me to do a commercial. When we got back to Chicago, Anna, who was working for Burrell Advertising, told me, "Jerry, I got this wonderful idea. McDonald's is coming out with a new sandwich called hot and cold. I want Aretha to do the hot and you, the Iceman, to be the cold." I liked the idea, and we eventually shot the commercial in Detroit. It was released during my campaign for the county board seat.

Celebrity does have its drawbacks, as I soon learned. Because I was a well-known entertainer, I was subjected to the equal time provision, the law that requires broadcasters to grant the same amount of time to all candidates running for political office. Maybe it was because some of the other candidates objected or the TV and radio stations were playing it safe, but the "Hot and Cold" commercial was pulled off the air.

"You Oughtta Be in Church!'"

politician (pol'i-tish'en) n 1 a. One who is actively involved in politics, esp. party politics; b. One who seeks personal or partisan gain, often by cunning or dishonest means.

Having been actively involved in the political arena for the past fourteen years, I have a vastly different view of politicians than the compilers of the *American Heritage Dictionary* who wrote the above definition of a politician. My definition of a politician is one who sees injustice and does something about it—or at least tries to do something. The *best* politicians, I believe, are those who have the persuasive ability to move people to take action, not through some demagogic trickery but as a reasoned appeal from one human being to another. The late Adam Clayton Powell, Jr. was like that. So was Harold Washington.

I don't recall exactly when I first met Adam (we were on a first-name basis from the day I met him). He just showed up backstage at the Apollo Theater one evening and introduced himself. I believe it was in 1964. After that, we would run into each other from time to time when I was in New York or Washington, D.C. But these were infrequent and, for the most part, brief encounters.

I was always impressed with Adam's style, his openness. Here was a guy, a congressman, in the heart of Harlem, with junkies and thugs all around, who could walk right up to anybody and say, "Hey, baby! How are ya? Goddamn, you oughtta be in church!"

I can still see him now, as I saw him that day in 1968, shortly after the release of "Only the Strong Survive," bursting into my dressing room at the Apollo, waving his ever-present stogie, saying, "Jerry, you've got to come around to my church. I'm going to preach a sermon. The title of that sermon is 'Only the Strong Survive.' I want you to come around and hear me."

I had planned go to his church the following morning, but didn't. I was just too tired after the show. I'm sure the sermon was a success, though. Knowing Adam, it had to be. Everything he did in those days was successful—or if not successful, stylish. From the day he exploded onto the national scene in 1932, administering a church-sponsored relief program for thousands of Harlem's homeless and unemployed, he impressed everyone with his inimitable style, a kind of in-your-face arrogance tempered with a heavy dose of chutzpah. Adam didn't just challenge his adversaries; he defied them.

In 1936, seven years after succeeding his father as pastor of Abyssinian Baptist Church, Adam was elected as an independent to the New York City Council, where he immediately clashed with Mayor Fiorello La Guardia over social issues. In what was to be his approach throughout his career, he used picket lines and mass meetings to demand reforms at Harlem Hospital, which had dismissed five black doctors from its staff because of their race.

He was elected to Congress in 1944, representing New York's newly created Twenty-Second (later Eighteenth) District. Soon after his arrival in Washington, Adam challenged the informal regulations forbidding black representatives from using Capitol facilities reserved for members only. Following the lead of Illinois congressman Oscar De Priest, he took black constituents to dine with him in the "whites only" House restaurant and ordered his staff to eat there whether they were hungry or not.

On the House floor, Adam often clashed with John E. Rankin of Mississippi, one of the chamber's most notorious segregationists. Adam introduced legislation to outlaw lynching and the poll tax and to ban discrimination in the armed forces, housing, employment, and transportation. He attached an anti-discrimination clause to so many pieces of legislation that the rider became known as the Powell Amendment.

In 1961 Adam became chairman of the Committee on Education and Labor and began the most productive and satisfying period of his congressional career. The committee approved more than fifty measures authorizing federal programs for minimum wage increases, education and training for the deaf, school lunches, vocational training, student loans, and standards for wages and work hours, as well as aid to elementary and secondary education and public libraries. This legislation constituted much of the social policy of the Kennedy and Johnson administrations. Adam received little recognition for his efforts.[1]

In late 1966, Annette and I were invited to go deep-sea fishing in Bimini by Bahamian boxer Yama Bahama. While there we ran into Adam.* He was sitting in this little restaurant, wearing Bermuda shorts and a tee shirt, enjoying a stogie. Except for the people who worked for the little hotel we stayed in, it appeared that no one else was on the island. I don't know what it's like now, but back then, it truly was *the* place to get away from it all.

And Adam had a lot to get away from when we ran into him. He had recently come under fire from his House colleagues, who had threatened to censure him for, among other things, his womanizing, his failure to pay damages to a Harlem woman he had libeled, and the misuse of funds in connection

---

* I read somewhere that Bimini was Adam's favorite hideout. This slightly remote island, which began as a rendezvous for rum runners and wreckers, also was favored by novelist Ernest Hemingway, presidential hopeful Gary Hart, and psychic Edgar Cayce, who believed that Bimini is a part of the legendary lost continent of Atlantis.

with trips overseas taken by Adam, some family members, and office staff. Seeing him in Bimini during that time, laughing and backslapping with everyone he met, you would never have thought that he was facing such problems.

On March 1, 1967, the House voted to "exclude" Adam from the 90th Congress, formally denying him the seat he had legitimately won in the November election. As expected, Adam did the unexpected: He appealed to the judiciary to inject itself into an "internal matter" of Congress.

Adam won a special election on April 11, 1967, to fill the vacancy caused by his exclusion, but did not take his seat. He was reelected to a twelfth term in the regular November 1968 contest, but the House voted to deny him his seniority. He declined to take his seat when the 91st Congress convened in January 1969.

In June 1969 the Supreme Court ruled that the House had acted unconstitutionally when it excluded him from the 90th Congress, and Adam finally returned to his seat, although he lost his twenty-two years' seniority.

Adam unsuccessfully sought renomination in the June 1970 primary, losing to Charles Rangel by the narrowest of margins.

Apparently heartbroken over his defeat, Adam in 1971 announced his retirement as pastor of Abyssinian Baptist Church and returned to his beloved Bimini, where he planned to write a book about his life. He was stricken with prostate cancer, and on April 4, 1972, in Bimini, he suffered complications from prostate surgery and was flown to Jackson Memorial Hospital in Miami, Florida. He died that night.

A funeral was held several days later at Abyssinian Baptist Church. Adam's body was taken to the Bahamas and cremated, and his ashes were scattered over the waters off South Bimini.[2]

Induction into the Rock and Roll Hall of Fame

The Impressions were inducted into the Rock and Roll Hall of Fame on January 16, 1991. The gala event, held in Manhattan, also saw the induction of LaVern Baker, the Byrds, John Lee Hooker, Wilson Pickett, Jimmy Reed, and Ike and Tina Turner.

What should have been a festive time for me was marred by three incidents: first, the ongoing conflict among the Impressions over who should be called "The Original Impressions"; second, the tragic accident that had left Curtis Mayfield paralyzed from the neck down; and, third, the military air assault on Iraq that same evening that became known as Desert Storm.

It was the battles—the war between the two sides in the Impressions dispute and the Desert Storm war—that left me sad and confused: Why, after thirty-three years, were Fred, Sam, Arthur, and Richard Brooks still holding on to their anger? I wanted to say to them, shout at them, "Let it go, guys! Let it go!" I think I did at one point. It was sad watching Fred and Sam sitting at one table and Richard and Arthur at another. But that was part of the bargain we had struck with Hall of Fame officials, who stipulated that in order to receive the award, all of the original members had to be present at the ceremony. Separating the warring factions was the only solution. I played mediator and sat with Annette at a table between the two groups. Curtis was unable to attend because of complications stemming from his accident a year before.

As for Desert Storm, I couldn't understand the logic of risking American lives in another foreign conflict that had very little to do with the price of butter—or oil. America imports less than 5 percent of its oil from the Gulf Region around Iraq. So why were we ostensibly "protecting our national interests" in a region where we had no apparent interests to protect? Like kids drawing lines in the sand, Saddam Hussein and George Bush appeared to put their political interests ahead of their respective countries' interests.

So when we were called to the stage to accept the award, it was with sadness that I said, "There are two things that happened tonight that I didn't think I would live to see: one, that I would be inducted into the Rock and Roll Hall of Fame, because I never considered myself to be a rock and roll singer; and two, that America would be in another war." I did not make reference to the mini-war being waged by my former singing partners, because it was too embarrassing, on the one hand, and too sad, on the other.

Over the years, Fred, Sam, and Curtis had become the Impressions. But Arthur and Richard had never given up their rights to the name—or at least their claim to the name. They were using the name "The Original Impressions" in some parts of the South, while Fred, Sam, and Curtis are recognized as the Impressions who recorded major hits like "People Get Ready," "It's Alright," and "Choice of Colors." All except Curtis lived in Chattanooga. Yet they never spoke to or saw one another; they never did anything together—until that night when they wound up in the same room, and I was the only one talking to both sides. It was weird.

To some extent, I can understand both sides of the argument. In contrast to my situation thirty-three years ago, when I left the group, I didn't keep anyone from making a living. And that's what it all came down to: Who's going to get the money? Or, rather, who's going to get the plaque?

Seven years later, in April 1998, after the Rock and Roll Hall of Fame had moved into its newly built 5,482-square-foot theater and museum in Cleve-

In 1983, past and current member of the Impressions went on tour to mark the 25th anniversary of the founding of the group. *From left:* Vandy "Smokey" Hampton, Curtis Mayfield, Sam Gooden, Nate Edwards, Jerry Butler, and Fred Cash.

land, I was invited to perform. I performed solo. It would have been nice, I think, if all of the original Impressions had been there with me to commemorate something special.

The Rhythm and Blues Foundation: Where Do We Go from Here?

I've seen it happen at least a dozen times: My contemporaries, my friends, once again in the spotlight, hearing appreciative, heartfelt applause, perhaps for the last time. For many of them, it is their first appearance before an audience in more than a decade or two, and it becomes too overwhelming and they break down, crying. It happens every year.

It was no different in 1996. That was the year when Betty Everett, overcome with emotion, said through tears, "This is the first time anybody has given me anything." Phil Upchurch, saying almost the same thing, cried in '97. It happened again in '94, the year I received my Pioneer Award. I don't remember if I cried (I probably did), but I do recall Earl Palmer, one of my co-recipients,

WITH JERRY BUTLER

Curtis Mayfield and the Impressions

"'He Will Break Your Heart' topped the Billboard R&B chart for seven consecutive weeks, and marked the beginning of a remarkable creative run which lasted well into the 1970s."..PAGE 14

poking me in the side and saying, "Everybody in here will be crying before it's over." What triggered his remarks was the unsolicited audience response to the Shirelles' Doris Coley when she sang the first notes of the group's gigantic 1958 hit:

Betty Everett and Jerry Butler backstage after her induction into the Rhythm and Blues Hall of Fame in 1996.

> This is dedicated to the one I love . . .
> Each night before I go to bed, my baby . . .

Most of the people in the audience that night, upon hearing those words, probably went on a nostalgia trip back to the days when they were just teenagers—I know I did—as they rose en masse and sang along with the Shirelles. Later, backstage, the surviving members of the Shirelles—Shirley Owens, Beverly Lee, and Doris (Micki Harris is deceased)—embraced each other and wondered why they broke up in the first place.

Receiving Pioneer Awards with the Shirelles, Earl Palmer, and me were Otis Blackwell, Clarence Carter, Don Covay, Bill Doggett, Mable John, Ben E. King, Johnny Otis, Little Richard, Irma Thomas, the Coasters, and the Robins.

The Rhythm and Blues Foundation annually bestows Pioneer Awards on artists "whose lifelong contributions have been instrumental in the development of rhythm and blues music." Award recipients are nominated and selected by the Foundation's Board of Trustees, Advisory Board, and Artist Steering Committee.

Other past recipients have included the Flamingoes, the Spaniels, Bobby Womack, Johnnie Taylor, Big Jay McShann, Johnny "Guitar" Watson, William Bell, Clarence "Gatemouth" Brown, Gene Chandler, Lloyd Price, the Moonglows, Cissy Houston, Arthur Prysock, Inez and Charlie Fox, Little Milton, Gary U.S. Bonds, Junior Walker and the All Stars, the Marvelettes, and the Spinners.

The Ninth Annual Pioneer Awards ceremony, held February 26, 1998, at the Imperial Ballroom of the Sheraton New York, was typical. Seventy-four-year-old award recipient Faye Adams got things started singing her 1954 hit "Shake a Hand." There was hardly a dry eye in the place when she finished.

Another recipient, Screamin' Jay Hawkins, dressed in white tie and tails and carrying a bone and a skull, performed his hit from 1956, "I Put a Spell on You," and then strolled over to a podium to accept what he said was the first award of his career.

"My mom told me, 'Son, you know, you got a big mouth,'" he said. "But for the first time I don't have any words."

Others who received awards with Jay were Kim Weston, who won fame with her Motown hit "Take Me in Your Arms"; Ernie K-Doe of "Mother-in-Law" fame; Bobby Byrd; Atlantic Records cofounder Herb Abramson; saxophonist David "Fathead" Newman; the Five Satins; Faye Adams; the Harptones; the O'Jays; and Tyrone Davis, who said, "I've been in this business thirty years, and I never had nobody give me nothing."

For the second year in a row, Smokey Robinson was master of ceremonies. Among those in the sold-out crowd of 1,500 were Stevie Wonder, the Artist (formerly known as Prince), and George Clinton of Parliament-Funkadelic. "It's like backstage at the Apollo here," quipped Clinton.

Bobby Byrd, James Brown's long-time collaborator, said as he accepted his award, "Once I wrote a lyric that said, 'I've been pounding this beat for a long time and I know I paid my dues.' It seems I'm getting paid for it tonight."

Gladys Knight and the Pips received the Ray Charles Lifetime Achievement Award, joining in that category past recipients Aretha Franklin (1992), Little Richard (1994), Antoine "Fats" Domino (1995), Bo Diddley (born Otha Ellas Bates McDaniel) (1996), and the Four Tops (1997).

Accepting her award with the Pips, Gladys was near tears as she recalled her early days on the road. "We were out there when [black people] weren't allowed to stay in hotels and . . . eat in restaurants," she said. "The young people don't know about this."

To remind young musicians and performers of some of those hardships and to make them aware of the pitfalls they may encounter on their way to stardom, the foundation has begun a series of informational programs on the black-oriented Web site Netnoir as well as on its own Web site. In addition to providing historical information, the sites invite applications for aid.

The Rhythm and Blues Foundation began operations in 1988 following a long and bitter battle between a group of rhythm and blues artists headed by "Miss Rhythm" herself, Ruth Brown, and Atlantic Records. At issue were royalty payments the artists claimed Atlantic owed them, dating as far back as twenty-five years.

The R&B group was aided in its fight by a young, energetic attorney from Columbus, Ohio, named Howell Begle, who, because of his deep appreciation of R&B and artists such as Ruth Brown, took on the case pro bono.

After requesting and reviewing hundreds of documents from Atlantic, Begle surmised that the company may have been in violation of the Racketeer Influenced and Corrupt Organizations Act (RICO). RICO allows individual plaintiffs to privately sue corporations—and win—if they can prove that the corporation engages in activities that organized crime normally gets involved in, such as larceny, extortion, and mail fraud. In the case of Atlantic, Begle was convinced that the record company knowingly sent out false royalty reports to Ruth Brown and others through the U.S. mail.

Faced with the prospect of a RICO suit filed against it, Atlantic, while admitting to no wrongdoing, recalculated its past royalty payments, settling on a figure of $1.5 million, which would be paid in the form of tax-free grants to the newly formed Rhythm and Blues Foundation. The grants, in turn, would be distributed to artists in recognition of their contribution to R&B music.

The foundation's first Board of Trustees, a real powerhouse, consisted of Dan Ackroyd, Howell Begle, Judy Belushi (John's widow), Ray Benson (Grammy award–winning singer/songwriter), Jay Berman, Michael Douglas, Tom Draper (vice president of Community Relations at Atlantic), Ahmet Ertegun, Phyllis Garland (professor of journalism at Columbia University), Gerri Hirshey, (freelance music writer), the Reverend Jesse Jackson, Congressman Mickey Leland, David Marsh (feature writer for *Rolling Stone*), Joyce McRae (Sam Moore's wife), Kendall Minter (entertainment attorney), Bill Murray, "Doc" Pomus (songwriter and lyricist), Bonnie Raitt, David Sanborn, Isaac Tigrett (founder of the Hard Rock Cafe), Dionne Warwick, and Louise West (music publisher).

As Ruth Brown pointed out in her autobiography, *Miss Rhythm*, R&B pioneers "were purposely excluded during the early stages of the foundation, to avoid conflict of interest when grants policy was on the agenda."

That policy held until shortly after I received my Pioneer Award in 1994.

Begle and Jim Fifield, then CEO of EMI, asked me to run for chairman of the board. At first I declined, citing my busy schedule performing and my county commissioner duties, as well as serving on a half-dozen or so other boards. But they persisted, and I finally said yes. I ran for the office and won.

I was reelected to a second term in August 1998 and preside over a board consisting of Ray Benson, Ed Bradley, Ruth Brown, Ahmet Ertegun, Jim Fifield, Richard Foos, Harvey Fuqua, Phyl Garland, Angela Harris, Chuck Jackson, Etta James, David Nathan, Kay Pierson, Frances Preston, Lloyd Price, Bonnie Raitt, Sylvia Rhone, Ernie Singleton, Terry Stewart, LeBaron Taylor, Judy Tint, Billy Vera, and Charles Wimbley.

The foundation currently provides performance grants and subsidizes live shows by longtime rhythm and blues singers, as well as emergency assistance to musicians who need medical treatment, help with rent, or other aid. The foundation has given out more than $2 million in aid, disbursing 87 cents of every dollar it receives.[3]

Since 1988 the foundation has held its annual ceremony the day after the Grammy Awards, taking advantage of the gathered representatives of the music business to pay tribute to rhythm and blues performers from the 1940s through the 1960s. Tickets for the event are $50 to $500.

Unlike a Grammy Award or a Rock and Roll Hall of Fame citation, the Pioneer Award comes with a check: $15,000 for a solo performer, $20,000 for a group (or at least $5,000 per original member), and $20,000 for the lifetime achievement award.

Not enough can be said about Bonnie Raitt, who made a substantial monetary gift to the foundation and helped us over many rough spots during the initial going. The same can be said of Howell Begle, who resigned from the board in spring 1999, and Ruth Brown. With their help, we were able to assist people like Big Joe Turner and LaVern Baker, who, before she died in 1998, was getting around her apartment on artificial legs. The foundation helped with her medical bills.

In another tragic case, the foundation, together with Diana Ross, Rod Stewart, and Bruce Springsteen, was also able to help Mary Wells before she succumbed to throat cancer. Mary, who had the first number 1 hit at Motown, was receiving eviction notices before Diana and the foundation stepped in.

The foundation has quietly distributed more than $500,000 over the years for medical emergencies, rent emergencies, and burial expenses. But former foundation executive director Susan Jenkins is the first to say that these are Band-Aids. "Not surprisingly, then the Foundation frequently finds itself debating how to help," said Jon Pareles in an article in the February 28, 1998, edition of the *New York Times*.

For aging artists, as for anyone, the best protection against disaster is medical insurance. But most artists have none, and it's generally agreed that the best way to get them some is to qualify them for the American Federation of Television and Radio Artists (AFTRA) plan.

This requires earning at least $7,500 year in royalties, however, and most R&B artists don't reach that threshold, often because they signed contracts many years ago for 1%, 2% or no royalties at all.

But if labels raised that rate to a now-standard 10%, hundreds more might qualify.

That's why, two years ago, many of the artists in the Foundation urged that it become an advocate for royalty reform—which EMI, Atlantic, MCA and others have to various degrees implemented.

This proposal was rejected, however, by a coalition that argued that helping artists challenge record companies could jeopardize the Foundation's image, mission and fund-raising.[4]

These opponents included labels whose financial support is considered vital to the foundation's existence and which thus carry considerable weight. As foundation chairman and a plaintiff in a massive class action royalty recoupment suit myself, I don't think it's the foundation's role to get involved.

"That leaves some people frustrated, the same way some are frustrated that the Foundation holds a lavish awards gala and gives grants to well-off artists like Smokey Robinson instead of channeling every cent to those in need," wrote *New York Daily News* critic-at-large David Hinckley.[5] Hinckley added, "The Foundation's answer about the dinner is that class deserves class, and that the grants are recognition for pleasures rendered—not charity. Ruth Brown, cofounder of the Foundation, argues that the trickiest part of helping pioneer artists is doing it in a way that doesn't destroy anyone's dignity.

"So the discussion continues, inside and outside the Foundation, and if it's sometimes frustrating it's also good, because anything that keeps pioneer artists on the mind of the music business is good. Atlantic Records, for instance, is reportedly about to announce it is raising royalty rates to 10 percent for all artists, 1948–1969, and that's not the kind of move that usually happens because an executive wakes up one morning with a sudden whim to do the right thing."

Screamin' Jay Hawkins

Seeing Screamin' Jay Hawkins in 1998 at the Ninth Annual Pioneer Awards ceremony in New York reminded me of just how original it was for an act to make his entrance onstage in a coffin. In recent years, however, he had

Screamin' Jay Hawkins

modified the act so that it resembled a magic act, complete with electronic smoke, a small skull sitting on a pole, and eerie music. I saw both acts over the years, and they were as hilarious and fresh each time as the first time I saw them.*

"This crazy business has done one thing to me that I have never been able to shake," said Jay, who was born Jalacy Hawkins July 18, 1929, in Cleveland, Ohio. "It made me into some kind of black voodoo artist. When I came into this business, I was trying to be an opera singer and a piano player." But a song he recorded for Okeh Records in 1956 changed those plans—in a hurry. "I Put a Spell on You" was Jay's first—and only—hit, proving once again that you don't need hit recordings to continue entertaining people year after year. You just need appreciative audiences—and a good booking agent.

* Jay died as this book was going to press.

It was disc jockey Alan Freed who talked Jay into using a coffin in his act. At first Jay hesitated. "I told him that black people don't get into coffins, because they might not be able to get out."

But that didn't deter Freed, who reached into his pocket and pulled out a wad of one hundred dollar bills and began peeling them off. "By the time he got to twenty-five hundred," said Jay, "I said, "Well, I'll try it just this once." From that point on, I became this black, voodoo, witch doctor, crazy, rock and roll person."

In 1947 he was a Golden Gloves boxer and won the middleweight championship. He entered show business in 1951 as a valet to guitarist Tiny Grimes. He recorded with Grimes for Gotham and Atlantic records for a year and a half. This was followed by a recording for Timely Records, "Baptize Me in Wine," a hint of what was to come.

In the sixties he recorded such tunes as "Alligator Wine," "Feast of the Mau Mau," and "I Hear Voices," and he appeared in the 1978 film *American Hot Wax*. In 1980, he opened for the Rolling Stones at Madison Square Garden. Keith Richards helped Jay in a remake of "I Put a Spell on You." Jay had a profound influence on Arthur Brown, who copied his style. The rock group Black Sabbath also tried to replicate his famous stage act, which one critic described as being on the "surrealistic borderline."

"When the curtain opens, there's the coffin," said Jay, describing the opening of his act. "When I hear the people go 'oooooh!' I know it's time to come out, and I raise my hand." During one performance, however, things didn't quite work so smoothly. "The coffin didn't open and I got scared. I knew there were only three minutes of air in the coffin." Complicating matters, his prop for that night's performance was a coffin borrowed from a funeral parlor. Its previous occupant had been transported elsewhere, leaving behind some embalming fluid.

Jay continued: "So I'm in there smelling this embalming fluid and something says, 'If you don't get out in three minutes, you're gonna be dead.' I thought about all the bad things I had done and I started praying to the Lord. I said, 'Lord, give me a chance.' Tears were coming out of my eyes.

"Then, all of a sudden, my bladder broke. Then my bowels broke. I had this white tux on. I kept knocking, and the coffin finally fell off the stand and opened. I came up gasping for air, and the people thought it was part of the act. I was all wet in the front and brown in the back. The band was cracking up. They were saying, 'How can he top that?'"

He couldn't. And neither could dozens of imitators, including Creedence Clearwater Revival, who covered "I Put a Spell on You." Compilations of Jay's

Screamin' Jay Hawkins. Photo by Charles McMillan.

recordings were issued on Edsel called *Frenzy* and on Red Lightnin' called *Screamin' the Blues.*

"Everybody started using coffins and electric smoke," said Jay. "Nina Simone saw me do 'Spell.' She fell in love with it and did a version of it. She said, 'I was so moved by the way Screamin' Jay Hawkins did it.' Three years ago she wrote her autobiography and titled it *I Put a Spell on You.* In the book she gave credit to Alan Price, the white boy. I saw him do 'I Put a Spell on You' and I got angry. How could this white boy get credit for this black boy's song? I finally told myself, Jay, shut up. Relax. What goes around comes around. In time it will happen."

It did happen. At age sixty-nine, Jay, with his electronic smoke, white suit, and skull, performed "Spell" at the Pioneer Awards ceremony. An appreciative, thoroughly entertained audience gave him a standing ovation. He finally received some of the recognition he deserved.

Epilogue

If I were to ask the Creator to reassess my life and choose for me the perfect time and place to have been born, I'm almost certain that He would choose this time and this place: December 8, 1939, in Sunflower County, Mississippi. What can be more perfect than to have lived one's life in the greatest country on earth and, thus far, in the most prosperous and productive period in human existence? Truly, I have been blessed.

I also have been blessed to have witnessed the tremendous growth in maturity of the American people. In 1939, African Americans living in the South could not vote or sit beside white Americans in movie theaters, restaurants, schools, churches, and public facilities. Blacks could not perform alongside or play on sports teams with whites. In the workplace, whites were paid twice as much as blacks. As late as 1968, vestiges of a bygone era lingered on in public signs that read "White Only" and "Colored" and "Negroes need not apply," the latter most prevalent in help wanted ads in northern newspapers. In almost all instances these inequities were enforced by law.

Since 1968, however, there have been few, if any, cases in America of overt segregation, and absolutely no cases of segregation laws being enforced. Americans today live, work, travel, and worship together, without regard to race, color, or religious belief. A shining example of that occurred in the summer of 1998, in the displays of sportsmanship by baseball stars Mark McGwire and Sammy Sosa. This I witnessed also.

The American people—all Americans—deserve credit for this phenomenal turn of events, this great leap forward in human progress, for without the examples of Martin Luther King Jr., Viola Liuzzo, Michael Schwerner, Andrew Goodman, James Chaney, Medgar Evers, and others—people of different races and religions who gave their lives for freedom—I doubt if much of the foregoing would have occurred.

Also during that time span, some startling technological innovations took place. In 1939, for example, Americans generally traveled to Europe on ships that would take anywhere from a week to ten days to reach their destination. Now they can travel by Concorde jet and arrive in Europe in about three and a half hours. What's more, once they reach places like Europe and Japan, they can travel on a bullet train and arrive at their destination in a fraction of the time it used to take to travel the same distance.

In my lifetime I also witnessed humans land on the moon and steer spacecraft to outer space.

Closer to my heart, I saw how recording technology went from using cumbersome four-track machines to sleek digital technology. This affected not only the sound of music but the sale. By that I mean that you no longer have to go to a record store to buy a record. You can sit in the comfort of your home and download music off the Internet or order a CD from a computer screen. Is that amazing stuff or what?

Yet despite all of the technological marvels and progress in human relations, there remains that nagging "problem" of what to do with those who grew up in the midst of all of these great and wonderful things but now find themselves in the position of not being able to benefit from any of it. I of course am referring to the many great musicians and performers who helped create rhythm and blues, who suffered through America's growing pains, and who made it possible for many of today's whiz kids and recording moguls to stand back with smug indifference, shrug their shoulders, and say, "I had nothing to do with that. It wasn't my fault."

Is it enough to construct monuments and museums to honor the memory

Jerry Butler and Jesse Jackson

of those pioneers, say thank you, and then be on our way? I think we owe them more than that.

I was at a club about three years ago, and Jesse Jackson came in. People were lined up around the block. Jesse said, "Jerry, can't many people from your era still do this."

I ran into Bobby Womack in an airport in Memphis in 1998, and in the course of our conversation he said, "I've got a new album out, and I just played to five thousand people last night. But nobody in there had heard it."

"Why?" I asked.

"Because I can't get it on the radio."

"That's tragic, man."

"Yeah, but imagine that," he said, shaking his head. "I played to five thousand people last night and can't get my record on the radio."

What Jesse and Bobby were alluding to, of course, was that so many artists and performers of my day still have an audience who will come see them per-

Bobby Womack at the 1997 Pioneer Awards banquet. Photo by Charles McMillan.

form and buy their records. But the record companies and radio stations have written them off.

Look at the Isley Brothers. They have been able to survive and thrive in my generation as well as the present. But they still don't get the acceptance at the radio level. The same goes for Ray Charles and Aretha. They're still out there making music, getting play, and doing things on the Grammys. But it's because they are so big. The force of the record companies is behind them to the point where they can't be overlooked.

Those are the exceptions. There are so many artists still performing who have made contributions but can't get airplay. The Dells, for instance, went to Texas recently and sold out the auditoriums they played in, but couldn't get their records played. Marshall and the Chi-Lites play to packed houses all over Europe. Can't get their records played.

Why, after forty years, do people still line up to see me perform? I don't know. My guess is that I always give people a good show. I always give them what they come to see. When people stop coming to see you, I think it's because the artist has gotten tired of performing, not that the people are tired of seeing the artist. When artists get tired of performing, they become lackadaisical. That's why so many artists get on drugs; they need that artificial stimulant. They can no longer get that high that they used to get when they had a love affair with the audience. So much of it becomes work. As B.B. King says, "The thrill is gone."

I still enjoy performing and enjoy the people enjoying the performance. The only reason I haven't been recording is that the radio stations have written me off as well. Radio programmers say, "If you're old, we'll play your old records because that's your audience—people from thirty-nine to fifty-nine."

But kids like those records, too. I was looking at my little nephew a few weeks ago watching Jackie Wilson on television. He doesn't know that Jackie is dead. All he knows is that he likes Jackie's moves and his singing. He doesn't know that that was forty years ago. To him it's right now, just like his cartoons are right now. He doesn't know that Mickey Mouse and Minnie Mouse have been around for more than seventy years.

Rhythm and blues music survives because the soul survives. As long as people sing and perform from the soul, the music will go on, burning like an eternal flame. This book is an attempt to keep that flame alive, as well as to raise consciousness about what came before. In another sense, it is my way of saying thanks to all of those who made this time and this place so magnificent. But, nevertheless, *aluta continuum*. The struggle continues.

Notes

Introduction

1. Excerpt from Internet review of William Strauss and Neil Howe, *Generations* (New York: William and Morrow, 1997): "The Silent Generation," http://www.csulb.edu/~wwwing/Silents/

Prologue

1. "The physical setting itself is striking. Visiting this bedeviled and beguiling area a year after Till hopped off that train, Robert Penn Warren noted the sad and baleful beauty of the Delta," with "its ruined, gaunt, classic clay hills, with the creek bottoms throttled long since in pink sand." Stephen J. Whitfield, *A Death in the Delta: The Story of Emmett Till* (Baltimore: Johns Hopkins University Press, 1991), p. 13.

2. Miriam Di Nunzio, "No R-E-S-P-E-C-T for Serious Music," *Chicago Sun-Times,* March 1, 1998, p. 38.

1. The Beginning

1. E. Marvin Goodwin, *Black Migration in America from 1915 to 1960: An Uneasy Exodus* (Lewiston: Edwin Mellen Press, 1990).

2. Kenneth L. Kusmer, ed., *Black Communities and Urban Development in America, 1720–1990,* vol. 5: *The Great Migration and After, 1917–1930* (New York: Garland, 1991), p. 4.

3. Michael Haralambos, *Soul Music: The Birth of a Sound in Black America* (New York: Da Capo, 1974).

4. Mississippi Department of Archives and History, *All Shook Up: Mississippi Roots of American Popular Music* (Jackson: Mississippi Department of Archives and History, 1995).

5. Richard Zoglin, "When Chicago Was Heaven," *Time,* February 13, 1995.

6. Daniel Wolff with S. B. Crain, Clifton White, and G. David Tenenbaum, *You Send Me: The Life and Times of Sam Cooke* (New York: William Morrow, 1995).

7. William D. Piersen, *Black Legacy: America's Hidden Heritage* (Amherst: University of Massachusetts Press 1993), p. 74.

2. Starting Over in Sweet Home Chicago

1. Richard T. Enright, *Capone's Chicago* (Lakeville, Minn.: Northstar Maschek Books, 1987).

2. The 18th Amendment to the Constitution—passed by Congress in 1917, and ratified by three-fourths of the states by 1919—prohibited the manufacture or sale of alcoholic beverages within the boundaries of the United States. "Lecture 17: The Politics of Prohibition—The 1920s," History 102, University of Wisconsin.

3. "On the afternoon of July 27, 1919, Eugene Williams, a black youth, drowned of exhaustion off the 29th Street beach. A stone throwing melee between blacks and whites on the beach prevented the boy from coming ashore safely. After clinging to a railroad tie for a lengthy period, he drowned when he no longer had the strength to hold on. . . . This was the finding of the Cook County Coroner's Office after an inquest was held into the cause of death. But false reports that he had been stoned to death led to five days of rioting in Chicago that claimed the lives of a total of 23 blacks and 15 whites, with 291 wounded and maimed. . . . Those findings, reported in the Coroner's Report of 1919 are followed by his recommendations to deal with the festering social and economic conditions that were the precipitating factors leading to the riots."

3. Learning the Basics

1. LeRoi Jones, *Blues People: The Negro Experience in White America and the Music That Developed from It* (New York: William Morrow, 1967).

4. Reality Sets In

1. Percy Bysshe Shelley, *Adonais*, st. 39. These lines, written for John Keats, were recited by Mick Jagger on the death of fellow Rolling Stone Brian Jones, in London's Hyde Park, July 5, 1969.

5. What's in a Name?

1. Bob Merlis and Davin Seay, *Heart and Soul: A Celebration of Black Music Style in America, 1930–1975* (New York: U.S. Media Holdings, 1997).

8. Learning Experiences

1. "We ended up splitting up. Some moved to Detroit to live with their relatives. Of course, I still lived in Cabrini-Green. That's when I got my first job, with Alfred Dunhill, a cigar store. So I delivered cigars up and down the Gold Coast [the wealthy lakefront area on the North Side] for Alfred Dunhill." Curtis's response to Robert Pruter on the breakup of the Impressions, in *Chicago Soul* (Urbana and Chicago: University of Illinois Press, 1991), p. 138.

9. Making My Mark

1. Despite the lingering myth that JFK was a strong proponent of civil rights, his administration saw no major civil rights legislation. It was actually brother Robert Kennedy, JFK's attorney general, who was passionately committed to civil rights. JFK, afraid of losing the always tenuous support of southern Democrats, put civil rights on the back burner once he was in office. "Lecture 25: Eisenhower & Kennedy," History 102, University of Wisconsin.

2. After the events in Montgomery, Alabama, and Little Rock, Arkansas, some liberal whites in Congress introduced the Civil Rights Act in 1957. It received no help from President Eisenhower, who stated, "I personally believe if you try to go too far in this delicate field, that involves the emotions of so many millions of Americans, you're making a mistake." "Lecture 26: Civil Rights in an Uncivil Society," History 102, University of Wisconsin.

3. "Teenage movie-goers, who were a part of the new post-war materialism, became jaded and were looking for something new to grab their attention. Nothing could have been more exciting to overindulged, immature teenagers than the idea of living on the edge as glamorized in movies such as *Rebel Without a Cause* starring James Dean, Natalie Wood, and Sal Mineo." Harry Turner, *This Magic Moment: Musical Reflections of a Generation* (Atlanta: AGM 1994), p. 34.

4. "Though a roughneck with no evident musical ability, Vastola had a number of years' experience in the music business. . . . And he was an owner of Queens Booking, a big agency mostly for black acts in the sixties." Fredric Dannen, *Hit Men: Power Brokers and Fast Money inside the Music Business* (New York: Vintage Books, 1991), p. 54.

5. Dick Clark and Fred Bronson, *Dick Clark's American Bandstand* (New York: Collins, 1997).

6. In 1986 RCA became part of BMG—Bertelsmann Music Group—when the West German media conglomerate Bertelsmann took it over. They were called major labels because they did their own nationwide distribution. Dannen, *Hit Men*, p. 112.

7. Ibid.

8. Francis Davis, "The Man from Heaven," *Atlantic Monthly* 279, no. 6, pp. 100–109.

9. Ibid.

10. A Little Help from My Friends

1. Another great rhythm and blues tune performed by the band between 1961 and 1962 and sung by John is featured on the first anthology, *Leave My Kitten Alone*. This had been an R&B hit for Little Willie John in 1959 and Johnny Preston in 1960. The Beatles' first hit in England in 1962, "Love Me Do," borrowed heavily from both skiffle and rhythm and blues. Mike Leyland, "The Influences of Black Music on the Mersey Sound," found on the Internet.

2. Daniel Wolff with S. B. Crain, Clifton White, and G. David Tenenbaum, *You Send Me: The Life and Times of Sam Cooke* (New York: William Morrow, 1995), p. 217.

3. Ibid.

4. Whitfield, *A Death in the Delta.*

5. Joel Selvin, *Sam Cooke's SAR Records Story (1959–1965).* Internet review, 1998.

6. David Nathan ("the British Ambassador of Soul"), U.S. Editor, Blues—Soul contributing writer, *Billboard* and NetNoir.

7. "During the week at the Apollo I got into some arguments with Jerry's percussionist and band leader Jamo Thomas, about what I don't remember, but it bothered Jamo enough that he asked Jerry Butler to dismiss me." Don Taylor, *Marley and Me: The Real Story, As Told to Mike Henry* (New York: Kingston Publishers, 1994), p. 40.

8. Mike Pinfold, *Louis Armstrong: His Life and Times* (New York: Universe Books, 1987), p. 88.

11. The Producers

1. Local engineer Joe Tarsia took over a mediocre local studio named Sound Plus, changed the name to Sigma Sound, and was lucky enough to talk Gamble, Huff, and Bell into giving it a shot. Nelson George, *The Death of Rhythm & Blues* (New York: Plume, 1988), p. 143.

12. "Kill or Be Killed"

1. Nancy Zaroulis, *Gerald Sullivan: Who Spoke Up? The American Protest against the War in Vietnam, 1963–75* (New York: Holt, Rinehart and Winston, 1984).

2. Stanley W. Beesley, *Vietnam: The Heartland Remembers* (Norman: University of Oklahoma Press, 1987), p. 15.

3. James E. Westheider, *Fighting on Two Fronts: African Americans and the Vietnam War* (New York and London: New York University Press, 1997), p. 18.

4. Vietnam Veterans Oral History and Folklore Project, Department of Anthropology, Buffalo State College, Buffalo, New York, 1991.

5. Westheider, *Fighting on Two Fronts,* p. 18.

13. Changing the World with a Song

1. Lloyd Sachs, "A Harmonious Twist of Fate: Destiny Calls on Guitarist One More Time," *Chicago Sun-Times,* November 5, 1996, p. 27.

2. Patti LaBelle, *Don't Block the Blessings: Revelations of a Lifetime* (New York: Boulevard Books, 1996), p. 219.

14. You've Got What it Takes

1. *Record Row: Cradle of Rhythm and Blues,* a 60-minute PBS documentary narrated by Rock and Roll Hall of Famer Etta James, is a production of the Chicago Production Center/WTTW, divisions of Window to the World Communications, Inc. Michael McAlpin, Producer; Shelley Spencer, Executive Producer.

2. "Comedian Bill Cosby is helping launch a new TV show. He's here to narrate a sales presentation for the pilot of singer Jerry Butler's 'The Soul of the Matter' program. The comic also took time to engage Max Davidson in a rousing tennis set at the East Bank Club. . . . " Item in Kup's Column, *Chicago Sun-Times,* January 21, 1982, p. 74.

3. "Toward the end of Dinah's career, she began missing her club engagements and acting rudely toward her audience. Because of her ongoing battle with excessive weight, she started taking prescription drugs for weight loss, then other drugs including sleeping pills. By 1960, she was also taking mercury injections to induce weight loss through dehydration. Along with her heavy drinking, the prescription drugs and mercury finally took their toll. Dinah Washington died of an overdose of sleeping pills, diet pills, and alcohol on December 11, 1963." William Barlow and Cheryl Finley, *From Swing to Soul: An Illustrated History of African American Popular Music from 1930 to 1960* (Washington, D.C.: Elliott and Clark, 1994).

15. Summing Up

1. Daniel Rapoport, *Inside the House: An Irreverent Guided Tour through the House of Representatives, from the Days of Adam Clayton Powell to Those of Peter Rodino* (Chicago: Follett, [1975]), p. 168.

2. Charles V. Hamilton, *Adam Clayton Powell, Jr.: The Political Biography of an American Dilemma* (New York: Atheneum, 1991), p. 478.

3. "Last year was a good one for the foundation, which received $772,000 in a new round of contributions and pledges from the music publishing agencies ASCAP and BMI, the trade publications *Billboard* and *Radio & Records,* Jobete Music Co., MTV

and the labels BMG, Def Jam, Polygram, Rhino, Sony, and Vee Jay." Richard Harrington, "R&B Foundation Hopes to Help Out," *Washington Post, Chicago Sun-Times,* June 23, 1993.

4. Jon Pareles, "With Dues Long Paid, Musicians Reap Awards," *New York Times,* February 28, 1998.

5. David Hinckley, "The R&B Foundation's Annual Cash Awards Help Put the Focus on Pioneers," *New York Daily News,* March 2, 1997.

Bibliography

Aletti, Vince. "Jerry Butler." In *The Rolling Stone Rock 'n' Roll Reader*, ed. Ben Fong-Torres, pp. 123–32. New York: Bantam Books, 1974.

Alexander, Michael. "The Impressions." *Rolling Stone*, December 27, 1969, p. 29.

Barlow, William, and Cheryl Finley. *From Swing to Soul: An Illustrated History of African American Popular Music from 1930 to 1960*. Washington, D.C.: Elliott and Clark, 1994.

Barry, Dave. "Play Some Oldies, but Don't Turn My Stomach." *Atlanta Constitution*, August 23, 1992, p. B1.

Berry, Chuck. *Chuck Berry*. New York: Crown, 1987.

Broughton, Viv. *Black Gospel: An Illustrated History of the Gospel Sound*. Poole, England: Blandford Press, 1985.

Brown, Charles T. *The Art of Rock and Roll*. Englewood Cliffs, N.J.: Prentice-Hall, 1987.

Brown, Marcia L. "Jerry Butler: The Ice Man Keeps On Rolling Along," *Black Stars*, September 1974, pp. 11–16.

Burns, Peter. "Billy Butler: Nearly a Decade of Writing and Recording." *Blues and Soul*, June 8–21, 1973, pp. 24–25.

Clark, Dick, and Fred Bronson. *Dick Clark's American Bandstand*. New York: Collins Publishers, 1997.

Cowdery, Ray R. *Capone's Chicago*. Lakeville, Minn.: Northstar Maschek Books, 1987.

Dannen, Fredric. *Hit Men: Power Brokers and Fast Money inside the Music Business*. New York: Vintage, 1991.

Denisoff, R. Serge, and Richard A. Peterson, eds. *The Sounds of Social Change*. Chicago: Rand McNally, 1972.

Escott, Colin. *Good Rockin' Tonight*. New York: St. Martin's Press, 1991.

Frith, Simon. *The Sociology of Rock*. London: Constable, 1978.

Gaines, Steven. *Heroes and Villains*. New York: NAL Books, 1986.

George, Nelson. *The Death of Rhythm & Blues*. New York: Plume, 1988.

Gillett, Charlie. *Sound of the City*. New York: Pantheon, 1983.

Goldman, Albert. *Sound Bites*. New York: Turtle Bay Books–Random House, 1992.

Gunther, Mark, and Bill Carter. *Monday Night Mayhem*. New York: Beech Tree Books/William Morrow, 1988.

Guralnick, Peter. *Feel Like Going Home*. New York: Vintage, 1981.

Haralambros, Michael. *Right On: From Blues to Soul in Black America*. New York: Da Capo, 1974.

Hemphill, Paul. *The Nashville Sound: Bright Lights and Country Music*. New York: Simon and Schuster, 1970.

Henderson, David. *'Scuse Me While I Kiss the Sky: The Life of Jimi Hendrix*. New York: Doubleday, 1978.

Hotchner, A. E. *Blown Away*. New York: Simon and Schuster, 1990.

Jackson, John. *Big Beat Heat.* New York: Schirmer, 1991.

Jones, LeRoi. *Blues People: The Negro Experience in White America and the Music That Developed from It.* New York: William Morrow, 1967.

Keil, Charles. *Urban Blues.* Chicago: University of Chicago Press, 1966.

LaBelle, Patti, with Laura B. Randolph. *Don't Block the Blessings: Revelations of a Lifetime.* New York: Boulevard, 1996.

Marcus, Greil. *Mystery Train.* New York: Dutton, 1976.

Merlis, Bob, and Davin Seay. *Heart and Soul: A Celebration of Black Music in America, 1930–1975.* New York: Stewart, Tabori and Chang, 1997.

Pinfold, Mike. *Louis Armstrong: His Life and Times.* New York: Universe Books, 1987.

Pruter, Robert. *Chicago Soul.* Urbana and Chicago: University of Illinois Press, 1991.

Quarles, Benjamin. *The Negro in the Making of America.* New York: Collier, 1969.

Rowe, Mike. *Chicago Breakdown.* New York: Drake Publishers, 1975.

Sawyer, Charles. *The Arrival of B.B. King.* New York: Doubleday, 1980.

Strauss, William, and Neil Howe. *Generations.* New York: William and Morrow, 1997.

Taylor, Don. *Marley and Me: The Real Story, As Told to Mike Henry.* New York: Kingston Publishers, 1994.

Turner, Harry. *This Magic Moment: Musical Reflections of a Generation.* Atlanta, Ga.: AGM, 1994.

Waller, Don. *The Motown Story.* New York: Charles Scribner's Sons, 1985.

Westbrooks, Logan, and Lance Williams. *Anatomy of a Record Company.* Los Angeles: Westbrooks, 1981.

White, Charles. *The Life and Times of Little Richard.* New York: Harmony, 1984.

Wolff, Daniel, with S. B. Crain, Clifton White, and G. David Tenebaum. *You Send Me: The Life and Times of Sam Cooke.* New York: William Morrow, 1995.

Discography

This discography is indebted to *Goldmine* #407 by Robert Pruter, March 1, 1996, pp. 48–60, and *In the Basement,* edited by David Cole, published by ASTRASCOPE, 193 Queens Park Road, Brighton, East Sussex BN2 27A, UK.

All chart listings here and throughout the book are from Joel Whitburn's *The Billboard Book of Top 40 Hits* (New York: Billboard Publications, 1987) and his *Top R&B Singles, 1942–1988* (Menomonee Falls, Wis.: Record Research, 1988).

Label	Record#	Title	Year

Singles

Jerry Butler and the Impressions

Label	Record#	Title	Year
Vee Jay	280	"For Your Precious Love"/ "Sweet Was the Wine"	1958
Falcon	1013	"For Your Precious Love"/ "Sweet Was the Wine"	1958
Abner	1013	"For Your Precious Love"/ "Sweet Was the Wine"	1958

The Impressions featuring Jerry Butler

Label	Record#	Title	Year
Abner	1017	"Come Back My Love"/ "Love Me"	1958

The Impressions

Label	Record#	Title	Year
Abner	1023	"The Gift of Love"/ "At the County Fair"	1959

Jerry Butler

Label	Record#	Title	Year
Abner	1024	"Lost"/"One by One"	1959
	1028	"Rainbow Valley"/ "Hold Me Darling"	1959

	1030	"Couldn't Go to Sleep"/	1959
		"I Was Wrong"	
	1030	"Couldn't Go to Sleep"/	1959
		"Don't Take Love"	
	1035	"A Lonely Soldier"/	1960
		"I Found a Love"	
Vee Jay	354	"He Will Break Your Heart"/	1960
		"Thanks to You"	
	371	"Silent Night"/	1960
		"Oh Holy Night"	
	375	"Find Another Girl"/	1961
		"When Trouble Calls"	
	390	"I'm a Telling You"/	1961
		"I See a Fool"	
	396	"For Your Precious Love"/	1961
		"Sweet Was the Wine"	
	405	"Moon River"/"Aware of Love"	1961
	426	"Isle of Sirens"/"Chi Town"	1962
	451	"Make It Easy on Yourself"/	1962
		"It's Too Late"	
	463	"You Can Run (But Can't Hide)"/	1962
		"I'm the One"	
	475	"Theme from Taras Bulba"/	1962
		"You Go Right through Me"	
	486	"Whatever You Want"/	1963
		"You Won't Be Sorry"	
	526	"I Almost Lost My Mind"/	1963
		"Strawberries"	
	534	"Where's the Girl"/	1963
		"How Beautifully You Lie"	
	556	"Just a Little Bit"/	1963
		"A Woman with Soul"	
	567	"Need to Belong"/	1963
		"Give Me Your Love"	
	588	"Giving Up on Love"/	1964
		"I've Been Trying"	
	598	"I Stand Accused"/	1964
		"I Don't Want to Hear It Anymore"	

Betty Everett and Jerry Butler

Vee Jay	613	"Let It Be Me"/ "Ain't That Loving You Baby"	1964
	633	"Smile"/"Love Is Strange"	1964
	676	"Since I Don't Have You"/ "Just Be True"	1965

Jerry Butler

Vee Jay	651	"Good Times"/"I've Grown Accustomed to Her Face"	1965
	696	"I Can't Stand to See You Cry"/ "Nobody Needs Your Love"	1965
	707	"Just for You"/"Believe in Me"	1965
	711	"Moon River"/ "Make It Easy on Yourself"	1966
	715	"For Your Precious Love"/ "Give It Up"	1966
Mercury	72592	"Love (Oh How Sweet It Is)"/ "Loneliness"	1966
	72625	"For What You Made of Me"/ "You Make Me Feel Like Someone"	1966
	72648	"I Dig You Baby"/ "Some Kinda Magic"	1967
	72676	"Why Did I Lose You"/ "You Walked into My Life"	1967
	72721	"Mr. Dream Merchant"/ "Cause I Love You So"	1967
	72764	"Lost"/"You Don't Know What You Got Until You Lose It"	1967
	72798	"Never Give You Up"/ "Beside You"	1968
	72850	"Hey Western Union Man"/ "Just Can't Forget about You"	1968
	72876	"Are You Happy?"/ "I Still Love You"	1968
	72898	"Only The Strong Survive"/ "Just Because I Really Love You"	1969
	72929	"Moody Woman"/ "Go Away Find Yourself"	1969

	72960	"What's the Use of Breaking Up"/ "A Brand New Me"	1969
	72991	"Don't Let Love Hang You Up"/ "Walking Around in Teardrops"	1969
	73015	"Got to See If I Can't Get Mommy"/"I Forgot to Remember"	1970
	73045	"I Could Write a Book"/ "Since I Lost You Lady"	1970
	73101	"Where Are You Going"/ "You Can Fly"	1970
	73131	"Special Memory"/ "How Does It Feel"	1970

Jerry Butler and Gene Chandler

| Mercury | 73163 | "You Just Can't Win"/ "Sho Is Groovin'" | 1970 |
| | 73195 | "Ten and Two"/ "Everybody Is Waiting" | 1971 |

Jerry Butler

Mercury	73169	"If It's Real What I Feel"/ "Why Are You Leaving Me"	1971
	73210	"How Did We Lose It Baby"/ "Do You Finally Need a Friend"	1971
	73241	"Walk Easy My Son"/ "Let It Be Me"	1971

Jerry Butler and Brenda Lee Eager

Mercury	73255	"Ain't Understanding Mellow"/ "Windy City Soul"	1971
	73301	"Close to You"/ "You Can Always Tell"	1972
	73395	"Can't Understand It"/ "How Long Will It Last"	1973
	73422	"The Love We Have Stays on My Mind"/"We Are Lovers We Are Friends"	1973

Jerry Butler

| Mercury | 73290 | "I Only Have Eyes for You"/ "A Prayer" | 1972 |

250

Mercury	73335	"One Night Affair"/ "Life's Unfortunate Son"	1972
	73443	"Power of Love"/"What Do You Do on a Sunday Afternoon"	1973
	73459	"That's How Heartaches Are Made"/"Too Many Danger Signs"	1974
	73495	"Take Time to Tell Her"/ "High Stepper"	1974
	73629	"Playing on You"/"Me and You against the World"	1974

Jerry Butler

Motown	1403	"The Devil in Mrs. Jones"/ "Don't Wanna Be Reminded"	1976
	1414	"I Wanna Do It to You"/ "Don't Wanna Be Reminded"	1977
	1421	"Chalk It Up"/ "I Don't Want Nobody to Know"	1977
	0007	"Chalk It Up" (12 inch)/ flip: Smokey Robinson	1977

Jerry Butler and Thelma Houston

| Motown | 1422 | "It's a Lifetime Thing"/
"Kiss Me Now" | 1977 |

Jerry Butler

PIR	3656	"(I'm Thinking about) Cooling Out"/"Are You Lonely Tonight"	1978
	3673	"Nothing Says I Love You Like I Love You"	1978
Fountain	400	"All the Way"/"No Love without Changes"	1982

Albums

Jerry Butler

Abner	2001	*Jerry Butler, Esq.*	1959
Vee Jay	1029	*He Will Break Your Heart*	1960
	1034	*Love Me* (same as Abner 2001)	1961
	1038	*Aware of Love*	1961

	1046	*Moon River*	1962
	1048	*The Best of Jerry Butler*	1962
	1057	*Folk Songs*	1963
	1076	*Need to Belong* (or *Giving Up on Love*)	1964
	1119	*More of the Best of Jerry Butler*	1965

Jerry Butler and Betty Everett

Vee Jay	1099	*Delicious Together*	1964

Jerry Butler

Mercury	61105	*Soul Artistry*	1967
	61146	*Mr. Dream Merchant*	1967
	61151	*Jerry Butler's Golden Hits—Live!*	1968
	61171	*The Soul Goes On*	1968
	61198	*The Ice Man Cometh*	1968
	61234	*Ice on Ice*	1969
	61269	*You & Me*	1970
	61281	*The Best of Jerry Butler*	1970
	61320	*Jerry Butler Sings Assorted Sounds with the Aid of Assorted Friends and Relatives*	1972
	61347	*The Sagittarius Movement*	1971
	7502	*The Spice of Life*	1972
	648	*Introducing the Ice Man Band*	1973
	689	*Power of Love*	1973
	1006	*Sweet Sixteen*	1974

Jerry Butler and Gene Chandler

Mercury	61330	*One and One*	1971

Jerry Butler and Brenda Lee Eager

Mercury	660	*The Love We Have, the Love We Had*	1973

Jerry Butler

Motown	850	*Love's on the Menu*	1976
	878	*Suite for the Single Girl*	1977
	892	*It All Comes Out in My Song*	1977

Jerry Butler and Thelma Houston

Motown	887	*Thelma and Jerry*	1977

	903	*Two to One*	1978
PIR	33510	*Nothing Says I Love You Like* *I Love You*	1978
	36413	*The Best Love I Ever Had*	1980

Albums and CDs

Jerry Butler

| Fountain | 2-82-1 | *Ice 'N Hot* | 1982 |

CDs

Rhino	75881	*The Best of Jerry Butler*	1987
Chameleon	74807	*He Will Break Your Heart*	1989
Street Gold/ Ichiban	4131	*Street Carols* (one cut: "Little Red Shoes")	1991
Vee Jay	700	*The Ice Man*	1992
Urgent/ Ichiban	1151	*Time & Faith*	1992
Mercury	968-2	*Iceman: The Mercury Years*	1992
Valley Vue	22006	*Simply Beautiful*	1994

Index

Page numbers in italics refer to illustrations.

BOOK AND JACKET DESIGN: SHARON L. SKLAR
COPY EDITOR: JANE LYLE
COMPOSITOR: L. CHRISTINE WILLIAMS
TYPEFACES: ADOBE CASLON AND BLACKOAK
BOOK PRINTER: MAPLE VAIL BOOK MANUFACTURING
JACKET PRINTER: JOHN P. POW COMPANY